Damien Brown is an Australian doctor based in Melbourne. He began writing seriously after his last humanitarian posting, encouraged by readers of a blog he kept while working for Médecins Sans Frontières in Africa. This is Damien's first book.

BAND-AID
FOR A
BROKEN
LEG

BAND-AID
FOR A
BROKEN
BEING A DOCTOR
WITH NO BORDERS
(AND OTHER WAYS
TO STAY SINGLE)
LEG

DAMIEN BROWN

ALLEN&UNWIN

First published in Great Britain in 2013 by Allen & Unwin

This paperback edition published in 2014

Allen & Unwin
c/o Atlantic Books
Ormond House
26–27 Boswell Street
London WC1N 3JZ
Phone: 020 7269 1610
Fax: 020 7430 0916
Email: UK@allenandunwin.com
Web: www.atlantic-books.co.uk

A CIP catalogue record for this book is available from the British Library.

ISBN 978 1 74331 665 8

Printed in Italy by ☙ Grafica Veneta

10 9 8 7 6 5 4 3 2 1

Text design by Lisa White
All photographs by Damien Brown
Maps by Brittany Britten

Dedicated to all those
whose stories fill these pages.

'Here, it is like this . . .'
—Dominga, our Angolan cook

CONTENTS

AUTHOR'S NOTE

All incidents described in this book are true. The names of patients have been changed to protect their confidentiality, but many of the names of staff have been left unaltered. Like Toyota, for example. I couldn't have come up with a name like that—not for a person.

This book was written in the months after the events took place, and as such all dialogue has been recreated to the best of my memory. Any errors or misquotations that could be attributed to characters in this book are purely mine, and mine alone. I bear full responsibility for any and all inaccuracies. While editorial constraints have meant that some minor scenes have been compressed, or combined, this was never done to alter the integrity of the account as a whole.

At the time of writing, I had no association with Médecins Sans Frontières, and it had no editorial input. My respect for the organisation remains high, but I hope this book will be seen neither as a specific endorsement of any one organisation, nor as a rebuke, but rather as what it was intended to be—a story about people, and of the difficult conditions they happen to live in.

AFRICA
(SELECTED COUNTRIES SHOWN)

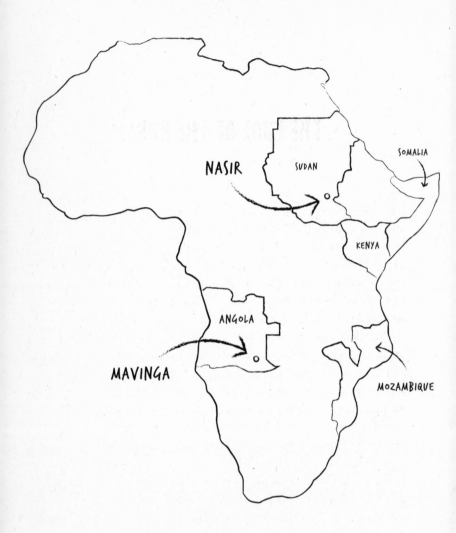

NASIR

SUDAN

SOMALIA

KENYA

ANGOLA

MAVINGA

MOZAMBIQUE

THIS MAP WAS CORRECT AT THE TIME THE AUTHOR WAS IN THE REGION. IN JULY 2011,
FOLLOWING A REFERENDUM, SOUTH SUDAN WAS GRANTED INDEPENDENCE,
DIVIDING SUDAN INTO TWO SEPARATE NATIONS.

I. THE EDGE OF THE WORLD

I arrived yesterday, dropped off by a little plane that promptly turned and rattled down the dirt runway, taking with it any semblance of a link to the outside world as it left me in this town. *If* you'd call this a town, that is. Seems more like a village to me. A dusty, isolated, mud-hut-filled outpost of a village, hidden in this far corner of Angola—a war-ravaged country in south-west Africa. It's like nothing I've ever seen, and is my home for the next six months.

But right now I'm trying not to think about it. Pretending there are no landmines. No crowded hospital. No ward with malnourished children; poster-kids from a Bob Geldof appeal who sit listlessly, wide-eyed, rubber feeding tubes taped to their cheeks, and for whose medical care I'm about to be responsible. Or that I'm to be the only doctor, for that matter, left working in the middle of a region once dubbed '*O Fim do Mundo*'—The Edge of the World—by the Portuguese colonists. And I'm hoping desperately that the immediate task at hand—choosing a gift for tonight's local wedding, to which the six of us Médecins Sans Frontières volunteers have been invited—will provide at least some respite, some fleeting distraction, from the incomprehensible, pitiful, frightening universe that begins just beyond these walls.

• • •

Three of us stand in our storage tent. Tim, the Swiss-French co-ordinator of our MSF project; Toyota, the Angolan logistics operator who supervises this storage site; and me—a junior Australian doctor on my first posting.

'Well?' asks Tim. 'Any ideas?'

Toyota looks up from his stock list. He's a tall African man with sharp eyes and a broad smile, and he's clearly untroubled by the after-noon heat. Thick blue overalls drape his solid frame and a pair of rubber gumboots is pulled near to his knees even though the dry, dusty savannah of the region suggests it hasn't rained for months.

'Oh, yes,' he grins. 'I found a very good gift. Just in here.'

'Great,' says Tim. 'But in *here*?'

'Oh yes. And believe me, you two will love it!'

Toyota drops his stock list and walks to the far corner of this space. It's a large enclosure—far larger than any room in the hospital, anyway. Yellowing canvas is hitched tightly over a high, arching metal frame beneath which our mine-proof vehicle is parked, yet there's still ample room for the rows of aid supplies along each wall. At one end, hundreds of plastic buckets form colourful columns that lean towards silver drums of cooking oil, the latter bearing the image of two hands shaking in a gesture of friendship, with the statement: '*Gift: Not to be sold or exchanged.*' Towards the other end, blankets, soap, high energy biscuits, and milk formula for the malnourished are piled in discrete mounds, while sacks of maize interlock neatly along both nearer walls. A family of cats, too; they're squatting somewhere in here—you can smell it, along with old cardboard, chlorine and diesel.

Tim shrugs. 'I know,' he says. 'In here, huh? But Toyota's the person to see about such matters. He looks after all the non-medical stock and has contacts all over town, so he can usually find what you're after. If not, he'll try to make it for you—he's good in that little workshop behind us.'

Tim would know. He's a veteran of several MSF projects in Africa and he's been in this town, Mavinga, for almost two months. Six-foot two and in his early thirties, he appears remarkably unruffled by the context; a man who, in glaring contrast to my current mental state, projects an air of calm authority. So I'm sticking closely to him these first days.

Toyota returns.

'This!' he declares. 'This is what you should bring.' He hands Tim a small package, about the size of a paperback. Some type of white cloth wrapped inside a film of clear plastic, I think, and like everything in town it's coated in a veneer of honey-coloured dust.

Tim looks up. 'Toyota, is this—?'

'Just open it!' laughs Toyota. 'You must feel it for yourself to know how good it is.'

Tim smiles, regarding the item from several angles. '*Merda*, Toyota. Is this what I think it is?'

'How can I know what you are thinking?' chuckles Toyota. 'I cannot possibly know. But I *do* know that you will like it. And I am telling you, this one you must feel. Feel it before you say anything.'

Tim opens the plastic at one end, pulls out a small piece of the fabric and fingers it lightly. He laughs. 'My God! Are you serious?'

Toyota looks surprised. 'What are you talking about, *Coordenador*?' he asks.

'There's no way we can bring this. It's supposed to be from the whole team, Toyota—and for a wedding! They'll be expecting something a little better from MSF, don't you think? What else have you got?'

'And why would you need something else?'

'Because we've given these things away for free in the past! They're worth, what—three or four dollars at most?'

Toyota's undeterred. '*Coordenador*,' he says, shaking his head adamantly. 'I do not agree. Why does this price matter? It is the *quality* of this that matters, and the quality of these ones is very good. I am telling you. You must feel it properly to know. How can you know if you do not feel it properly? Feel it!'

Tim ponders the package again for a long moment, mumbling to himself. He unfurls the full length of fabric and turns to me. 'What do you think?'

I shrug, tell him I'm not sure what it is.

'A mosquito net,' he says.

'A what?'

'A mosquito net,' he repeats, straight-faced.

I suppress a laugh. 'Really?'

He nods. 'A nylon mosquito net. Insecticide-impregnated and all, same as those distributed by health agencies across the continent. So, would you be happy to bring it to a wedding?'

I look at the two of them, hesitant to say what I really think. They watch me expectantly.

'Well?' Tim asks. 'You want to bring it?'

I smile uneasily at the pair. Part of me suspects they're joking: two weeks ago I was looking at a hundred-dollar cheeseboard on a friend's bridal registry in Melbourne—one of the cheaper gift sugges-tions; now, a mosquito net? I watch Toyota, expecting him to break out of character at any moment and say, *Ha! As if!* But what if he *is* actually being serious? Who am I then to stand here, on my second day, deriding the apparent level of need in this country—a nation with the highest infant mortality rate on earth?

So I shrug. Again. No idea what to say. No idea even what to think, which has been exactly the problem since I arrived: I don't even have to walk the ten metres over the road to the hospital in order to feel lost, overwhelmed, out of my depth. I feel it everywhere I go. Like right here, standing in this tent, as I grapple with the absurdity—the reality!—that a mosquito net may in fact be a feasible wedding gift.

As for things in the hospital? Therein, my real source of fear. People are everywhere in there. In beds, under beds, across beds, between beds, in front of beds. Even five to a bed, or on the floor of those two tents, the large white ones pitched in the back courtyard. Others just sit outside, on the dirt that surrounds the tin-roofed wards. Who's a patient, who's a brother? I can't tell. Everyone looks feverish in this heat. Everyone looks a little on the skinny side to me. Everyone needs *something*.

'Are all these people your family?' I asked a woman on the ward this morning.

'Yes,' the answer. Her mother, her daughter, her three sisters—all on the one bed.

'And these four people next to it? On the floor?'

No—they were the neighbours of the patient in bed eight, the woman with some strange fever. They were here to wish her well, to cook and care for her. Their village was a two-day walk from here, so they wanted to please stay with her a while.

'And that man? Why is he sitting in a tent, outside?'

'Oh, he is always there,' said one of the health workers. 'He has been here since the hospital opened four years ago. He came when the war finished. We think he was injured in the fighting—injured in the head—but we cannot know because he only says "Toto", so that is what we call him. Try it, Doctor—ask him anything. Try! You will see it. He will only say: "Toto".'

I tried. He did.

And then there was this morning's wake-up call. An urgent summons to the hospital, and a glaring, screaming reminder that this is all going to be unlike anything I've experienced.

I'd not yet fallen asleep when I first heard the footsteps. Was still lying under my own mosquito net and a mountain of musty blankets, hiding from the harsh chill of these savannah nights—something I'd not expected—while contemplating the hundred-and-sixty-something days ahead. Then, approaching footsteps. 'Doctor?' called a voice. I fumbled for my torch. The firm bang of a fist on my tin door followed; a ricochet of echoes around the dense silence of my spartan brick room.

'*Sim?*'—Yes?

'*Emergencia!*'

Jesus, no need for coffee because there can't possibly be a more powerful stimulant in the world than that single word. I was up in a flash, heart thumping as I knocked over my bedside candle, scrambled to pull on yesterday's clothes and jogged quickly to the hospital. No—I ran back: I'd forgotten my stethoscope. A sprint back to the hospital. No—back again: I needed the other doctor. I can't go anywhere without Tim or the other doctor because I don't know where anything is or how to—

'Sofia? Hospital! Quickly!'

She was on her way.

A jog, but not too fast this time because I didn't want to get there long before Sofia. Out the front of our living compound, straight across the dirt road to the hospital entrance not ten metres away where a wooden cart stood hitched to the fence post near the front gate. The animals were still panting. The patient's transport? *This is how people get to the hospital?*

I ran past the oxen, across the hospital's sandy front yard and into the first room, where a small battery-powered lamp threw a gloomy light at the brick walls. A group of people were lifting a man onto the single assessment table—three men and two women that I could see, but I still don't know who actually works here and who doesn't because there're fifty-something people working in this hospital for MSF, another fifty working outside of it. Far too many to remember but I'll need to figure it all out before Sofia leaves this place on Monday.

'We don't know what happened,' said one of them as I ran over. The beam of my headlamp zigzagged across the patient as I tried to make a quick assessment. He was a middle-aged African man, drowsy and dehydrated, numerous lacerations on his face and forearms. His clothes were tattered, stiff with dried blood. The injuries were at least a day or two old and the distinctive smell of infected flesh filled the room. He urgently needed fluids and antibiotics.

'Let's give him—' I began, but I still didn't know what drugs we had here. Or where we kept them. 'You—please, an IV line,' I tried.

'Sorry?'

'An IV line,' I repeated.

'Uh—'

Sofia ran in. Glanced over quickly and assembled some equipment from the cupboard, then directed one of the women to insert the IV. We opened the man's shirt to examine him properly. 'What happened to him?' she asked. 'Anyone know what happened?'

The Angolan nurse couldn't find a good vein for a needle. I knelt beside her to search for a spot on his forearm that was neither cut nor infected—a difficult proposition given his injuries. We tried. Fumbled. Tried again and got it.

'Someone—please,' repeated Sofia. 'I need to know what happened.'

'We cannot be sure,' said an elderly African man behind us. 'We do not know what happened,' he said, stepping forward and removing his old cowboy hat, apologising for the intrusion. An old business jacket and trousers hung loosely from his body, a torn blue shirt showing beneath. No shoes. 'We found him outside of town. We were getting firewood outside Rivungu village, far from here, and we saw something move near the track. I thought it was an animal. It was very slow and made no sound. My son said maybe we could get meat so he got down, but I was worried. But when he got closer he called to me and said it was a man.'

The first bag of IV fluid went up but the patient still lay with eyes closed, breathing softly. Sofia tried to rouse him. 'Sir?' She touched his chest gently. 'Can you open your eyes?'

Only a mumble.

The man with the hat apologised again. 'Can I say, he slept in the cart. He slept all the time. We tried to give him a little water because he looked very weak, but otherwise we did not disturb him. We just came straight to Mavinga. But he did not tell us what happened.'

We ran the fluids in as fast as possible, and under the light of my headlamp Sofia and I examined the wounds more closely. His injuries were numerous, concentrated around his head and upper limbs. Worst were a series of lacerations above his right eye and along both forearms, a few going deep into muscle. Several puncture wounds, too—small, as if he'd been stabbed with something round, not just slashed—although fortunately sparing his abdomen and chest.

'Someone get a vial of morphine,' said Sophia. 'Here, take my key. And get antibiotics.'

We hung the second bag of fluids and squeezed it in fast. Next, IV dextrose to raise his blood sugar level. The two cart-drivers stood close by, concerned and apologising all the time. 'We came as fast as we could,' said the younger man. 'We are sorry—we tried to bring him here faster, but it took most of the night. That road is very bad. There was a lot of sand, and the moon was with us for only some of the time.'

The first nurse returned with the drugs and Sofia sent her back to find an anti-tetanus dose in the fridge of our living compound. Gradually, the man's conscious state improved and with help he was able to lift his head a little to sip water. 'What happened?' we asked again, but he only mumbled softly.

'You must tell us,' said the health worker. 'We need to know so we can tell the police. This, what has been done to you—it is terrible.'

The patient shook his head and said something about it being okay, no police.

'But who did this?'

He took his time. Another sip of water, then the words he whispered brought the room to a halt.

'A leopard.'

Everyone paused.

'A *leopard*?'

'Yes.'

'You sure?'

A nod.

'In *town*?'

'Outside,' he whispered. 'Away from Rivungu village. To the north.'

Murmurs rippled through the room.

'But he could attack again!' cried the nurse with the syringe. 'He will come back! This hasn't happened for years—we must let the police know to hunt him.'

The patient shook his head. 'No,' he whispered. 'It is okay.'

'How?' asked the younger man from the cart. 'Did you injure it?'

The patient asked for another sip of water. The nurse filled a cup from the yellow jerry can beside the desk and helped him drink, propping him up gently on the foam mattress. 'It happened in the dark,' he began, slowly. 'I did not know . . . I did not see it coming. It was very quick. I covered myself . . . here, my arms, like this, over my face . . . but it carried on.' He stopped to take another sip of water and shut his eyes, then described the hissing of the animal as the attack continued, saying that he didn't know how long it all went on for—one minute, maybe fifteen. At some point he'd managed to get free. 'It must have gone,' he said. 'I do not know why, because before it was angry, very strong . . . But I am lucky—I found my knife. I found it before he came back.' Another long pause. No movement in the room as everyone stood frozen. 'I was frightened,' he continued, in time. 'I pushed this other arm, here, into him when he came. Into his face. I tried to keep him from my eyes, my neck . . . With my free arm I got it. Many times . . . Anywhere.'

The Angolans looked on in disbelief.

'With your knife?' asked the younger man. 'Got him with the knife?'

A nod.

'It is dead?'

Another nod.

'You sure? Can you be *sure*?'

'Yes.'

'You saw the body?'

He nodded again. We'd have hoisted this man—this real-life Rambo!—into the air in celebration had he been in any state for it, but for the moment he needed treatment. Someone was going to have to debride and explore the wounds, trim away the dead, infected tissue at the edges of the lacerations, clean them, and make sure there were no deeper collections of pus. In the meantime we gave him antibiotics and the nurse wiped his wounds with antiseptic. Sofia drew up a dose of morphine to give in anticipation of further treatment, but the patient shook his head.

'It's only for the pain,' she explained. 'You'll feel better for it, then we can clean those wounds properly.'

'Thank you,' he said, 'but no. It has been two days already. Two days since I was attacked. I have been travelling since then . . . walking, lying in the bush, and now the pain is gone. I do not need that medicine.'

• • •

So began my first full morning, just hours ago. But for the moment we're still debating the net. Still discussing the pros and cons of cheap mesh, although the conversation—as with every other exchange I've had out here—is in truth clumsier, far more circuitous, because it requires another expat to interpret for me: I can't speak Portuguese. It's no small issue. None of the Angolans I've met here speak English, and there's no translator for hire. So for now Tim interprets, I stare confusedly, and Toyota waits patiently. Tim insists that we need to find something special to bring, and Toyota laughs.

'*Aqui?*'—Here?—he asks. '*Eh!* Look around!'

We do. It's a valid point. Suggestions to bring chocolate—we have a modest supply in the expat compound beside this tent—are met with equal disapproval. 'You cannot bring something that many people have never seen,' Toyota says, 'and expect that the couple can keep this for themselves.'

'Why not give money?' I ask.

'Even worse!' laughs Toyota. 'This they will spend on little things. Things like soap and salt, or maybe batteries for a torch. They will not save this money. And what special thing, as you say you would like to give, can they buy with it? You have seen our market?'

I have. It's another valid point. Donated clothes and the goods Toyota mentioned account for most wares, so we continue to go in circles. Tim asks Toyota what he'd think if we arrived at *his* next wedding with only this net to give on behalf of the team, which clearly catches him off guard.

'This?' asks Toyota. 'For me?' He pauses, dissolving suddenly into laughter. Big whoops convulse his body, and whether he's laughing with us or at us I can't tell, but it's so utterly infectious that we both succumb anyway. His teeth are perfect; perfect white teeth in a chiselled face, and his skin, flawless, has the complexion of everyone here—a colour utterly dark, blacker than black coffee. His body seems designed for laughing, and when he does it's so loud and all-consuming and high-pitched and totally unexpected from his muscled physique that I don't even know why we started anymore but we carry on anyway, just swept up with him. And this, I suspect, is the difficulty with Toyota: his face, although handsome, is a thoroughly mischievous one. It seems impossible to take what he says seriously.

'Now listen,' says Toyota, regaining his composure. 'We can talk all afternoon like this, but I am serious about the mosquito net. I do not joke about it. It is a good gift for many reasons. For one, it will last them many years—these things do not fall apart. And even more important, it will protect them from malaria. And tell me, Doctor, is this not what we are all about? Keeping people healthy?'

I can't argue.

'So this is a gift that could even save their lives, this net that you laugh at?'

'Well—'

'It is! But I will tell you another truth,' he says, motioning us closer. He lowers his voice to near-whisper as his eyes sparkle, giggling excitedly in anticipation of his own point. We're now three boys huddled together in a locker room. 'Tell me this, you two,' he begins. 'Where do people make love?'

We stare blankly at him.

'It is in their beds, yes?' he prompts.

We agree.

'Of course it is! And now tell me this: where does this mosquito net hang?'

We shrug, unsure of his point.

'Over the bed!' he answers.

I still can't see what he's getting at. Neither can Tim.

'So imagine!' enthuses Toyota. 'Imagine that when they are making love—tonight, tomorrow, all the days after this—it will be under this net. Under *our* gift. And for years to come, all of us with MSF here in Mavinga—we will be in their hearts whenever this couple make love!'

And so, only hours later, sticking closely to the two roads we're cleared to use, we make our way to the wedding. With mosquito net in hand. And yet again I'm forced to concede how thoroughly lost I am. How am I to relate to, let alone live with, people from such a different world? How am I to supervise this entire hospital—this *only* hospital—on my own? And what exactly did I imagine I was going to achieve coming here, anyway? All questions that seemed infinitely easier to answer two days ago. But for the moment we arrive at the wedding venue itself; and here, I'm at last afforded some respite from these bigger issues by a more pressing one: the entire congregation—bride, groom, minister and a hundred guests—are waiting patiently, the wedding ceremony having been delayed, because we're late.

2. THE FIRST DANCE

Five kinds of people end up in places like Mavinga, the saying goes. The five Ms: Medics, Missionaries, Mercenaries, Misfits and Madmen—sometimes even a few categories in the same person. Me? I'll take Medic, if only by exclusion. As for *Mad*, not yet, although we'll see what six months on call in Angola will do. Ditto *Misfit*. And as for *Missionary* or *Mercenary*? Not in any sane applications of the words.

It's not quite clear to me how I've ended up volunteering, though. I can't recall any precise moment of decision-making. But there is history. Born during the latter years of the apartheid era, I spent the first fourteen years of my life in Cape Town, South Africa; a privileged middle-class childhood, albeit one largely cocooned from the rest of my country by race laws and attendant *Whites Only* signs. The wider realities of the region did occasionally reveal themselves to me, however, such as when the sprawling shanty-towns—oceans of poverty in which millions of my fellow countrymen drowned, their homes cobbled together from scavenged materials—blurred past our car window. But these were only ever fleeting objects of curiosity as we travelled fast between two wealthy areas, which was largely my experience of Africa in those days: a series of glimpsed images, of momentary encounters and half-baked impressions that seemed deeply contradictory.

The *real* Africa was in my mind a pitiful place, a thing to be mourned. 'Don't you dare leave those vegetables on your plate,' my grandmother would reprimand me, 'because there are children starving all over this continent!' Yet equally it seemed a place to be feared, avoided. Reports of violence filled the daily newspapers, while high-walled compounds and private security companies were the norm in many white areas. Nothing like life for those in the poorer black townships, though. Political unrest and police crackdowns resulted in numerous deaths there during those years, and gang-related crime was rampant; I'd heard it said that a girl growing up in these areas had a statistically greater chance of being raped than of learning to read.

But none of this directly affected my young life. For the most part such things happened *there*—outside the cities, in the townships, several of which could be seen from the sports fields of my school on a clear day but were as foreign to me as the *favelas* of Brazil. I never had black friends who could share their stories, and a state-controlled media and whites-only education system perpetuated my ignorance to a degree. Maybe I'm just making excuses; I did see street kids, ragged throngs of them begging in the city centre, or huddled from the cold of Cape winter mornings beneath sheets of newspaper, but I took this to be an inescapable fact of life on the continent. My overriding recollection of Africa is rather its profound appeal: stories of a childhood in rural Africa from my great-grandmother, whose two stuffed, mounted lions looked on from the corner of her lounge; hiking for weeks with my father along the rugged southern African coast, baboons climbing down the rock faces to rifle through our campsite for food; a family safari in Zululand, not far to the east of my grandfather's farm, with leopards well-fed and at a safe distance; and the gentle nature and easy laugh of the few black Africans I did meet.

Amid increasing political tensions in the early 1990s, my family migrated to Australia, where I went on to study medicine. It was the obvious career decision for a seventeen-year-old who'd been fascinated by the surgical procedures of the nearby vet, and who harboured a vague notion of 'helping'—maybe even of returning to Africa. But it wasn't until my university years that I had my first close-up, if inadvertent, encounters with poverty.

Backpacking with borrowed money during lengthy semester breaks, I travelled widely. In Kathmandu streets, I came across leprosy sufferers who begged from pitifully makeshift wheelchairs—wooden trays fitted with furniture coasters—on my way to trek in the Himalayas. En route to tropical beaches, I met children and elderly people working the busy intersections of South American cities, selling rolls of toilet paper, individual boiled sweets, even just a lone apple; in a town in the Andes I chatted with a young woman selling string by the metre to support her unwell mother. Health care was too expensive for them to access, she told me: the medication they needed would cost thirty dollars a month. What pensions would be available for these people to claim? What access to health care? Another day, a group of street children approached me, selling finger puppets. 'But mister,' replied one little girl when I evasively showed her the two I'd previously purchased, 'you have eight more fingers. You can buy eight more!'

And the only common denominators I could see in all this were opportunity and circumstance. That I was a medical student who spent time backpacking had more to do with the chance events of my birthplace and parents than any great effort or brilliance on my part: it could have been me staring into that car window from the edge of a shanty-town. So there was no religious compulsion, family pressure or career disillusionment behind my decision to volunteer. It wasn't about escapism, though I'll admit that the travel and cultural aspects of working in less-developed contexts were far from a deterrent. But I wanted to help. Or at least try, in some capacity.

Embarking on a whirlwind tour of duty in Australian hospitals after graduation, I gained as broad a range of medical experience as I could, rotating through various paediatric, obstetric, surgical, medical and emergency departments. After two years, I flew to Peru to study for a diploma in tropical medicine. A short stint volunteering in a clinic in Thailand followed—a brief but immensely rewarding experience. Mornings were filled by lengthy rounds in open-walled wards, treating Burmese refugees suffering from malaria, TB and HIV/AIDS, among other conditions. Many had crossed the border just to seek health care, fleeing ethnic persecution under a military regime that allocated only forty cents to each person in the annual health budget. In the afternoons I gave teaching sessions to the health workers, themselves Burmese refugees, who sat cross-legged for hours as I drew hearts and kidneys on the whiteboard, explaining the basics they'd never learned. And in the evenings I cycled past rice paddies to my teak guesthouse, where the neighbours were saffron-robed Buddhist monks, whose saffron-coloured laundry chequered the whitewashed monastery walls on sunny afternoons. Everything about the experience appealed to me, and I was sold. This work, I decided, was what I wanted to do with my life.

As for Angola? The position was the first to be proposed by MSF in the months following my application. It came at a good time; a new doctor had arrived at the Thai clinic, and the year I'd taken off for volunteer work was already halfway gone. Not knowing anything about Angola, though—such as where it was on a map—I called my parents.

'The irony . . .' Mum sobbed. 'I mean, we migrate from southern Africa, end up in Australia . . . We have every opportunity here, every-thing! Landed with our bums in the butter, as your grandma used to say, and now you want to go back to the region? And to Angola of all places? Good heavens, child . . . *Angola*? Speak to your father about this . . .' At which, a couple of octaves lower and with a thicker accent on a faulty cordless phone—

'*Ja*, hello? What's he . . . *Angola*? Shit! You know that I was there, don't you? You know I got sent to the border there during their war, just on the Namibian side?'

This I only vaguely recalled. Dad's stories of his conscription into the South African Defence Force seemed to revolve more around flipping truck tyres around compounds, dressed in full combat attire—punishment for having disrespected an officer, he'd joked—rather than any tales of battle per se, but by now there was again sobbing on the other phone because Mum had just remembered a high school friend.

'Cliff! Oh my God . . . you know Cliffie was shot there? He was so young, such a nice guy . . . Shot dead near the border. Somewhere in the south, I think . . .'

—so I decided not to disclose that my posting was in fact near the border, and in the south, too. But, their initial shock aside, my parents were unfailingly supportive.

'Just make sure you know *exactly* what you're getting into,' Dad cautioned.

Background reading revealed nothing reassuring: Angola had only recently emerged from a long, catastrophic, twenty-seven-year civil war. Images of Princess Diana touring minefields came up frequently during any internet search, outnumbered only by pictures of amputees and bombed-out buildings. Descriptions of the conflict and its aftermath were frightening. Far from any notions of a war with clear objectives and established fronts, a soldier recalled the confusion, as detailed in a book I came across, Ryszard Kapuscinski's *Another Day of Life*: 'You can travel the whole country and come back alive,' he'd said, 'or you can die a metre from where you're standing. There are no principles, no methods . . . Nobody knows where they really stand.'

The conflict began as an unfortunately common scenario of the era: a post-colonial scramble for the control of a newly autonomous country. Following Angola's independence from Portugal in 1975, several armed liberation groups, previously united in their struggle against the colonial government, turned immediately on each other. Capitals were declared in different parts of the country, and fighting erupted; no one was going to relinquish control of this vast, diamond- and oil-rich nation. Two groups eventually emerged as the major protagonists: UNITA (The National Union for the Total Independence of Angola), and the Marxist MPLA (The People's Movement for the Liberation of Angola), with other countries weighing in. The Soviet Union and Cuba supported the Marxist MPLA, the Cubans in particular sending tens of thousands of troops, while South Africa and the USA supported the opposing UNITA forces; these were, after all, Cold War years. And in the meantime, vast diamond and oil reserves helped fund the conflict's perpetuation as foreign companies continued to trade with the belligerents.

Only in 2002 did the war end, following the assassination of the UNITA leader. By this time roughly a million people had died, four million had been displaced, and landmines littered thousands of square kilometres of roads and farms. Infrastructure and health care were almost nonexistent; an average parent of the day could have expected one in three of their children to die from malnutrition or disease.

This was the disaster into which MSF and other aid groups arrived to provide assistance, and Mavinga, the town I'd been offered a post in, was reputedly one of the worst affected areas. It had now been four years since the ceasefire although it sounded as if little progress had been made in town. Health care was still provided solely by MSF, and landmines remained problematic. There'd be no possibility of transferring patients, I was told, nor any prospect of moving outside our small security perimeter. Adding to the pitch, MSF were also dealing with a cholera outbreak along the coast, and an Ebola-like virus was killing more than ninety per cent of infected patients in the far north of the country. But, as I read on, with none of this particularly reassuring, it became clear anyway that there was no decision to make. I was in from the start. Because really, fuck it: one could talk about maybe trying to help, of doing something like this in the coming years—when the loans are paid off, when the Master's degree is under the belt, or when a decent house deposit has been saved—and never actually make it happen. Now was the time. I was ready to roll up my sleeves.

Then I told my girlfriend.

And so, eight flights, two briefings, three continents and several teary goodbyes after leaving Australia, I sat, a single man, immersed in the intoxicating fumes of aviation gas and denial, bumping around in a charter plane. With no idea that the next day I'd be discussing the virtues of mosquito nets. And as we headed due east, leaving the Atlantic coast of West Africa behind us, I tried to correlate what I'd read with what I could see. It wasn't so easy—the absence of landmarks mandated a little imagination. So I gazed to the right, due south across dry plains, and tried to picture my father standing sentry at a military compound on the nearby Namibian border almost twenty years ago. I looked to the left, due north, and tried to imagine the Congo River snaking past (the setting for Joseph Conrad's famous novella, *Heart Of Darkness*, in which Kurtz speaks of 'The horror! The horror!') where it forms part of Angola's border with the Democratic Republic of Congo. There was little chance of seeing the river, though—it was well over a thousand kilometres away. Ahead? Only scrub. Flatness. *Nothing*. Zambia lay somewhere beyond all that, but below us it was just more of the same: an endless khaki plain, with gnarled trees and knotty vegetation forming a balding covering that thinned as we headed towards the south-east corner of the country. An occasional sandy road was visible, but I could see no other evidence of settlement. Difficult then to comprehend that a war took place for three decades down there, because from above it looked so serene.

We began descending.

'Already?' I asked the pilot.

He nodded.

'Where to?'

He gestured towards the horizon.

'But where's the town?'

He laughed. 'There—'

Jesus, it's nothing! Just mud huts! We descended quickly and soon made a low pass to check the dirt runway, a crowd of black faces gathering to watch all this, and as we came around and lined up to land I was forced to concede that despite my previous bluster regarding certainties, just getting on with it, I was actually quite nervous all of a sudden. I could see 'grids' cut into the bush around town—paths for the de-mining teams, the pilot explained—and there was the hospital, just beside the runway, and it was far bigger than what I expected, this town far smaller, and *My God* I was actually getting scared and maybe I wasn't ready for this after all. And of all the things I could think of at that moment—the violence in South Africa, for example, and whether or not as a white man I was going to be safe in the middle of this war-torn piece of Africa—what was bizarrely worrying me most was the note I had seen in the aviation office at the hangar where we boarded the plane; the note that was written in bold red on the *Important Information* whiteboard of the pilot's office. The words had caught my attention as the pilot stood metres away on a stepladder, fuelling the plane himself, the other end of the rubber hose dangling into a drum of avgas; it was a note that made my palms sweat and heart pound and head realise more than any of the documents I'd read that this was going to be another *world*, because really, where else would such words constitute the most vital piece of information for the pilot?

Mavinga—airstrip dry. Watch for stray dog.

• • •

If the wedding gift seemed unusual, the venue is no less so: a large metal shed, one of three, built to temporarily house refugees returning after the war. It's one of only a dozen buildings in town not made from mud. A dozen *intact* buildings, that is. The foundations of a few brick structures still peer from the bush in places, but they're bombed out, shelled, damaged beyond repair. A loose sprawl of huts accounts for most of what I see, their stick frames protruding like ribs through an emaciated mud-and-dung skin. The landscape—flat, dry, brown but for pockets of yellow grass and a defiantly green tree here and there—is broken only by a shallow river meandering past the southern end of town, along which women collect water and lethargic cattle graze. Gone, any resemblance to the Africa I'd known as a child.

We arrive at the shed door. All six of us volunteers—Andrea, a Swiss-German midwife; Pascal, an Italian logistician; Isabella, an Italian nurse; Sofia, a German doctor; Tim, the Swiss-French co-ordinator; and me. Tim's the one carrying the mosquito net. He gets nudged in first, but he darts straight back out.

'We're late,' he says, looking back confusedly.

'What?'

'Everyone's already in there, standing quietly. Like they're waiting for something.'

'For *us*?' asks Sofia.

This shouldn't be. We'd arrived earlier at the scheduled time— five—only to be confronted by an almost empty shed. Only one person was inside, a man atop a wooden ladder, fixing a length of wiring to the roof. 'Oh yes,' he'd laughed. 'The wedding is here. It is just late!' He'd suggested that we try again later, although exactly when *later* was he couldn't specify. We'd suggested eight. 'Sure,' he'd replied. 'Eight is very good. It should definitely be starting then!'

It's now seven-thirty. Ostensibly early, but a large group of Angolans are standing quietly beyond the entrance. They turn as we put our heads around the corner.

'Hi,' whispers Tim, in Portuguese. 'Don't bother moving—we'll stay here.'

They move. Tim gestures frantically. 'No, no,' he says, 'stay,' but the crowd parts to create a corridor into the centre of the room. We can now see the bridal party, the emcee, the pastor. They see us.

'Oh! *Boa noite!*' exclaims the emcee—Good evening! 'Ladies and gentlemen, it's our *expadriados*! Please welcome them!'

A hundred-and-something faces turn to look.

'Please, come to the front,' calls the emcee. 'We have been waiting for you. We would not want to begin without our friends from the hospital!'

Solemnly, deeply embarrassed, we follow Tim down this impromptu corridor. No one utters a word. Homemade paper-chains and a Fanta beachball dangle from the roof above, coloured fabric from the steel walls ahead. People press in and stare at us, although the fascination is mutual—for me at least. They're remarkably handsome, the Angolans; lean, with strong bodies and equally strong faces, their coffee-complexions accentuated by chiselled jawlines, prominent cheekbones and dark, intense eyes. Definitely no office-type physiques in this room. Many of the younger women are utterly gorgeous, too; curvaceous with beautifully shaped hips, their long limbs slim and toned like an athlete's, although this latter point is no surprise. Every woman I've seen during the day has been either carrying something—children, water, food or wood, often several of these simultaneously—or pounding grain.

We arrive at the centre of the room. A half-dozen plastic tables have been arranged around the bare concrete floor to create the ceremonial area, where the bride and groom are already standing. *Waiting.* Guests crowd closer, the women draped in ornately patterned traditional dresses in an explosion of colours—blues with pinks, reds against greens—their matching headscarves knotted elaborately to one side, although men wear a more eclectic range of Western garb:

trousers with any combination of mismatching shirt, jacket and tie, two noteworthy items being a T-shirt advertising a Dublin plumbing company, and what looks suspiciously like a pair of pyjama pants. Clothes that were undoubtedly once donated.

'Please, our *expadriados*,' says the emcee, who's making far too much of our arrival. 'Come, take your seats!' He leads us to a row of plastic chairs near the front—right next to the bridal party. The ceremony begins immediately.

The bride, who's no older than sixteen, wears a traditional Western gown and is standing before the African pastor, staring ahead nervously. The groom is in his early twenties and wears a neat black suit, appearing equally anxious beside her. I can't imagine where either of them got their outfits from out here. And I'd argue that this girl is far too young to be getting married, definitely too young to even contemplate motherhood and the risks of childbirth, but in a country where the median life expectancy is thirty-nine, and where a woman bears an average of six children, of which two will likely die before their fifth birthday, I imagine that people see little point in waiting.

The pastor speaks for an hour. Only the sound of a petrol generator drones in the background as it powers the bare bulbs above. No singing, no hymns, no laughter; it all seems remarkably austere. Not what I'd imagined of an African wedding. An arranged marriage, perhaps? The bride and groom stare solemnly at the floor and I see no stolen glances, no hand-holding, so maybe it is. But all of a sudden there's applause: the couple are man and wife!

'*Senhoras e Senhores!*'—Ladies and Gentlemen!—cries the emcee, bounding excitedly back to the centre. 'Please, let us congratulate our new couple!'

Enthusiastic cheers follow an awkward kiss.

'And now,' declares the emcee, 'our new couple will dance together. Please let us welcome them!' He leads them to the centre of the shed as onlookers step back, then nods to the DJ in the corner. What follows is a marvel of improvisation: with the flick of a switch and jiggle of a connection, tape player, speakers and car battery unite instantly, unleashing a barrage of crackly sound. A high-pitched wail of a man's voice fills the shed, the lyrics something about a man loving a wom . . .

Jesus, is this . . .?

It is! Mains electricity hasn't made it out here, neither plumbed water, sanitation, telephones, nor a school with a roof—but *this* has? *Michael Bolton?* I'd laugh but the moment is so sincere, the two of them are enjoying their first dance, and maybe this wasn't an arranged marriage after all because now the tension of the ceremony is over they're embracing, they do look to be in love. And maybe Michael Bolton is the newest thing here because I suppose they missed his heyday during the war, missed everything—did they even have weddings at that time? Possibly—but loud music? There's no way. This must surely be new, this celebrating and planning and doing what the rest of the world has been doing for the last three decades, without fear of another raid or conscription, or of starving to death like a thousand other Angolans on each of the worst days, or of being forced into the sexual servitude of a soldier three times your age as many girls were—

'Okay, *Senhoras e Senhores,*' chimes in the emcee over the second verse. 'I would like to ask our special guests to come up here, to join for the first dance!'

There's no way, I think, *there's absolutely no way I'm getting up there to*—but the emcee walks to our table and ushers me up, actually guides me by my elbow to the middle of the floor where he brings over one of the young flower girls to dance with me. And now he fetches my colleagues while a hundred pairs of eyes stare from around the room, fascinated by us foreigners—the only six in the entire region—as we begin to dance.

Michael Bolton finishes, which is fortunate: I'm not sure how to slow-dance with a six-year-old. But for this second song we're blaming it on the boogie with the Jackson Five, so I hold her hands somewhere above her head, below mine, and we step side to side but embarrassingly she does it with more rhythm than I do. Tim nudges me as he bounces past with his partner—a big, voluptuous African aunt of a woman, the first overweight person I've seen in here—and Andrea sashays across the concrete, swept around by our sixty-year-old head of Outpatients, who's really cutting up the floor—straight back, good rhythm, leading well despite his bookish appearance—but the rest of the shed stand transfixed. Children peer from between adults' legs; adults gape; there's nothing left to lose, so I go for broke—I pirouette my partner. The room laughs! She loves it, she giggles delightedly in her white frock and wants to go the other way, so we do. A round of applause this time!

'Okay,' calls the emcee. 'Everyone, on the dance floor!' And now people relax and this wedding is what it should be, and I've forgotten all about the hospital, all about those malnourished children and that leopard-attack survivor this morning, and I'm thrilled and excited to be here, and I imagine that this is what my life as an aid worker will be like from now on: gatherings on the weekends, events with the locals, beers, dinners—

'Fat chance,' laughs Tim, as we take seats at our undecorated plastic table. Fried pork knuckles and a handful of beers have been placed out for us. 'You will be at work most of the time,' he says, 'and at home you will want to kill your colleagues within two months, because it'll soon be just four of us. Sofia's off on Monday and Isabella in a week, and the conversation will quickly run out.'

Pascal and I are unlikely to run out of conversation anytime soon, however. Unlikely to start one either. He speaks Portuguese but no English, I the opposite, so we just clink beers and exchange a few words and laugh. He at least looks to be an amicable guy, bearing no small resemblance to a young Che Guevara. As for Andrea, the new midwife, we seem to get on well, and I suspect she's going to be very popular out here: attractive, easy laugh, and three male colleagues— all of us locked together in a small compound for six months.

Tim's whisked back onto the dance floor. Sofia pulls up a chair beside me, grabs a pork knuckle and tells me I'll settle in quickly— presuming I speak the language. 'How on earth did they send you if you can't speak Portuguese?' she asks, and I tell her that I speak a little Spanish and squeezed in five hurried Portuguese lessons before I left. 'But that's not good enough,' she replies. 'You need to be conversational. What will you do on the wards? Who will translate?'

Questions not lost on me.

'Tell me, Damien,' she asks next. 'Do you have a girlfriend?'

'Until a week ago I did. Now, well . . .'

'Because of this?' she asks. 'Because of this posting?'

'This was the final straw, I guess, but there had been—'

'You will absolutely get back with her!' says Sofia. 'You simply *have* to. Because out here there is little else to think about. You need someone to care about, Damien, a person to email in the evenings, because . . .' and now her eyes mist up, 'because the work out here can be . . .' *God, and now she's flat out crying!* 'It can be difficult,' she says. 'The people, the . . . I'm sorry. Wait—I shouldn't be saying this. I'm just tired . . . A patient of mine died two days ago, from eclampsia. I knew her well, and I've been up a few nights lately . . .'

I look for a tissue but see none. I instead see Tim waving on the dance floor, trying to get our attention as he gestures to the front, pointing to where the bride and groom are opening their small pile of gifts. I'd rather not watch. They're standing together, going through each package, counting out cash when they find it, slowly, meticulously, and soon enough they get to ours. Too late to change it now. *We even put our names on it!* Gently, they peel open the pages of the Italian gossip magazine we used for wrapping, and see the net. They open the plastic and unfurl it, then check the paper. They look again at the net. Check the paper once more, look around at us, and we're all thinking the same thing: *bloody Toyota!* Hopefully the couple will feel differently when they climb under it tonight, though—they fold it neatly enough, salvage the paper, and move on to their last gift.

Another dance, and we soon leave. We thank and congratulate a long line of relatives we've never met, and wave to those swaying to the Afro-Latin beats of *Kisamba* the DJ's found on the radio, hips grinding ever closer under the tangerine orb of that Fanta beachball.

We stroll across the grassless soccer pitch, and as we do I'm forced to contemplate the effectiveness of finding and clearing landmines using trowels. Three thousand have been recovered from town this way—two hundred in just this central square—and walking on it now I wonder how certain they are that they got them all out.

But we survive the crossing. Along the moonlit, sandy main road we wander, talking and laughing, breathing in the smell of wood smoke from the hundreds of cooking fires burning earlier this evening; a camping trip, maybe. *Yes!* That's what this is!—an adventurous weekend away with friends. One where you swap stories as you walk, and can see the night sky through the mortar holes in the town's school building there; where you greet the guard who sits sentry outside your living compound, hunched alone over his fire for the long, cold night, then bury yourself under a pile of musty blankets and fall asleep to candlelight, a teach-yourself-Portuguese book on your lap; and where you get to wake up in a day's time to make sense of, and somehow supervise, the most daunting, heartbreaking place you've ever walked into . . .

3. O NOVO DOCTOR

... because even this first patient after Sofia's departure, just this morning, worries me greatly.

He lies feverish, a halo of sweat darkening the sheets around his young body. His family watch closely; mother and two brothers from where they share his single metal bed, father from the floor where he's spent the night. They watch his chest rising slowly under a sheen of sweat, and they sponge him often with an old cloth. And they do it with such hopeful attention that they don't react to the dozen of us crowding around.

'How was he during the night?' I ask, as the father shifts their belongings for us—pot, enamel bowls, a box of matches.

'The same,' replies one of the health workers. Isabella, the blue-eyed Italian nurse, translates for me. 'He had some diarrhoea this morning, otherwise nothing. His parents say no change. He is not any better.'

'And his fever?'

The health worker flicks through the chart. 'It was down a little during the night,' he says. 'But now it is back up.'

The boy remains deeply comatose, unresponsive to any stimuli. His risk of dying from cerebral malaria, the condition we think he has, is significant. *If* that's what he's suffering from. It's a presumptive diagnosis—a likely one given the incidence of malaria out here—but without further tests we can't be one hundred per cent sure. The blood test that we have here for *falciparum* malaria, a plastic strip that looks and works not unlike a home pregnancy test, was positive in his case, although that in itself doesn't confirm the cause of his coma. Either way, we're treating him for severe malaria; the quinine infusion was started as soon as he arrived last night. I now pull out my tropical medicine handbook to re-check our dosages, making sure we've not forgotten anything. We haven't. We're doing everything—everything that we can do out here, that is, because consider the context: this boy is in *Intensivo*, our 'intensive care ward', which isn't too different from any ordinary brick room. Four single metal beds crowd along one wall, a hazy fibreglass window opposite. His quinine infusion hangs from a nail on an improvised wooden stand, and there will be electricity for lighting for just four hours this evening when Pascal runs the generators. There's little else. No machines, no oxygen, no electronic equipment—just a small cupboard with essential medicines. A little misleading then to call this *Intensivo*, I'd have thought, but the set-up means that patients can be watched more closely; two health workers will be able to concentrate on a maximum of four patients here, as opposed to the eight or more cases in each of the other rooms. Sofia assured me that's a big advantage. And what then of referral to a bigger hospital—like one with oxygen? No chance. The only hospital larger than ours in this province is in the regional capital, Menongue—a run-down, former ivory trading centre that's a two-day journey by road, and where the wards are even more poorly equipped. Flights too are out of the question. The little Cessna that MSF charters to fly us out here is a five- to ten-thousand-dollar round trip, even without medical equipment or nurses on board. There's no guarantee, either, that the family will be able to afford the cost of treatment elsewhere.

So for now we continue with the quinine. And cross our fingers, because we're this boy's only option for medical care. A thought that frightens me.

'His IV bag looks new,' I note. 'Has it just been changed?'

The health worker nods.

'Great. So how much quinine are we giving him through it this morning then?'

He rustles through the patient's papers. Along with eight other health workers, all men, he's one of the *clinicos*—the seniors that work at a level somewhere between a doctor and the *enfermeiras*, the locally trained nurses. He says nothing.

'It's on the drug chart,' I say. 'Manuel, isn't it? Your name? Good! It's on the drug chart from yesterday, Manuel. We wrote it at the top.'

Isabella translates, but Manuel says nothing.

'Does anyone know how much quinine we're giving him?' I ask.

No one replies.

'What about the *enfermeira*? The one who put up this morning's bag? Is she here?'

Again, nothing.

'So how can we be giving him the right dose if no one knows what the right dose is, or how much he's getting right now?'

Silence.

Why no answer? Perhaps I'm misunderstanding the work manner here. Sofia did this, though. She asked them things. I'm also sure she said that the *clinicos* looked after all the infusions and other aspects of treatment, the doctor having only a supervisory role, but we really didn't have long to spend on staffing arrangements during the handover. Seemingly endless files accounted for most of our time together—spreadsheets for drug orders, staff rosters, monthly reports, six-monthly reports, TB treatment registers, vaccine stocks and adverse outcomes reports, among others—so I'm not entirely clear as to the exact set-up on the wards. And maybe these health workers don't understand what I'm asking, because they'd surely know how to give an infusion. *Or would they?* Isabella thinks so, but she's normally in Outpatients.

'So who's supposed to be checking how much quinine we're giving him?' I ask.

Again no one answers.

'Someone must know. Please—this is not easy to set up, this drip. Someone's done it, and very well. They must know the dose.'

An awkwardness is growing but I'm not trying to embarrass anyone. I just need to know that this child is getting the right treatments. Malaria is one of the few tropical illnesses I have reasonable experience with—the clinic in Thailand was rife with it—and the issue now is that quinine is extremely toxic if given in too-high doses. Too little, and the malaria will progress.

'You are checking it, *Novo Doctor*,' says Sergio, the head *clinico* here. He's a short man with closely clipped hair and unusually soft facial features in comparison to those of other locals. *O Novo Doctor*—The New Doctor—is what people have been calling me since my arrival.

'You are checking the infusion,' he says.

'Sorry?'

He chats with Isabella for a moment.

'He says that of course you should be checking this,' she translates, 'because you are the doctor. He says that this is your responsibility. He says that surely this is why MSF sent you, and that you should know this.'

'Hang on, tell him I'm not pointing fingers. Tell him that I'm just trying to work out who does what on the wards. And tell him that I'm still a little confused, because if the *enfermeiras* give the drugs, and the doctor supervises treatment, what exactly is the role of the *clinicos*?'

It's an honest question that's immediately misconstrued. Sergio shakes his head and speaks with the others.

'I think something's getting a little lost in the translation,' Isabella says, winking to me. She adjusts the infusion herself. 'I'm not quite sure, but I think we may be stepping on toes here. Let's just move on for now, hey?'

We do. We review the two other patients in the room—an infant with pneumonia, and a woman receiving a blood transfusion for post-partum anaemia—and step outside.

• • •

The hospital itself is a series of freestanding, single-storey build-ings, dotted around a football pitch–size compound. Some parts are well planned, others an afterthought. Although clean and neat—the exterior of each structure is painted in either soft blues, pale yellows or dusty pinks, a welcome splash of colour against the dreary land-scape—it's likely only a few storms away from collapse.

Walls are sturdy brick, but doors are flimsy and roofing's a problem, the latter a greying, silver patchwork of metal sheeting fixed to a rickety wood-pole frame. Much of the basic structure had been here when MSF first arrived but had required extensive rehabilitation—a task duly carried out, albeit under the assumption that the project was short term. Four years later, it's still seeing three hundred patients admitted to its wards each month, another two thousand filtering through the outpatient rooms. The current plan is for MSF to close it at the end of the year and hand responsibilities for health care over to the town's Administration, who're working on a new hospital about a kilometre up the main road.

We step from *Intensivo* into the rear courtyard. A low sun and calls of *Toto!* greet us; our onomatopoeic resident is up. Clothed in bright red jumper and black pants, he's surveying the passing world from his tent, here in the sandy centre of this quadrangle of inpatient build-ings. The location appears to suit him well. His white canvas home,

MAVINGA COMPOUNDS

HUTS

DONKEYS

AIRSTRIP

LIVING COMPOUND

LATRINE

STORAGE TENT

BEDROOMS

BEDROOMS

MEETING AREA

OFFICE

DINING KITCHEN

SHOWER

ROAD

HOSPITAL COMPOUND

ISOLATION

OPERATING THEATRE

MATERNITY

SURGICAL PROCEDURES

LAB

TENTS

INTENSIVE CARE AND ASSESSMENTS

OUT-PATIENTS

NUTRITION

MAIN WARDS

KITCHEN

along with the identical one beside it—shared permanent residence of a blind albino woman who's riddled with skin cancers, and her demented mother—couldn't possibly be better positioned for people-watching.

Immediately ahead of Toto are the general adult and children's wards, a long, yellow building in front of which people congregate in the afternoons. Looming behind him are *Intensivo* and Outpatients—a single block of rooms that partially separates this space from the hospital's front courtyard, and around which new patients will shortly be queuing. To Toto's left, smoke curls gently from the tin-walled kitchen hut, beside which the malnutrition ward stretches, while to his right, a young mother feeds her infant on the steps of the maternity and delivery wards. All of which places Toto at the epicentre of hospital life. A fact he seems quite happy with, peering ceaselessly from his floppy white door.

The *clinicos* chat with him—

'Morning, Toto. Oh, yes, we are good. And how are you? Very good. Oh yes—it is cold.'

—carrying out something between imaginary conversation and normal dialogue as *Toto's* are called back in appropriately varying tones. There's calling from our right side, too, where Portuguese with a heavy German accent can be heard against the backdrop of periodic moaning: Andrea and the Angolan midwives are coaching a woman through labour. But we pass their pink building, step around Toto, and enter the first room in the long, yellow block at the back of the hospital. The general paediatric ward. And it's now that I brace myself for the inevitable: a punch to the sensory cortex. A wake-up call more powerful than a hundred coffees, and an odour so pungent it literally takes my breath away. The smell of unwashed humanity confined to too small a space.

Sixty or more people lie in this dim hall of a room this morning. Two dozen patients and their attendant relatives, all on or beside the two dozen beds along the walls. Mothers have shut tight the windows and doors overnight in an attempt to stave off the bitter cold, instead locking in the stale air of the crowd—many of whom are suffering from vomiting and diarrhoea. The air is thick, utterly nauseating. Sergio orders the windows to be opened.

People stir as we enter. Some are eating, others chatting, many lying listlessly, but mothers are all up, and breasts of all shapes and sizes have been urged from beneath layers of clothing to feed hungry mouths. Most children appear delighted with the novelty of a new, different *Branco* (white person) in their midst—this short, untanned, shaved-headed specimen—although not in all cases. A handful are frankly upset. Glances their way prompt only fearful moans, with one young boy opting for a more decisive bolt out the door.

'Little Pedro Neto,' begins the *clinico*, as we gather around the first bed. 'He is one year old, from the village of Seixta-Feira. He arrived yesterday. His diagnosis is malaria *moderada*'—moderate, as opposed to severe like the patient in *Intensivo*—'and diarrhoea.'

There's not much to see of little Pedro from here. Light seeps weakly through the few windows, and most of Pedro's face is hidden anyway by a colourful, oversized beanie, his body wrapped in several layers of baggy garments. His carer begins to undress him as we talk, and what's left a couple of minutes later is a pile of garments twice the size of the skinny body they covered. In fact, the dress in general is distinctly more Scandinavian than African in here. Staff too wear thick, warm tops over their lab coats, again in that mishmash of styles that seems to be the rule, with many in woollen hats as well. Patients and carers are often not as warmly dressed. Most wear Western clothes nearing the end of their days: pants that have been repaired and re-sewn, then re-worn and re-repaired with other pieces of fabric; shirts—torn and glued, now stitched to other bits of old shirt; and nylon ski-jackets, fluorescent and gaudy and completely out of place in the African savannah. Footwear is a luxury many do without.

We examine Little Pedro, who appears delighted with all the attention he's getting. No new problems overnight, says Carlos, who's looking after this ward today. Pedro's fever is down and his feeding up, so he'll likely be discharged tomorrow, after the last of his three days of curative artemisinin injections.

'And his mother?' I ask. 'Will she come here before then?'

Carlos looks confused.

'The mother,' I say. '*A mãe*. Where is she?'

Quizzical looks are exchanged among the staff.

'That *is* the mother, *Novo Doctor*,' says Carlos.

'Seriously? It can't be—she looks far too young! That's surely his sister, no?'

'It definitely *is* the mother,' says one of the *enfermeiras*. 'I know her family.'

'Really? How old is she?'

'Fifteen,' the answer.

But I'm right to ask the question. Many children are indeed being looked after by their older siblings here—brothers and sisters aged eleven or twelve—because the mother has stayed at home to look after others. I soon learn to stop asking the same question for the other end of the reproductive spectrum, though. 'Tell the grandmother ...' I begin on two occasions, only to be corrected that the heavily wrinkled, aged-looking woman in front of me is in fact the mother—and a mother in her mid-thirties at that. It appears that marriage followed closely by motherhood in one's mid to late teens, all the while tilling fields, grinding grain and ferrying endless loads under a tropical sun, is a potent accelerant of the ageing process.

For hours we continue like this: I ask questions, Isabella translates, confused looks shoot back. I stop to jot down things to address, and after two hours there's still more than half a hospital to see. But the paediatric cases at least appear straightforward. Chest infections, malaria, diarrhoea—or any combination of the three—account for most admissions, and almost all children appear to be responding well. Where treatment is being given appropriately, that is. What is particularly unusual though is that all those with diarrhoea, essentially the entire ward, have been prescribed an antifungal drug. A relatively safe medication, albeit a strange and entirely unnecessary one.

'We always use it for diarrhoea,' the *clinicos* explain. 'In Mavinga. Always.'

'Why?' I ask.

'Because we give it, and they get better. That's how it is.'

'But have we seen what happens if we don't give it?'

'Why would we do that?' asks Carlos. 'It works.'

'But what infection are we treating with it?'

Sergio sighs loudly. 'So many questions, *Novo Doctor!*' he muses.

'Sorry, Sergio—I'm just trying to understand all this.'

'And yet you have so many new ideas for us?' he says, a clear change in his tone.

'Not at all. I'm just trying to make sure I understand everything. No point me being here if I don't know what we're doing, yes?'

He turns to the others. 'And this is only the first week for *Novo Doctor*,' he notes. 'The very first day! Is every round to be like this, I wonder? Are we to be questioned about *everything*?'

I'd been cautioned about this. They warned me during my briefings in Geneva to avoid the compulsion to rush in and change things, or at least to wait until I had a good understanding of the context before doing so.

I back-pedal. I tell Sergio that he's right, but that I'm not blaming or accusing anyone. 'Many things here are different for me, Sergio. A lot of this is new and confusing, so I please need for you to explain it to me as we go, okay?'

Isabella translates. Chuckles ripple through the room as Sergio adds something quietly.

'What's he saying?' I ask.

'You're not going to like this,' she replies. 'He's saying that of course you're confused. He says this is because you don't speak their language.'

Vacillating somewhere between embarrassment and anger, I take her up on her suggestion of a short break.

. . .

By late morning the sun casts a welcome warmth over the compound. People move outside. Roosters wander in at the front entrance, but our guard shoos the goats away. Security is tight. And the hospital's really starting to come to life now; kids play while women hang colourful squares of laundry along available hospital fence, and a more substantial pall of smoke billows from the kitchen in preparation for lunch. Bath time, too: a young girl's being washed outside the malnutrition ward in a plastic tub, her head a turban of soapy bubbles.

I prefer it out here.

It's now our second break from the ward rounds, a couple of hours since we finished in paediatrics. Since then, I've fielded two requests for annual leave, marvelled at the leopard-attack survivor's progress on the men's ward, winced at the low rumble of a distant detonation by the de-mining team, and been called to the laboratory to ponder a finding.

'You see it?' asked our lab tech, a lanky, middle-aged Angolan. He works in a small room near the front entrance, equipped with only a single microscope and small shelf of supplies.

'See what?'

'The oval thing,' he prompted.

'Oval?'

'Yes.'

'Where?'

'All over. There are many of them.'

What I did see was a kaleidoscope of colours, shapes, and fibres of plant matter, glowing in the sunlight reflected by the microscope's mirror. Could've been modern art, for all I could tell. 'What's the sample?' I asked.

'Stool.'

'Ah.'

'Do you see the egg with the hook?'

'Um . . .'

'It is *Schistosoma*, I think.'

'Oh.'

'Do you agree, *Novo Doctor*? Do you agree that it is this?'

I agreed only to get my pathology book from the office and return after lunch.

For the moment I take a seat with Isabella, below the only tree in the compound, just near the dispensary, and contemplate this growing list of newly discovered roles. It's pleasant out here, a world away from the austerity of the wards, but it's not providing the desired respite. Because even this front courtyard, entered via the crooked gate to our right, a *No Guns* sign tacked above, is unlike anything I've seen. Traditional village, grim medical centre, happy child play-centre, last hope for the desperately poor—it's all of these, everything in between.

Ahead, a few dozen people sit under a large cloth awning, waiting for consultations with one of the four Outpatients *clinicos*. There'll be a hundred such people today. Every other day, too. At the front of this open-air waiting room, two toddlers are suspended loosely in linen harnesses that hang from scales. It looks fun. Just like a big swing, as if hanging there would be enjoyable, but these two aren't buying it. Not in the least. They're screaming loudly in protest; screaming at the rows of people on the log-roll benches in front of them—people with coughs, tumours, leprosy, leg injuries, malaria, and a man with a spine that's bent at improbable angles who's propping himself up with an old tree branch. Screaming at a young man who's clutching his belly with abdominal pain, a symptom that may be caused by schistosomiasis from the river in town, or may be due to any of the other thousand viruses, parasites and bacteria that thrive in this part of the world and that are going to necessitate my doing some serious reading. Screaming too at the boys kicking a half-inflated football near the gate and at the dozen people waiting for malaria tests; and at the two of us, Isabella and me, as their mothers and those on the benches chuckle at the pair's disapproval.

Unhappy little parachutists, caught momentarily in the weighing-tree.

'You were saying?' I ask Isabella. She's been trying to reassure me about things this morning, telling me I'll pick up the Portuguese. I'm going to have to; she leaves in a few days.

'With all that banter between you and Sergio,' she smiles, 'you'll get plenty of conversation practice.'

I ask her if I said something wrong on the rounds.

'Don't worry about it,' she says. 'Sergio gave the previous doctor a hard time as well, especially when she started. He's got quite the reputation around here. I think he's just trying to—what's a nice word?—*assert* himself, to establish his standing in the hospital. And that whole quinine issue was unnecessary. He normally does keep an eye on those things. That was sloppy on their part. But I think he just doesn't like being questioned, especially because you are new. Just give it back to him, though. Sofia did! She really clashed with him for a while.'

As we talk, three older women waiting at Outpatients walk over to us. 'How many children does he have?' the shorter of them wants to know of me, and then—'*Eh!* At his age! Why on earth not?' So I try to explain that this is normal for a twenty-nine year old where I come from, but the Inpatients *clinicos* wave to us; and as we join them and enter the women's ward all levity provided by recent moments is shattered and I feel ill, actually physically ill, because on the first bed is a woman soaked in urine, skeletal, barely—

Is she even alive? I watch her for a moment. She is. *Just.* Her face is a grimace, an unmoving paper-thin mask draped over the severe architecture of her skull. Her eyes, open and unblinking, seem untroubled by the flies gathering at their margin.

'She's been sick for many months,' says the *clinico*, speaking with the husband. 'He just brought her here. She had bad pain in her belly, and she cannot eat. Now the pain is everywhere.'

Her two children sit quietly beside her on the bed, and her husband leans over to gently wipe the flies from those big eyes. It's the saddest sight I've seen. I ask if I can examine her and her eyes turn to me, and the husband gives his permission so we gently pull up her dress and cover her lower half with a blanket. There's no need to really even touch her, though. An obvious mass, a firm fist of tissue, is visible low down in her belly, bulging from the deep concavity between her hipbones. Several smaller knuckles of tissue can be felt nearby, too. It's surely cancer. But whatever the exact condition, she's in the final stages. We can try to keep her comfortable, little more.

I cover up her belly and the husband grabs my hand, smiling warmly. The *clinicos* translate his words from Tchokwe, a local language. 'He says that he's grateful to us for helping her,' says Isabella. 'He says he knows that here she will become strong again. He knows we will fix her here. His family wait for this day.'

He can't really believe this. I ask him to come outside with us so we can speak in private, and in the far corner of the yard I explain that we will help her as best we can. 'But sir,' I add, 'she is already very weak. We can't ignore this.'

He nods, eyes downcast.

I explain that hers is not an illness we can cure. I wait for the translations, give him a few moments, then tell him that I think it's cancer. He's not heard of it before. He studies Isabella's face intently as she clarifies, the *clinicos* interjecting with explanations in his language. I feel awful telling him all this but he needs to understand. She's certainly going to die in the next few days; he needs to be prepared. His children meanwhile hold on to his legs, watching me with big smiles as I talk, fascinated by this white person who's chatting with their father in the yard.

'It's a very serious illness, sir,' I continue. 'A very strong illness. And I don't think that here, in Mavinga, we can possibly fix this. But I promise you that she will be comfortable while she is here.'

He speaks with the *clinicos* and shakes his head. His face softens and he grabs my hand between his, looks at me with eyes that scream hope. 'That is why we brought her here,' he says. 'We know you can help her. God has led us here, and God will show you. She will get better—she will be strong!'

What to say? Maybe I'm not saying the right things. I ask Isabella how they approach such things here, but she agrees: tell him we'll keep her comfortable. No false promises. So I try to explain that her recovery is out of our hands, but he excuses himself while the others begin to translate. 'I must be with her,' he says, and walks back inside.

I stay where I am. I'm not entirely clear if I've done the right thing. I'd have said the same at home, but one doesn't see people in this advanced state who don't already have a diagnosis, or at least some understanding of the nature of their illness. One of the senior *clinicos* steps forward as I talk with Isabella.

'I can operate,' he says.

'Sorry?'

'I can operate on her,' he repeats. Roberto's his name. He's a lean Angolan man, a good four inches taller than me. Sofia's told me much about him. He's the closest thing we have to a surgeon here—a health worker, trained in field hospitals by military surgeons during the war, who's proficient with limb amputations and less so with emergency laparotomies. But it was stressed to me that he's not a doctor. And it was made clear that he'd likely pressure me to operate, but that he was to perform only emergency surgeries—and only with my permission. Looking now at his imposing frame, telling him what he can and can't do seems somewhat hypothetical.

'I can take out the mass,' says Roberto.

'That whole thing?'

'Yes. This afternoon. Or tomorrow. When you're ready.'

I look at Isabella. 'Is he serious?' I ask. She looks at me uneasily, shakes her head and looks back at Roberto. His expression suggests he very much is.

'The husband wants us to help her, yes?' he says. 'So what then is your plan?'

'I'm not sure if there's much we can do, Roberto. There's no way she will survive an anaesthetic in her condition—not in America, not in my country, definitely not here. She's far too weak. And that cancer, or whatever her illness is—it's surely spread. We won't be able to cure her.'

'She is not in your country!' says Sergio, stepping forward. 'Or in America. She is in *Mavinga*. Do not compare us.'

I'm speechless. *Do these guys really think an operation is feasible?*

'And this nice family,' says Roberto. 'She has young children—did you not see them? How can you just do nothing? She will certainly die without this surgery. And yes, with the surgery she may die too, this is a possibility, but how can we not do something? How can you not at least *try*? Let us talk with the husband—let us see what he wants. But I tell you now, he will ask us to operate.'

I'm lost. No one back home would consider such a plan. *Surely!* Is this how they do things here? Maybe the husband would rather she died during surgery being given a last fighting chance; perhaps to just palliate patients out here is to admit defeat, regarded as weak. Un-African, even. Is it an insult to the husband if we don't operate, given that he's carried her here with their two children in tow? I have no idea. I'll call the medical advisor in Geneva this afternoon, but right now there's still other wards to see—not least those malnourished children. I tell the *clinicos* my plan and turn to head back to the wards.

'*Novo Doctor!*' Roberto calls out, walking towards me. I stop and turn back. He looks like a military commander as he strides towards me. A man's man, for sure. Am I really about to get involved in a stand-off with the local staff? *On day one?* And how am I meant to be the 'boss' out here, anyway? These guys are mostly ten to thirty years older than me, yet technically I'm the more qualified. I'd not expected any of this. I'd rather imagined arriving and just getting on with seeing patients, and that on at least some level people would be grateful for my having come here; that I'd learn from them, they from me, and in the process we'd all work as a happy team . . .

But this—?

'Yes, Roberto?'

'We are not finished talking,' he says, piercing brown eyes staring through me. 'You must not forget something very important,' he warns, voice calm, his face one of annoyance. 'Do not forget that you are very young, and I am sure have no experience in Africa.'

'Roberto—'

'Am I correct?'

I can think of nothing to say. I look away, watch patients queuing with bowls in hand for a serving of maize and beans from the kitchen nearby.

'We are from here,' he continues sternly. 'This is our home, and these are our people. *Our* patients. We all have worked here a long time. For years, even during the war. Long before MSF came here, we were looking after patients. And you? You have been here what—not even a week? You have only just arrived! You know nothing about us, about our medicine—nothing even of our language! You need to remember these things, *Novo Doctor*. Remember all of them when you are in this hospital, trying to tell us how we should manage our people, what drugs we should use, when we can operate on them. And when you do—when you understand and respect these things— maybe *then* we can work together properly.'

I stand, frozen, in the middle of the yard. He walks off with the others.

I've got no idea where to begin.

4. CONFUSÃO

The week grinds on in the hospital. More sick patients, more debates over management, and there's no point in heading to our living compound in search of any comforts. I find myself having to bolt at times for the shed in the far corner of our living area, just near the fence, in what's becoming somewhat of a routine. The flies whoosh past as I open the door, no doubt themselves keen to escape the smell in this little room. A plastic grate with a hole in the middle is its sum total of fittings, the outline of two feet on either side prompting confused users what to do. But I already know: *Squat. Squeeze. Flee.* You really don't want to stick around in here.

I'll get used to the latrine, Tim assured me, but he also said that our compound is one of the better MSF ones around. I'm yet to be convinced. Our bedrooms—cold, simple brick spaces—are furnished with only a metal hospital bed and small shelf, arranged along the two far sides of a dusty courtyard. Mine, to the left, has the dual luxuries of backing onto the logistics area—site of the recent wedding gift debate, and where our guard slaughtered a goat for the cook two nights ago—and of providing sweeping views towards this latrine. A dining room accounts for our communal space, just across from my bedroom, beside which a cold shower has been set up in a shed.

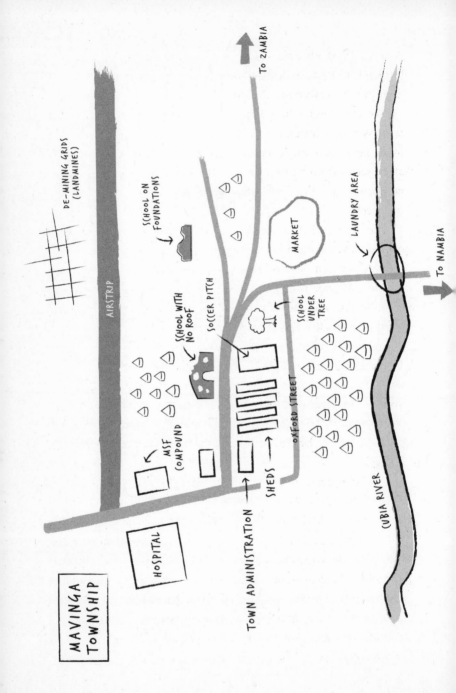

A garage-sized office block takes up the fourth side of the yard. As for our kitchen? Best avoided. So how we're going to survive the next six months in here, with just the four of us for company, I can't be sure.

Nor can I be sure how we're to survive *outside* the compound. In fairness I can't imagine a more authentic African experience than living here; there *are* redeeming features. Problem is that they can all be seen within a fifteen-minute walk—the limits of our security perimeter—and I've done so numerous times. Already, in only this first week.

The airstrip is our northernmost boundary, just behind the compounds, and the river our southernmost, about a kilometre away. Midway between these is the sandy main road—the only safe path we can use, aside from the airstrip and a short track to the water's edge. To the west, the main road curves between our hospital and expat compounds, then crosses the airstrip and continues north to the provincial capital of Menongue, about two days' drive away. To the east it flees straight for Zambia; the kilometre of this east–west stretch, between our hospital and the large tree that marks the limit of our perimeter, is the town centre—a barren cluster of two peach-coloured Administration buildings, the grassless football pitch, three metal sheds, and a handful of other buildings in various states of decay.

Our boundaries are absolute, imposed by MSF in Geneva, but at a glance seem over-zealous: locals appear to wander everywhere, and only to the north of the airstrip have I seen any of the red tape and '*Perigro, Minas!*'—Danger, Mines!—signs that mark uncleared fields. That said, I'm unlikely to go exploring. Photographs on our laptop show the aftermath of an accident four years ago, when an MSF LandCruiser struck an anti-tank mine on a road just outside town. Seven occupants were killed, pieces of the car flung high into nearby trees. And if that's not deterrent enough, the poster on one of our wards is: *How to exercise your stump following a limb amputation.*

So what then of any 'redeeming features'? They do exist. One need only get up a little earlier, or wait until evening, to encounter them. Times when Mavinga reveals her softer side.

Hours after confused roosters commence their ill-timed calls, a red toffee-apple of a sun rises and beams down the length of the east–west main road, flinging long shadows behind the groups of children heading to school. Hand in hand, wearing tops that are either far too long or not nearly long enough (an occasional patch of belly smiles through torn fabrics here and there) children walk with friends or younger siblings as smoke curls from cooking fires in dusty front yards. What I'd always imagined was an exaggerated cliché of African people, that they sing beautifully while going about mundane activities, is not so, here. They *do* sing—and beautifully. All the children. And even the soldiers, carrying out their morning drills on the far side of the airstrip, just hours after they were last heard having drunken brawls in their distant barracks.

By the time the sun climbs a little and burns off its scarlet hues, the wooden benches at Outpatients will be full. My next ten hours will be spoken for. Meanwhile, children will have set down their blue plastic chairs—it's bring-your-own furniture at school here—in one of the several makeshift classrooms, either the building with no roof, just opposite the wedding venue, or beneath one of the few trees, nearer the soccer pitch. Women will be hard at work. With goods balanced upon the head and a baby most likely swaddled to their back, they'll be filling a bucket with water or collecting firewood on the outskirts, or attending the ramshackle collection of stalls at the market, or perhaps washing their laundry at the river, where cattle will by now be being driven across the knee-deep waters by boys equipped with sticks. As for the men, I'm yet to work out what they do.

So I do my best to get up a little earlier. And the four of us will certainly wander into town sometime after work; sometime after the sun's dragged itself across this cloudless vault of a sky, slid behind the cooking fires at the opposite end of town, and resumed its deep blush to the west. Then we'll head to the river. We'll sit there for a while on the muddy bank, bask in these images of rural life, and, as I put another disastrous day on the ward behind me, I'll wish that I could spend the entire week beside that water.

But right now I need to enter this little shed. And not for the first time today, which makes me wonder if Tim's comment about getting used to this latrine was a warning rather than any kindly reassurance. Regardless, I again inhale deeply, step inside, and wish immediately I hadn't; and when I scramble out moments later, light-headed from battling the urge to breathe, it seems an appropriate time to take stock of this first difficult week in the hospital. The lists handed to me minutes ago seem a good way to try. The belated summaries of last month's presentations, prepared by each of the department heads, as I pull them from my pocket:

Outpatients
A neatly ruled table annotated in pencil by Senhor Kassoma, the man first seen whisking Andrea around the dance floor at that wedding last weekend. The numbers are impressive. Two thousand eight hundred patients attended last month, and were seen by one of four Outpatients *clinicos*. Eight hundred were under five years of age. Malaria accounted for twelve hundred cases—the majority of presentations for children, but less so for adults. Other diagnoses, in decreasing order according to number of presentations: respiratory tract infections, diarrhoea, chronic pain, sexually transmitted infections, skin infections, jaundice, meningitis, and the thoroughly nondescript category, *Others*.

Maternity
Twenty-six vaginal deliveries, two stillbirths and four miscarriages, documented in meticulous detail by Nene, the head Angolan midwife.

I'll pass the report on to Andrea, along with that for the dispensary, the other major department she looks after.

Dispensary
A long list of items given out or used this past month, including six thousand amoxicillin tablets, fifteen thousand paracetamol tablets, one thousand de-worming tablets, and fifteen hundred malaria treatment packs. They're also requesting five pens and a new torch. *Are they serious? Could we possibly use this many tablets in a single month?* This surely needs looking into.

Laboratory
A summary of tests performed. Two hundred stool smears, forty urine tests, fifteen hundred malaria tests, and a handful each of hepatitis B and C, HIV, and syphilis tests, and blood-typing for transfusions— the latter being single-use kits from Europe.

Surgical outpatients
The first I've heard of such a department. I double-check the name, flick the paper over, but it seems right. According to this, twenty-eight abscesses were drained, five plaster casts applied and a hundred-and-something wounds dressed in there. Says also that twenty-three teeth were removed. *We're pulling teeth? Here?* This place I'm going to have to find.

Tuberculosis program
Nine patients who live at home, and who return fortnightly for their medical review, new pills and a food ration to encourage their compliance. One, an elderly man, is currently living in our isolation ward—a pair of small rooms at the far corner of the front hospital yard. I've not met the others, but according to this, one of them died: a forty-two year old woman.

Surgical theatre

Operations performed last month: one Caesarean section, one appendicectomy, one hernia repair, and a leg amputation. No deaths.

Inpatient unit

The source of my ongoing difficulties, this unit, and one overseen by Sergio. Says here that two hundred and ninety-one patients were admitted last month, two-thirds being for malaria. Six patients died; three from malaria, and one each from TB, eclampsia, and pneumonia.

All of which begs the question: How to manage this? These numbers are staggering, no less given our limited resources. In an emergency department back home I'd see ten patients in a shift. Here, we have sixty-five on the ward—each of whom needs to be reviewed daily—and another hundred coming through Outpatients.

Most of the local health workers seem pleasant, at least from what I can tell via translations, although Sergio and Roberto remain difficult to work with. Sergio had wandered off on that first afternoon and busied himself with paperwork for a couple of days, but has since returned—grudgingly. Roberto's been far more direct. He's not missed a ward round, and continues to argue the case for operating on the woman with cancer even though the MSF surgeon has agreed with me via email: she's far beyond any hope of cure, likely to die either during or shortly after surgery. As per universal medical ethics, we're to First do no harm.

Roberto doesn't see it this way. 'How can you not at least *try* to help her?' he implores, in full view of her relatives and other patients. Quoting the advice from Geneva only provokes him. 'And where then is this man?' he asks. 'Am *I* not the one operating in Mavinga?'

I take some comfort in the recovery of the young boy with cerebral malaria, who's now sitting up and picking at a bowl of maize. And from the man who'd killed the leopard, who can be seen showing off his bandaged limbs to an entranced audience outside the men's ward. But overall I'm lost in that place. I'm thoroughly out of my depth, and I haven't mentioned those malnourished children. Three new admissions joined the nine already on the ward this week, and treating them is like trying to combine intensive care with homoeopathy. Drug dosages are minuscule (even the quantity of specially formulated milk they're given has to be exact, just so, not too little and absolutely not too much) and their progress is measured in *grams* each day. For some, a dozen grams makes for a significant improvement. For others, a few vomits or bouts of diarrhoea can be catastrophic. It's frightening. The entire hospital is frightening. And I've got a hundred and sixty-something days left in there. But right now our cook, Dominga, is calling us for lunch.

• • •

Tim's at our plastic dining room table, re-reading a month-old newspaper. I take a seat opposite him. Andrea's not here yet, but Pascal returns moments later from a trip in our vehicle, a large, mine-proof, ex-South African military personnel carrier. He's been to inspect the water point, a series of taps through which the town's only clean water is distributed. It's another site of interest on any walk; a constant queue of people wait out front of it, empty buckets under arms, while others carrying full containers stream out the other end. One hundred and twenty thousand litres are carried out like this each day, a bucket at a time atop the heads of women and children. The project is run and maintained by Pascal and his logistics team of around a dozen Angolan men, Toyota included, who are known collectively as the 'logs', and who are responsible for all the maintenance, construction, communications and supply aspects of the project.

'Two police officers pulled us over on the way back today,' gushes Pascal, standing at the dining room doorway. He has a mildly frantic appearance when he speaks, his wild eyes caught between an explosion of unkempt hair and a wispy goatee. He's immensely entertaining, even if I can't understand much of his Spanish-Portuguese mix. Tim clarifies. 'Toyota was driving the truck,' Pascal tells us, 'and the police asked for his licence. So Toyota laughs. He asks them who has a licence in this place anyway—does anyone?—but the police make him get out of the truck. So now we're on this dirt road just five hundred metres from here—I mean, how far is this fucking water-project anyway? A kilometre?—and there is no car in any direction, no cars all week in any direction, and we stand on the sand next to the truck when a donkey cart goes past with kids on the back of it, these kids poking the donkey with a stick every now and then—like this!—slower than walking speed, and Toyota asks the police if the kids have a licence to drive that. So then the police start getting funny with him, because even these two officers don't have a car—I mean, they walked across the road to pull us over, because our thing does what, twenty kilometres an hour on this shitty road? So I try to apologise and make it all right, but Toyota—he knows them well, he told me afterwards—he stirs these guys. The police say we should know that Jamba is the only one on the team with a valid licence, but then Toyota points to Jamba, who's sitting in the back seat, and teases him, saying that Jamba is an alcoholic these days so he thought it was safer if he drove. So now Jamba and Toyota are in hysterics, and I'm trying hard not to be disrespectful to the police, but I mean, these cops don't even have tickets or anything—what were they going to do?'

'Shoot you,' notes Tim.

Pascal contemplates this.

'Seriously. They'd all be ex-soldiers.'

'Okay, maybe this is a possibility,' laughs Pascal. 'But by the end they were laughing. But I mean, what the fuck—we drive twice a week for ten minutes, and now we get stopped for licence checks?'

He pulls up a chair, looks into the three pots on the table. 'This is it?' he asks. 'Peas? And *pasta*?'

Tim looks unfazed. 'Probably.'

Pascal heads to the kitchen. He seems troubled when he returns. 'There's nothing else in there. Dominga still here?'

'Gone home for lunch.'

'But this can't be right. Peas? On *pasta*? And look at this,' he says, running a spoon through one of the pots. 'Never mind malaria—we will all die of heart attacks before we leave!'

He may well be right. Dominga's fondness for oil knows no bounds. Today, pasta glistens in a viscous lake of orange. Yesterday it was chicken, bobbing in the same. The day before, heavily fried goat.

'If you want variety,' says Tim, 'we'll need to come up with new recipes for her. She's only been cooking a few weeks. Before that she was the hospital cleaner.'

Andrea joins us, also not overly impressed with lunch. She's looking a little ruffled, too, having been up most of the night with a delivery. Isabella flew out hours ago.

'You guys can say all you want,' says Tim, 'but believe me, you'll be wishing for peas with tomato sauce when the wet season arrives. It's only been a week now since our last food delivery. Wait until the rains begin. Wait until flights get cancelled, and it's been three weeks since the last flight. *Then* you will dream of peas and—'

WHOOOOMFFFFF!!!

A noise we feel as much as hear.

What the fuck was that?

Windows rattle and dust drifts from the roof as my adrenal glands swiftly dump a year's supply of the hormone into my circulation.

Jesus—is this an attack?

A dense silence follows.

Tim asks Pascal to turn up his walkie-talkie. We sit. Frozen. No chance that sound was the de-mining team—we hear their controlled detonations most mornings but they're never this close. Or loud. This is something else.

'*Tim?*'

'Wait,' he says. 'We stay here for instructions. If it's a mine, we don't respond first. If it's an attack, no fucking way.'

I'd been cautioned in briefings that landmines are deliberately arranged in clusters in order to maximise casualties. The would-be rescuer risks the same fate as the victim. Only the HALO Trust's de-mining technicians are to respond to blasts in town, and we're to provide backup when called. *If* this is a landmine.

A long moment passes. We stare wide-eyed at each other. Someone suggests that maybe there's an innocent explanation for all this but that's unlikely: a thin pall of smoke rises from behind our wood-pole fence. The walkie-talkies suddenly burst into life and several voices speak at once. Police, de-miners, the army—all say it wasn't them. The chatter settles and we hear screaming from behind our fence. It quickly gets louder.

'*Tim?*'

'HALO Trust,' crackles the radio. 'We're en route. We can see the site—centre of town, near hospital end . . . Some casualties.' A pause. 'Uh, beside the main road. Access is definitely safe. MSF—come in.'

'MSF here.'

'Proceed to site immediately.'

Andrea and I grab the emergency medical kit from the entrance. Pascal grabs more handsets. We run out the gate following Tim but there isn't any need to go to the scene because before we can get even fifty metres a crowd of Angolans are heading towards us, some with injured people slung over their shoulders, and they're heading straight for the hospital. *Christ. It's the real thing.*

We change direction and run back to the hospital. People pour in behind us, straight into the small assessment room, but there's only one bed in here so they lie the injured on the floor.

A young girl bleeding from her cheek.

A man bleeding from his neck.

A woman, crying, laid down in the corner.

Others arrive. They sit against the wall and people step around them and shout, more squeeze in, this room is far too small—

'Wait!' I call to Tim. 'Tell them to stop bringing people in here. We'll see them outside. In the yard.'

—but they keep coming in, now a man with a bloodied shirt that's torn open, and the ferric smell of wet blood is strong in the little room so we need to assess people quickly. Carlos runs in with two *enfermeiras*, and I ask him where the rest of the staff are. He says they've all gone home for lunch.

'All of them?'

'Yes.'

Jesus, what timing!

'We need to clear beds quickly. Let's put the *intensivo* patients in the tent,' I say. 'We'll see the injured in *Intensivo*. And in here. No, outside. There's too many. Okay, no—let's triage them outside, under the tarp. No more in here.' The staff stare confusedly at me. I'm speaking English. I've forgotten any Portuguese I know. Andrea and Tim come over and explain.

More people rush into the room. It's impossible to tell who's injured and who's not, and there's more blood on the floor from someone.

'Pascal—can you get some stretchers and set them up outside?' I ask him. 'And bags of fluid. In the cupboard, there. Lay out bags of fluid. And bandages—'

A woman with a red headscarf yells, and I break off although I have no idea what she's saying. One of the *enfermeiras* has stopped to bandage a small hand injury. 'No!' I say. 'Tim—tell her we need to assess everyone first. We'll treat later. Ask her to set up IVs.'

Another young boy arrives, bleeding from the scalp, then another boy with a facial laceration. Police rush in. The woman with the red headscarf is still yelling and she grabs me—

'Pascal!' I call. 'Can you send someone in the car to fetch the *clinicos* from wherever they are. And—'

Wait, is that blood on the woman's head? Is all that blood? I pull off her headscarf to check but I can't see an injury, and she won't follow me next door so with no respect for privacy the *enfermeira* and I lift up her dress and look at her limbs and torso to make sure we're not missing a serious injury. We're not. We think she's yelling for her child so the *enfermeira* takes her outside.

Health workers run back from lunch and recognise many of the injured—family members, neighbours, friends—and head straight to them. Everyone begins doing their own thing, seeing patients anywhere and bandaging injuries and getting suture kits to sew lacerations.

'No one is to treat minor injuries yet,' I ask Tim to relay. 'We've got to do this systematically. All non-injured, wait on that side. Only injured on this side. One relative can stay with them. First thing is to check vital signs and make sure no one's bleeding heavily. Anyone with an injury gets an IV line inserted. Everyone else must stay out of that room—'

No one listens.

People are frightened and in shock and want their relatives seen immediately. More spill in through the gate, the front yard is boiling with people. Pascal returns with Toyota and a handful of the logs and we use them as crowd control, but the *clinicos* are still doing their own thing in the yard, the front room, against the outside walls, so Andrea and I walk between all patients to quickly assess wounds. A basic triage for major incidents: who needs immediate intervention, who can wait a little while, who can safely wait hours? We make a first pass around the yard then back into the assessment room, but by the time we've finished our staff have moved patients—

'Where's that boy with the facial injury gone?'

—and there are new faces everywhere. We start again.

Back outside. Through all the rooms. The yard. Within minutes we think we've seen everyone. If no more patients arrive we'll be okay; most injuries seem minor—facial and limb lacerations that appear dramatic as blood seeps onto light clothing or trickles down faces, but that are easily manageable. Two people have chest injuries but their breathing sounds normal and blood pressure is good—for the moment. They could have life-threatening internal injuries, but who knows how deep the wounds go, or into what, because we don't have an X-ray out here, so for now we're just going to have to—

Shouting at the gate. Two policemen arrive, carrying a colleague who's slumped and dragging his feet. We lead them straight through to *Intensivo* but the injured policeman refuses to sit. He's slurring and lashes out confusedly at his colleague, and I stand dumb as the two colleagues wrestle him to the bed and remove the gun from his belt. We pull his hat off and examine his head but find only a small injury, about half a centimetre long at the back. 'Was there metal?' I ask. 'Any shrapnel?'

'Everywhere,' says Andrea, speaking with the police. 'They think it was a grenade.'

How to treat a head injury here? I've seen pictures of burr holes drilled into skulls to relieve certain types of clots on the surface of the brain. I watched a neurosurgeon perform it in theatre—once. *But out here?* I don't think the man's a candidate anyway. It's the wrong type of injury. 'Where's Roberto?' I ask. 'We need him!'

'Injured,' says Carlos, tending to someone new behind me. 'One of our *enfermeiras* saw him. The guard has gone to fetch him.'

Jesus Christ, the one man in Mavinga who can deal with this stuff is injured?

We restrain the policeman to insert an IV. We give some diazepam to sedate him, then antibiotics for the wound. Andrea heads back outside. Carlos shows me the patient he's dealing with, a boy of about ten with an open jaw injury. He's lying on his own and looks impossibly calm, no tears, and he nods when we tell him we're going to rinse the wound to have a better look. I inject local anaesthetic and Carlos pours saline through the entry wound, a long jagged gash above the left jawline, but Carlos stops abruptly when smaller bone fragments from the boy's mandible begin flushing from a second laceration beneath his mouth. No way we can manage this out here. Carlos applies bandages and gives antibiotics. We'll come back to him.

Back outside. Andrea's dealing with a man who has a cut to the side of his neck, and I see Roberto limping towards her. We help him to the stairs outside the assessment room, sit him down and roll up his trousers where they're torn. 'It's small,' he says of the gash to his right lower leg. 'Show me the patients.'

'Roberto, we should—'

'*Leave it.*'

Pascal finds him a crutch. Andrea and I show him around, and maybe half an hour passes without more people arriving. Things seem to be settling. All staff are back and now working systematically. Only two patients appear to be severely injured—the policeman, now losing consciousness, and the young boy with the jaw injury— and all others have relatively minor injuries: that neck laceration, a breast wound, several limb and facial lacerations, and two men with chest wounds.

We organise the beds that are needed. We give antibiotics and tetanus cover and spend the remainder of the afternoon exploring wounds, trying to assess their depth and retrieve shrapnel, but without X-ray it's largely a fishing expedition. Hard to tell how many fragments there are, or how deep, so we retrieve them where we can;

for others, we leave the wounds open but bandaged, hoping the metal will extrude itself in coming days.

By evening there's little evidence of the disaster. Patients have been admitted or discharged, and onlookers have dispersed. In a lucky co-incidence, the police have a supply plane arriving tomorrow and offer to fly out their injured colleague and the boy with the jaw injury. The de-mining team have meanwhile dug extensively around the site, and their suspicion is that a small fire had triggered a forgotten cache of explosives, either grenades or an anti-tank mine, buried deep beneath a hut. No one had ever checked for explosives *beneath* existing homes, it seems, only around them; those who'd been injured had merely been walking past the hut at the wrong time. A sobering reminder of the difficulties these people live with, the experience of war felt even years afterwards.

Later, I find Roberto on the wards, still hobbling between patients. With some trepidation I insist that we treat him; with an equal measure he allows me. We head to the operating theatre where I inject local anaesthetic into his leg, and the *clink* of my surgical forceps against metal soon reveals shrapnel lodged in the muscle. It's easy enough to remove, although I don't recall ever being so nervous about treating someone.

'Take some days off, Roberto,' I suggest. 'Rest that leg.'

He says nothing.

'Roberto?'

He nods slightly. Then gets up, limps off on his crutch, and returns at seven-thirty the next morning for ward rounds. By which time the policeman is dead.

5. TESTIMONIALS

Friday morning, and a small milestone: I've made it to two weeks out here.

I leave the hospital and cross back to the expat compound, doing my best to avoid our resident wildlife. Lurking behind my towel, a hamburger-patty of a spider in the bathroom shed. I freshen up quickly. In our courtyard, one of the storage tent cats is crouched behind a bush, dreamily eyeing a rooster at least triple its size. I step past them, into the kitchen, although even this room is not for the faint-hearted: the hind quarters of a goat are poking from a plastic tub on the bench—hoofs, hair, flies, and attendant smell—at a little after eight in the morning.

'*Pequeno-almoço?*' I ask Dominga—Breakfast?—and she giggles.

I light our gas stove and fill a pot of water to boil as she fishes out the first of the limbs, laying it on the uncovered wood table, then pull out my Portuguese flashcards to practise phrases with her. We've been doing these drills daily this second week. Dominga's our cook and cleaner, a sturdily built Angolan grandmother, and she's turning out to be the mother figure of our compound. In every sense, a large woman: expansive mood, broad smile, wide hips, gleaming round *Krugerrand* eyes, and ample bosoms that jiggle wildly when she laughs—which is frequently. I'd known a similarly proportioned African woman years ago, who'd delighted in wearing a far-too-small T-shirt with the print, stretched across her chest, boasting: *'All this, and brains too!'* I'd like to think it was made with Dominga in mind.

Dominga asks me how the hospital's going. Her neighbour's child is currently in *Intensivo* with pneumonia, but I report that she's a little better this morning. 'And you?' I ask. *'Como vai?'*

'Muito frio!' she smiles—too cold. It gives her back pain, she says of the chilly weather (the consequence of our elevation on the Central African Plateau, over a thousand metres above sea level), so I promise to bring her some paracetamol. She nods, then looks to the flash-card in my hand. Ignoring the half-carcass between us, I read out the first phrase.

'Bom,' she says, massaging onion onto the meat—good. She's not quite so sure about my next attempt, though. *'Eh?'* she asks, leaning over to follow the card with her pink-wet forefinger. *'Não! é assim!'*— It's like this—and corrects my pronunciation, which is my real struggle with this language. Vocabulary I'm okay with; memorising lists of relevant words isn't too difficult. It's the understanding and being understood where I come unstuck. People here don't say words, they *eat* them. Each word rolls into the next before it's completed, and a strong nasal twang muddies things further. What's written seems to bear little resemblance to what's spoken, so I've created lists of simple, closed questions for the ward rounds. If I can get people to answer me with only a *Yes* or *No* for the remaining five months, I've decided, I may just be fine.

Dominga listens as I try another phrase, and another. Nonchalantly, she thumps a cockroach as it scuttles across the table, then flicks it, wipes her hand on the apron over her green dress—all the while listening—and resumes rubbing salt into the goat meat. *The source of my frequent latrine visits lately?* Quite possibly. I'll be sure to ask Tim to bring up food hygiene with her when he passes on those new recipes. Not that I'm being lazy in avoiding the issue directly with her. It's just that Tim's the overall staff supervisor, and for the moment I'd hate to spoil this dynamic between Dominga and me. Because this mother to seven children, grandmother to two more, is the only Angolan I'm getting to know outside the hospital. And unexpectedly, her presence is prompting a torrent of long-forgotten, warmly pleasant memories of my South African childhood.

It's not just Dominga, though. There are other things out here, too, seemingly unremarkable cues that prompt film strips of memory when I least expect it. The beers we drink in the evenings, the only brand sold by the little stall near the market, are Castle, 'Premium South African Lager', driven in from Namibia and last seen by me in the door of our fridge in Cape Town. The heavy cast-iron pots in which women boil maize flour here, set over evening fires, are the same black *poitjies* we'd used for traditional stews, brewed slowly over a barbecue on Sundays. And the earthy smell of these huts evokes strong images of the labourers' cottages on my grandfather's hobby farm in the north of South Africa—little brick buildings in which a handful of workers lived, the surrounding landscape of yellow grass and dry soils itself not unlike corners of Mavinga. But none stirs my memories as much as Dominga. So I sip a coffee, ignore the cockroaches, and take my time as I practise Portuguese in her bizarrely familiar, strangely comforting presence.

• • •

Tim's in the office. Cigarette in hand, he's trawling through the slew of daily emails forwarded via our satellite link with MSF in Geneva. His job confines him here for most of the day as he handles the work contracts, staff salaries, communications with various MSF offices and the Angolan government, and develops strategies for the project's future. This morning there's a warning about possible unrest following Angola's loss to Portugal in the football World Cup, he tells me, and a message from my ex-girlfriend. (Our email is communal—we can't access the internet here, only an MSF-based account in Geneva—and there are no passwords.) 'You like me to read it out?' he smiles. 'Because if I have to read another bullshit forward from head office . . .'

Andrea looks no more impressed with her job. She's at the plastic medical desk, immersed in a pile of stock lists as she tries to put together our next pharmacy order. 'They're in four languages,' she says. 'Look at this. These lists are all over the place. Urinary catheters: French, Italian, Portuguese, and here—English! And none of the numbers add up.'

I'll take the travails of the hospital any time over trying to manage that pharmacy. Just yesterday a large amount of medical stock was flown in, and this next order should've been emailed off already— it'll take the supplies three months to be shipped here from Europe. Compiling it is no easy task, though. The pharmacy is a warren of shelves in a large brick room behind our storage tent, stocked to the roof with an impressive range of supplies. Antibiotics, painkillers, surgical kits, obstetric sets, catheters, drains, tapes, pens and even blank medical charts fill the space, but layout is haphazard. As well, numerous requests from the hospital dispensary arrive on her desk daily, creating an almost full-time job in itself.

My bigger worry this morning isn't the late drug order, though. It's the semi-conscious twenty-year-old man lying in *Intensivo*. He arrived yesterday, and we've since performed all the tests that we can—a malaria check and lumbar puncture—but both were negative. Or at least the lumbar puncture appeared to be when I held the sample up to the sun, about the sum total of what we can do with it. So for now I'm checking the textbooks again, which is how I spend most of these mornings between the handover and longer ten o'clock ward round. And, much like Andrea, my tasks are also often hampered by linguistic issues, our three shelves of medical references filled with books from various countries. Cholera outbreak? Here's a yellow guide covering every aspect of management, from building the treatment centre to diluting chlorine for disinfecting the bodies; problem is I'll need to learn French to read it. Same too for obstetrics, although Spanish is what I'll need for paediatric surgery. But it's the tropical medicine books I'm after, and they're fortunately in English. I pull them out, along with the nearby *Medical Resources* folders I've not yet browsed, and squeeze onto the desk beside Andrea.

The files are an interesting distraction. A mixed bag: medical reports from 2002; guidelines for a haemorrhagic fever outbreak; someone's team photographs in a plastic wallet; a review of malaria; and a thick document, containing what looks to be transcriptions of an interview. I flick through it for a moment.

'Tim—you seen these things?' I ask.

'Which things?'

'Testimonials, I think. Taken here after the war.'

'*Oui*. I have. You should read it, but sometime when you're in a very good mood. It's heavy stuff.'

I nudge Andrea, but she's only up to *Ampicillin ampoules* on her encyclopaedic list, so a little distracted. I nudge her again. 'You seen these?'

She shakes her head.

'Listen for a second.' I read the first entry, that of a middle-aged civilian:

A friend warned me that [the government MPLA forces] were going to come and lock me up, and so I left. I hid in the forest with all my family. I started to teach my children in the forest. We went all the way to Mavinga. From 1977 until 1979 I walked, for two years. I bought food, or exchanged my clothes for it. We got to Mavinga and stayed until 1992 . . . It was an area controlled by UNITA and there was a school there. After, I went to [my previous home]. In 1994 my house was destroyed by the bombs so I fled. I had a good rest . . . the aeroplanes didn't come as far as there. Then a bomb fell on my new home. We set off again, at random, running always from the bombs that were just behind us. We walked and walked, to the right, to the left, always in the bush. We passed villages empty of people . . . During the whole time we slept in all of our clothes, afraid that we would have to flee without being able to take anything. I even slept with my tie on.

'That was taken *here*?' asks Andrea.

Tim nods. 'MSF do it after many conflicts or big disasters, part of the whole *témoignage* process,' he says, referring to a French term that translates roughly as 'bearing witness'. It's one of the organisation's core principles, along with impartiality, neutrality, and the uphold- ing of universal medical ethics. 'But I'm telling you,' he adds, 'this is heavy stuff. Read it when you're feeling very happy with life, not when you're about to start three hours of ward rounds. Believe me.' He gets up and heads outside for a moment, but I'm too absorbed to stop. What I've read of the war has been mostly in drier briefing documents, but this is from people here, some of the stories told in our hospital. I read on.

This from a young mother:

If UNITA attacked one day, then you had to expect the [govern- ment] to turn up the day after. Most of the time we hid in the bush while UNITA pillaged our houses, and then we stayed there throughout the [government] offensive. Sometimes we stayed two weeks in the bush. We lived like animals. We led that life for many years, but in 1998 we couldn't continue any longer. My two nephews were forced, on pain of death, to join UNITA's army. Around that time the [government] gave the order that people must get into their trucks unless they wanted to be killed. So we did. We've been crammed [into a disused factory] for two years now. People are dying like flies. We used to have everything . . . a small piece of land which gave us onions, sweet potatoes, sometimes tomatoes.

And another young woman:

I was captured when they attacked our village. I came to Mavinga. I studied in the high school [at the UNITA base]. Life was just suffering. They put us in the houses of the grown-ups, the officers. There, we had to work, washing the clothes, but they didn't give us anything, no clothes, no food. Some of the officers raped the young girls, so they ran away. My parents were also captured. They were taken to the [food supply] base in Mavinga, where they farmed. My husband had to go to work and he never came back. The [government] attacked us. I ran and hid in the bush, there was a big group of us. We were just running all the time. The pregnant women were also running, but if they couldn't keep it up they handed themselves to the [government army] . . . My child fell ill in the bush; he had malaria and diarrhoea and we had no medicines, so the nurse gave him some roots. He died. A lot of children died, every day three or four died. A lot of children were also lost when we were running away and were never found again.

Such testimonies go a long way to explaining the nonchalant response of our staff to that fatal explosion four days ago. My attempts to initiate a debriefing session the next day were met only with confused looks. 'We were not hurt,' they'd replied, 'so why would we want to talk about it?'

Why would they? They'd have dealt with far worse. Not so for us expats, though, who're running on adrenaline for days. In two years of working in Australian hospitals, I'd not ever come across a gunshot wound, let alone the victims of an explosion. And for all the political unrest during my time in South Africa, the most harrowing incident I recall is having a gun pulled on me by a white businessman when my friends and I sprayed his sports car with water pistols: 'You ever point a gun at me again,' he'd threatened, *'plestic* or not, and I'll fucking shoot you.'

So then, are we safe here? I think so. I take heart in Tim's reassurances that no staff have been killed since that 2002 explosion, and that there's never been an accident in areas that the HALO Trust have cleared. Guns don't seem overly prevalent, either; extensive disarmament took place after the war, and only police and soldiers seem to carry them.

The bigger question for me, though, after my reading, is how I can possibly go back to work and pull staff up over trivialities, such as the treatment of diarrhoea, when *this* was happening four years ago—

To kill our thirst, when there was no water, we chewed on leaves. For two months we would eat one day, then not eat for two days, like that.

As I read on, it worries me what role some of the people here, the men, may have had in the events described. Because UNITA, which in Mavinga had an almost exclusive supporter base, and for which many of our staff worked, was clearly no innocent participant.

. . . it was like someone had just slaughtered goats, blood everywhere and all the people lying dead, right there in the middle of the road. It was just women and children that lay dead in the middle of the road with blood everywhere.

For years, UNITA was considered a viable political party by outsiders. Their leader, Jonas Savimbi, was an articulate, charismatic man who'd begun studying medicine in Portugal before switching to political science, and who was deemed a great political thinker by many. He dined at the White House and was openly supported by the CIA and the South African government, portrayed as the archetypal African freedom fighter. As for the MPLA, the current government, they were led for the first years of the war by Agostinho Neto, an acclaimed poet who'd also studied medicine in Portugal, and who was widely respected across Africa as an anti-colonialist hero. Hard then to reconcile that idealism with all this mayhem.

... I was woken up by the sounds of shooting—fway, fway, fway!—and bombs: Bwow! I just ran. Some this way, some went that way, others went that way. I ran ... Then I started to look for my family.

I can't finish. It serves me better not to think too much about what has taken place here. About who was a victim, who may have been a perpetrator, and that some of these people—on either side—could be on our staff. The hospital is just metres away; through the office window I can see a group of kids kicking a semi-inflated football near Pascal while he works on the fence; and I think: this could've been them just four years ago. So I stop at these last words as I close the file. Words from a nine-year-old orphan, interviewed during her treatment in the feeding centre in Mavinga.

My family is dead. I ate sand. What will I do now?

• • •

'It is very hard for us *clinicos* to work like this,' laments Sergio, addressing the group of staff. It's later this same Friday, and the weekly meeting with the heads of the various departments is being held. 'We cannot work properly,' he goes on. 'Not like this—not with someone who cannot speak our language. It is very difficult for us all.'

This last point I don't doubt.

'And let me say that this language thing, *Coordenador*,' he continues, as a dry breeze coughs hot air at us, 'that this is just part of the problem. Because it is also the work. For example, we have had a very sick woman these last two weeks. And before, we have operated on such patients. Many times we have helped them. But now—' he stops as he looks around the open-walled hut, here in our expat yard, eyeing the dozen staff seated on wooden benches around the circular shape, '—this *Novo Doctor* won't let us do this!'

'Move on, Sergio,' says Tim. 'This is not the place.'

'I disagree, *Coordenador*, because this concerns everyone. Our hospital is not good at the moment. *Novo Doctor* questions things he does not understand. And let me please just say this one thing.'

On he goes. I'd almost enjoy his speech if I wasn't the topic. He's remarkably dramatic, gesticulating, pausing, staring, pacing, contemplating, and shaking his head ruefully, enunciating each point. Andrea interjects with whispered translations from my left, but they're largely unnecessary. The gist is clear.

'Two weeks ago we had a nice mother arrive,' he continues, describing the case of the woman with cancer, 'and we did nothing. Roberto wanted to operate, but still we did nothing. And just yesterday, this woman died! With *still* no treatment from us. How can this be?'

The woman had held on far longer than I'd imagined, although she'd been unconscious for much of this second week. I arrived for work yesterday morning to find her children clinging to her body. The husband said nothing, just quietly wrapped her in a blanket and carried her out the gate, two young sons in tow.

'*Novo Doctor*?' calls Sergio. 'Tell us. Tell us why we did nothing for her!'

He takes his seat. There is nothing I can think to say. The Angolan staff look just as uneasy; Sergio's a senior, technically their boss, and as MSF expats we're the employers. Most look away in silence. Next to Andrea sits Senhor Kassoma, the head of Outpatients, who's for some reason making notes on all this in his diary. Beside him are Pascal, Tim, and Toyota—still dressed in his blue overalls and thick gumboots; Vasco, our head guard—who's more likely to charm someone out of entering the compound than physically prevent them; Theresa, the forty-something head of nursing, with whom Andrea's been having her own run-ins; Jamba, our affable driver, who's afflicted with an unfortunately large goitre; Nene, the head of midwifery, today outfitted like a West African queen in flowing blue dress, matching headscarf and large hoop earrings; and Roberto, who's not missed a day of work since his injury. Also present are the heads of cleaning, water distribution, and the hospital dispensary.

'Sergio, I've made this clear before,' says Tim. 'These are not medical meetings. This is not to happen again.'

'Excuse me, *Coordenador*,' interrupts Roberto. He stands slowly, leans his crutch against the wall of the hut and straightens his checked business shirt. 'It is not just Sergio,' he says. 'Okay, I do not think it is fair to suggest that *Novo Doctor* caused the death of this woman. She was very ill, and I think this is unfair. But I could have tried to help this woman. This is the thing: we could have *tried*. It is what her family wanted. But *O Novo Doctor*—who has been here for what, two weeks?—he has been refusing such things. And now there is another young girl on the ward—'

'The point's been made, Roberto,' says Tim. 'The four of us can meet afterwards.'

Sergio's back on his feet. 'But must we go through this *every* time a new doctor arrives?' he asks. 'Always, these new questions, these different rules. What if this new patient dies as well? What if she—'

'Enough!' calls Tim. 'We will talk afterwards. Now—Pascal, logistics issues this week?'

I need to seriously question the reality of staying in Mavinga. This is absurd. *How has it all so quickly deteriorated into this?* There's a deep irony in my having left the Thai clinic to come here, too—maybe someday I'll appreciate it. The difficulty of working there had been in getting the mild-natured, soft-spoken Burmese to actually speak up to me at all!

Pascal fills us in on stock issues, and as I watch him speak I want to trade places. Having previously spent a year in Angola with a women's development agency, he's a fluent Portuguese speaker, and gets along effortlessly with his team. And what a job *he* has. Just yesterday our six-monthly logistics order arrived spectacularly in a giant, Russian-built cargo jet, an event overseen by Pascal. The sound of the ageing Antonov bearing down on our dirt runway, just metres from the hospital, was almost apocalyptic as it screamed its reverse thrust into the quiet African morning, the scene equally surreal: a marvel of twentieth-century engineering parked on the dirt as an ox-drawn cart trundled past. A group of local kids quickly gathered to inspect the plane, giving the tyres a firm *thump* with a fist, *whack*ing the fuselage with a small branch. The logistics team meanwhile unloaded and inspected the tonnes of supplies—fuel, chlorine, medical equipment and maize, and the sundry other items including wiring, cement, sand and bricks for new projects: every conceivable thing we're likely to need in coming months—and it's this logistical aspect of the project that I find most fascinating. That here, in the midst of The Land at the Edge of the World, a bubble of modern infrastructure has been created, allowing the hospital and water system to function at a level not otherwise possible. All the technical aspects fall under Pascal's responsibility, and when not dealing with flights he can be found tinkering with the generator, adjusting the satellite communications equipment, fiddling with plumbing, or getting driven around in the mine-proof vehicle. So I also want to be a log, I've decided. I want Pascal's job. An organised one, with quantifiable, visible results, and a team of light-hearted Angolans to boot.

'Anyone else with something to add?' Tim asks.

'Yes, *Chefe*,' begins Sergio. 'There is now *another* patient—'

'Right,' Tim interjects. 'Meeting's over.'

The others leave. Only Tim, myself, Sergio and Roberto remain. We stay on our benches at opposite sides of the hut.

'This is a huge problem,' begins Tim, sitting forward. He runs a hand through his dark, close-cropped hair, and asks the two *clinicos* to explain their sides of the story. For a quarter of an hour the duo speak passionately. It's a bitter pill, listening to their complaints as Tim relays them. 'We do want to get on well with the doctor,' Sergio concludes. 'We need a doctor to lead the team. But this situation . . .'

'Thanks for your honesty,' says Tim. 'Now for my input. You know that I'm not a medical person—my background is in project management—so it's not for me to give a medical opinion. But I know that our doctor has been speaking with the surgeon in Geneva, and he's following the advice he's been given. Advice also from the medical coordinator. These people are my bosses, too, so if they suggest that we don't operate on certain patients, then we don't.'

Roberto glances my way. Sergio stares off into the distance, looking bored. I'm still not sure what to make of these two. I was told in briefings that several of our staff were formerly UNITA seniors, but senior *what*? Health workers? Politicians? Teachers? Or military commanders? Christ—were some of these guys involved in what I'd just read about? *Responsible even for such acts? Am I quibbling with people who ran guerrilla armies?* I know I shouldn't entertain such thoughts. I understand that in circumstances like those everyone was a victim, people were forced into situations to survive and did what they had to, and all are equally deserving of care—it's the very premise of this organisation. Our staff seem well respected by the local people, too, which must count for something, and I can only assume that MSF looked into their backgrounds before employing them. I'd ask Tim, but I'd rather not know.

'I don't want to have to get involved in clinical issues,' Tim finishes up, 'because it's not my job. But if this goes on we're going to have to lay down clear rules via the medical advisors. You all have to work together for another half year, so you need to please find a way. Any more issues, you come straight to me. Okay?'

Sergio and Roberto get up and leave the compound quickly. I stay where I am.

'Having a tricky time, huh?' smiles Tim.

'I expected to be pushed a little, mate, but seriously . . .'

'You should have a good read of the old medical reports in the office,' he says. 'Sergio's been like this for years. He's very good with coordination staff, but in his mind this is his hospital. As for Roberto? Well, he has a background in war surgery, and you don't. You also look very young, my friend!'

I ask him how the previous doctors managed.

'The one before you was good with surgery and obstetrics,' he says, 'so she spent a lot of time on that side of things, maybe less on the general wards. I never met the other doctors—I've only been here a few months—but I can tell you that it's not uncommon for new staff to get tested when they arrive. I even saw local staff strike in another project once, just because they refused to work with certain expats.'

We walk the few metres to the dining area and grab Castle beers from the vaccine fridge, slump into plastic chairs. The mechanical drone of the generator begins. It feels out of place here, an unwelcome intrusion, but the most delightful sound can still be heard coming from just behind our fence, where children from the nearby huts are playing. Hands clap, little voices sing, and through our open door I can see the sky, blushed with streaky pinks where a setting sun slid past only minutes ago. *The softer side of Mavinga*. Sitting before us, though, cubes of this morning's goat, suspended in a puddle of orange.

'You have to put yourself in their shoes,' Tim continues. 'These guys get a new doctor every six months, sometimes more often, and all of you try to change things when you arrive. After a few months the next guy arrives, and he does the same. I've seen that list you carry, too, my friend . . .!'

Touché. It's now a small booklet of issues I'm hoping to address.

'We are all guilty of this,' Tim laughs. 'The thing is, this project has been going for years. Staff are close, and you're another outsider. But you need to be on those wards all day.' He stops, takes a long sip and stares quietly out the window. 'You know, this is a difficult time for them. In six months we're handing this hospital to the government. The MSF presence in Angola is ending. All projects are closing, and the health workers may well be working on their own after that—if they're working at all. This is the last few months of formal support they'll have from MSF, maybe the last time they'll have a doctor, so you need to teach. And find the problems. So stand your ground with Sergio. Do what needs to be done. As for Roberto?' He leans across and clinks beers with me. 'Good luck with *him*.'

Pascal bounds through the doorway, covered in dust. 'Fucking hell!' he declares. 'Listen to this. Okay, so Jamba is in the tent just before, working through this big order. It's going to take us days, by the way, this thing. Big fucking mess, lots of stuff missing.'

'Stolen?'

'For sure. Some boxes were cut open and resealed, almost perfectly. Only the expensive items are missing—lots of medicines. But anyway, this is for tomorrow's problems. So, Jamba opens this box and he looks closely inside for something, his head down—he's concentrating hard—but Toyota comes up from his side, quietly, like this . . .'

Tim and I laugh as Pascal mimics Toyota creeping, but before he can finish the story, a distraction occurs, a comprehensive derailment of thought: three heads pivot in unison like carnival clowns, mouths agape, because, wrapped in only a figure-hugging towel, Andrea has just stepped out of the shower and she's making her way across the yard to her bedroom.

('*Fucking hell!*' notes someone beside me.)

It's going to be an interesting few months.

6. MAVINGA IS DIFFERENT

Another windy morning. The red and white MSF flag sketches colour into a burned-out sky above the hospital entrance; below, one of our guards reclines in his plastic chair, struggling to light a cigarette. I pass him at the gate but a young girl stops me.

'*Tire uma photo!*' she says brightly, a phrase I've come to know well from walks into town. She wants me to take a photo. Her older sister chimes in as well. '*Por favor, Branco,*' she begs—Please, White Man—leaning on a wooden crutch that she's long outgrown, her left leg hanging limp and withered—polio, I suspect. The disease still occurs out here, and she's old enough to have caught it during the war. A time when an entire generation would've missed out on vaccines.

I tell them I don't have my camera with me. I pat my empty pockets to prove it, but bashful little eyes peer back from bowed heads, and soft voices go up a pitch. No choice now. I fetch my camera from the office and return to a waiting chorus of squeals and little jumps on the spot, only the other half-dozen children nearby are just as excited, nudging and pushing each other to be at the front.

I ask the other kids to wait. First the sisters, then everyone else, I say, but it's impossible to compose a shot with even just two of them. They're in constant motion, wriggling forward incessantly, stopping only when their faces are almost on the lens as if it's a peephole they desperately need to see through.

I inch back.

They inch forward.

'*O que e isso?*' I ask, trying to ready the shot again—What's this?—because the younger girl's cradling a brown bottle, holding it between the two of them for the picture. She hands it to me gently. It's a bottle of Windhoek Lager, another Namibian export. 'What on earth are *you* doing with beer?' I laugh.

'*Não é cerveja,*' she replies, shaking her head earnestly—It's not beer. But it definitely *was* beer, only now it's empty, a tuft of coarse, black hair jammed into its top.

'Why this?' I ask, pointing to the woolly clump. '*Porque este?*'

She smiles, takes back the bottle, and with all the dignity of a little princess—a princess wearing a torn, shapeless dress, the colours long since massaged out on the riverbank—she replies: '*É a minha boneca.*' It's my doll.

I'd laugh, if only she wasn't serious. It's like that wedding gift we'd been advised to take. Or the way that people here salvage *everything*—bottles, plastic bags, old cloth; or the pieces of twine they'll fashion into jewellery and the lengths of wire they'll use as a belt. Poverty *this* extreme can't be quantified. It's a state of existence. Hollow cheeks, four skinny limbs and a belly swollen with parasites; patches of ringworm causing bald spots all over these kids. And it's why I'm here, I've decided. For the sister that should never have had polio. For this young girl, proud as punch with her hairy, eyeless beer-bottle doll. And for the countless others, sleeping on cowpat floors in smoky huts, for whom the hospital represents the only hope when their kid gets malaria or their partner develops TB.

So fuck it: I'm not about to be bullied out by a chubby health worker. Nor his non-chubby, highly imposing, war surgeon of a colleague, although I'll be honest that he does frighten me. So I step in, this third week, and confront my accusers on the ward. Because surgery isn't the only issue here.

• • •

'To see the doctor,' says Manuel, the *clinico* looking after the women's ward today.

'That's the management plan?' I ask.

'Yes.'

'Nothing else?'

'No.'

'You're not giving any medications?'

'None.'

It's an often-had conversation as we review new patients on these lengthy mid-morning rounds. 'But what's the patient's diagnosis?' I ask. 'What's her actual illness?'

Manuel loosens his lab coat, tilts his head and scratches the skin under the collar of his brown plaid shirt. It's the only shirt I ever see him in. 'The notes don't say a diagnosis, *Novo Doctor*,' he says. 'Just: *to see the doctor.*'

'Yes, but that's what the Outpatients *clinico* wrote,' I say. 'You're looking after her now, Manuel. What do *you* think the problem is?'

'Uh . . . not so sure,' he replies. The three *enfermeiras* and five other *clinicos* stand patiently behind him, shuffling on the stained concrete floor. 'Her malaria test was negative, and she does not have a cough.'

'Okay. So it's probably not malaria, maybe not a chest infection. But she's got a fever and it's got to be coming from somewhere, Manuel, so we need to look for a source. What other infections could it be?'

'It could be anything, *Novo Doctor*. Anything at all!'

He's right. It really could be: bacterial, viral, fungal, parasitic— most infectious diseases I've come across in the textbooks seem to exist in this part of the world. Thousands upon thousands of unpronounceable, obscure, hard-to-diagnose rarities I've not ever seen, if heard of.

'I agree, Manuel. So it's important that we take a proper history and examine her from here,' I say, pointing to the patient's head, 'to here,' pointing to her feet, because mime is now an integral part of my communication strategy on the ward. I have my vocabulary sheets on hand, too, and Andrea's usually available when I get stuck. 'So you need to examine everywhere, Manuel. Did you do this?'

'No.'

'Why not?'

'Because she is waiting to see you, *Novo Doctor.*'

'I know this, but *you* can still examine her, Manuel.'

'But there is no point—the plan is already here.'

'Where?'

'Here.'

'There isn't a plan there!'

'There is.'

'Where?'

'Here: *To see the doctor.*'

And it's not because staff are incompetent that this happens. Many of the *clinicos* have years of experience. Sergio, for all his bluster, is very clinically astute, as are many of the older health workers. They've dealt for years with illnesses that I've never seen at home. The real problem is this . . .

'Manuel,' I say, 'we talked about this yesterday. I want *you* to assess these patients,'—and now I run to get Andrea to help explain these next bits, because a gallery of querulous eyebrows meets me as I try— 'because you are health workers, not paper clerks. You are not here to just write what I say. You have medical knowledge and medical experience, no? You must use it, Manuel. I want *you* guys to come up with the diagnoses and suggest plans, and then we can discuss them together afterwards. Okay?'

It's not okay.

It's all too confusing, the *clinicos* lament. Another doctor wanted them to make the decisions only after hours, not during the day, but the doctor before that forbade them from initiating any treatment until she'd seen the patient. Then there was the doctor who forbade them from prescribing for children, but not for adults. As well, this lack of continuity has clearly led to a lack of accountability: who is actually responsible for the patient?

We move on to see the eight other patients in the women's ward. The presumed diagnoses, left to right: typhoid fever, gonorrhoea, a severe skin reaction to an anti-leprosy drug, undifferentiated abdominal pain, period pain, back pain, and a kidney infection. And this young woman—Maria, a twenty-nine year old with breast cancer. Her tumour is ulcerated and has a foul-smelling discharge weeping constantly from it, and there's a large abscess in her armpit that's likely associated with a metastasis. Yesterday we drained the abscess. This morning, says Manuel, her blood pressure is seventy.

'*Seventy?* You sure?'

Sabino double-checks the chart over Manuel's shoulder. He's a tall health worker with a wide gap between his front teeth, a black leather baseball cap shadowing his boyish face. 'Yes,' he says, sheepishly. 'It says so here.'

'But she's in shock then—this is severe! Why did no one start treatment? It's been like this since yesterday afternoon, according to the chart. Who recorded it?'

'I did,' admits an *enfermeira*.

'You must tell someone, though, Veronica. This is an emergency—there's no point writing it down and just leaving.'

And then, as IV cannulas and bags of fluids are hastily gathered, the finger-pointing begins. 'I wrote it on the front of his chart, in red,' opines Veronica. 'The *clinico* should have seen it.'

'Look at the time it was written,' Sabino defends. 'I was at lunch then. Carlos was in charge.'

'I was in charge of the whole hospital then!' cries Carlos. '*Every-one* was at lunch. There were sixty-five patients, and that man in *Intensivo* was going crazy. Why didn't the night-shift *clinico* see this?'

'Because he sleeps,' quips the nearby cleaner.

'No, because he admitted four patients,' defends Therese. 'Ask *Novo Doctor*—he came for two of them.'

'But *Novo Doctor*,' sighs Sergio. 'You are in charge of this hospital, no? We have had this conversation. *You* must check these things.'

They're all fair points. And they're largely the result of differing backgrounds, I suspect. While I was being guided through eighteen years of structured, formal education, these people were surviving war. Many health workers have also been promoted quickly, well above their level of training, in a region where literacy and numeracy skills are an advantage shared by few.

But all of this needs to be addressed. I've got only five months left, although I'm confident that if we concentrate on the common medical conditions, consistently and repeatedly, with clearly allocated responsibilities on the ward, there'll be at least some benefit to patient care. I'm not the first to try—an office folder bulges with the handouts from lessons given by previous expats—but if I'm to be the last volunteer doctor here, it's essential that this hospital soon runs at a competent level, and independently. Our aim as volunteers, in my mind at least, should be to make ourselves redundant: to leave self-sufficient, sustainable facilities when we pull out.

First thing to address is those malnourished children, by far the most fragile patient group. Beneath the battered metal scale that we weigh them in each morning, three treatment protocols sit, dog-eared and smeared with high energy milk. Two are in Spanish, one in Portuguese, and all are different. So I work on summarising a single up-to-date guideline, then translate it with Tim's help.

Next, I plan some formal sessions with the health workers. Easy enough: an MSF handbook outlines standard treatment policies for key illnesses in all projects. All I need to do is to learn Portuguese. So I watch Dominga massage onion into goat legs after morning handovers for the following days, running through some phrases with her. Then, with Tim's help, I script a first teaching session. I rehearse it, practise it again, and review it with Dominga.

And now, just days later, on this third Friday, I take my place in front of the health workers in the larger Outpatients room. It's a tough crowd. The twenty or so Angolans stare silently, but I'm quietly optimistic. I did exactly this in Thailand, and it became the watershed moment of my stay. For hours, forty Burmese health workers had sat cross-legged on a hard floor, peppering me with polite questions and asking when I could give the next lesson—'Maybe two more this week, Doctor?'—and there's no reason Mavinga will be any different. We're going to all work better because of this, I think to myself. Patients will benefit, health care will improve and morale will soar, because all that's been missing from this project is the enthusiasm and fresh-eyed approach of a young, inexp—

'Does anyone know what *Novo Doctor* is saying?'

'I'm saying that—'

'We cannot understand you well, *Novo Doctor*,' says Sabino, looking to me sympathetically from the front row.

'What if I speak more slowly?' I try.

'No,' says Sergio. 'This will not work. We cannot go through a whole lesson like this. We just cannot. No way.'

I run to Maternity to find Andrea to translate, but she's dealing with a premature baby who's hypothermic, wrapping it to mum's chest with a silver-foil blanket. 'We've got twenty-something women waiting for antenatal clinic,' she apologises. 'I'm going to be here for hours.'

I jog over the road to find Tim, who's working on a letter to the Angola Ministry of Health. 'Sounds too interesting to miss,' he says, and as we walk to Outpatients I explain that I want to address a therapy that's both medically inappropriate and a waste of resources. Tim nods. Now, back in front of the health workers, firmly in position on my pyre at the front of the room, I throw the match: 'So really,' I say, 'we need to stop this use of antifungals for all diarrhoea here.'

The flames erupt.

'What is he talking about?' shouts Sergio, as Tim translates.

'Why?' asks Senhor Kassoma, the partially hoarse director of Outpatients. 'Why is he saying this? This makes no sense!'

Hands are thrown in the air. There's a snort of incredulity from the back. Roberto shakes his head, and I see now that I've made a huge mistake—it's far too soon for me to be telling them what they should or shouldn't be doing. We should've just revised a straightforward medical topic, but the damage is done.

'He doesn't know what he's talking about,' says Kassoma, eyeing the room from behind his far-too-large corrective glasses. 'He has no idea! We have been doing this here for years. He does not know our diseases.'

How to get out of this? I look over at Tim but he just shrugs, no longer translating. I run back to our compound and return carrying several textbooks, opening them to the relevant sections of each. 'Look,' I try. 'Here: diarrhoea in children, and there's no mention of antifungals.'

The din is now a low roar.

'And this one,' I say. '*Manson's*. It's the bible of tropical medicine. And look—forty pages on diarrhoea and there are no recommendations for routine antifungal treatment.' I thumb through others, hold up tables, show charts, but it makes no difference.

'None of these books were written about Africa, *Novo Doctor*!' states Senhor Kassoma, who actually looks offended. Who'd have believed that this was the same elderly man who'd whisked Andrea around that dance floor so gracefully? 'And besides,' he adds, 'you haven't worked in Africa before!'

I point out that two of the books *were* written about Africa, and a third has an African editor. He doesn't miss a beat.

'Well, none of the books were written about Mavinga!' he says.

'That is true, Senhor, but they are written about *tropical* Africa. And we are in Africa, and in the tropics, not so?'

'No! We are in *Mavinga*! It is not all just the same. Maybe to you *Brancos* it is. For us it is very different. You cannot tell me that a man from Zambia will have the same illness as a man in the Congo. Things are different here in Angola. The war has changed things. And besides, Doctor Lorenzo who was here last year—he was happy for us to use this drug. He was a very good doctor, and a very experienced doctor.'

The rest join in, jumping onto this newly assembled bandwagon. 'Mavinga is different,' agrees Senhor Calvino, one of the four Outpatients *clinicos*. He's a large man, the only obese person among our hundred staff members. 'It is not like other places anymore,' he says.

I should've known that there was another expat behind this treatment. Why should they now believe me? As they talk, my mind torpedos back to those testimonies I'd found, and I recall reading elsewhere that the battle for Mavinga had been one of the most violent confrontations of the entire war; and here I stand, not even two decades later, picking an argument over diarrhoea.

A few health workers get up to leave. Tim asks me what I want to do, and in a fit of desperation-induced inspiration I make a proposal: we could conduct a demonstration for a few weeks. All children admitted on certain days will be given the antifungal treatment, while all children admitted on the other days will receive only fluids, as per the guidelines. We'll alternate the days to keep things balanced, monitoring recovery times to see if there's any difference. Tim's intrigued. He translates, though perhaps he shouldn't have.

'Now he wants to do *experiments* on our people?' shouts Kassoma. 'Absolutely not! *Nunca!*'

'It's a demonstration,' I say, 'not an experiment, Senhor. And the books say that what I'm suggesting is safe and effective—I'm not doing anything dangerous.'

The room simmers with conversation.

'And if any of the children get worse on my treatment,' I add, 'we'll stop immediately.'

Kassoma leads the discussion among the *clinicos*. Interesting to watch the dynamic of them all together like this; Kassoma's clearly the leader, Roberto deferred to as well, but I'm not too sure about Sergio.

Kassoma turns back to me. 'And if our children recover quicker,' he asks, 'we will keep using antifungals?'

I hope dearly that this isn't going to backfire. It's far from rigorous. 'Okay,' I say. 'But if there is *no* difference, we stop using it altogether. Deal?'

Excited deliberations take place. Roberto and Sergio are opposed, many others just amused by the afternoon's turn, but Kassoma seems to be for it. He stands up to face the group. 'No, what *Novo Doctor* is suggesting is interesting,' he says. 'Let us try this for a short while. Let us prove that he is mistaken.' He turns, and with pointed finger he cautions me. 'Because you will see this, *Novo Doctor*,' he says. 'You will see it. And you will understand that Mavinga is different!'

• • •

Saturday's a half-day. Outpatients closes at lunchtime, but the wards keep us busy until late afternoon. By early evening, patients' families begin lighting cooking fires around the yard, just a few of the hundreds being lit all over the region, and the soft haze of smoke that characterises these chilly evenings blankets the town. Blood-red sunsets are a welcome consequence, although walking for a little fresh air seems an ironic pursuit after work: the smog is at its thickest by then. But distractions remain few, a stroll to the river supreme among them. It's not to be missed.

'We delivered twins today,' Andrea tells me, as we head left onto the main street. Tim and Pascal have chosen instead to stay home and finish their game of cards. 'First I've delivered in ages,' she continues. 'It's crazy—you have no idea there's a second baby until you've delivered the first. I thought I could feel two bums through mum's belly, but I really wasn't sure. Always quite the surprise!'

I've come to look forward to these debriefings with Andrea after work. Pascal tells me they're poorly disguised attempts at flirting; either way, she's the only other medical expat, a valuable source of support. Having previously spent a year working in an orphanage in Brazil, she's a confident Portuguese speaker, and her competence in the maternity section is an asset to the hospital. Together with the Angolan midwives she looks after all the obstetric services in the hospital and community. Their morning antenatal clinics are my favourite—a wonderful spectacle: the heavily pregnant bellies of a row of expectant mothers bulge beneath bright dresses as they sit side-by-side on the wooden benches, looking like vibrantly coloured fruit ripening on a branch. Unfortunately though, due to the distances travelled, many of these women will never reach us in time to deliver, instead going into labour at home. That's an extremely risky thing to happen out here: one in thirty mothers will die from pregnancy-related complications in their lifetime. Now that the war is over, giving birth is the most dangerous thing a woman here can do.

We fill each other in on other patients as we pass the school building (just look for the '*Escola*' sign on a pockmarked façade, no roof above, and broken pieces of blackboard glued to the front wall), where a handful of boys are playing with wooden tops—crudely carved cones that they spin on a point, flicking them with a strip of linen to maintain the motion. Meanwhile, the evening rush hour weaves past us on the main street: the last of the day's hundred and twenty thousand litres of clean water, sloshing about in tubs balanced on heads; a handful of roosters, scuttling neurotically between bald yards and steering wide of the crudely constructed pig pens; thin goats, skittish and nervous, nibbling at any object (mostly thorny scrub, although a discarded truck tyre has the attention of one); a group of young girls who'd like to please touch Andrea's blonde curls; three policemen, still with no car; and two oxen, guided by a young boy who's whistling instructions from atop the wood cart they're dragging, the truck axle beneath it squeaking to the plodding rotation of its wheels.

But what we mostly see is kids. Dozens of them. Hundreds, even. And really, this is the highlight of evenings here: children own the town at this hour. They account for half the population anyway, more than double the proportion in my own country, but now, with adults having gathered around fires or settled against the crumbling walls of their huts, the kids lay an even more conspicuous siege to the township. No track is devoid of a group of girls skipping, singing, or chasing someone around, while boys, if not being chased, push cars made of soft-drink cans and plastic containers, or kick footballs— often a tight bundle of paper or plastic—where space allows.

We turn right. Down a deeply rutted track, past the market, and we soon arrive at our destination: the mighty Cubia River. Two metres wide and knee-deep at best, it's a silty, lethargic and slightly funky stream, slowly dribbling its way towards the Zambezi River, which ultimately traverses the continent to discharge off Africa's east coast. The unimpressive-looking stream may be the only water source for the town, but to dismiss it as mere water supply would be to horribly belittle its role: the very heart of Mavinga. Just five minutes here, and any doubts as to what I'm doing in this town disappear.

The Cubia's banks are the hub of social activity, a place where people sit and chat about the weather and who knows what else. It's the town laundromat, where teenage girls scrub garments over smooth boulders, eyeing the teenage boys who bathe in the shallow pool upstream, behind the reeds. The far side is a favoured fishing spot, where simple rods made of a stick dangle hooks into a small pool that yields the occasional *tilapia* fish; the dating spot, where young men come to flirt with young women, and the malaria-laden mosquitos do the same with their kind; and I suspect it's also the sometime-latrine, the *I really hope that kid didn't really just do that in there* place, although the cattle wallowing in nearby stretches surely don't observe toilet etiquette anyway.

It's all of these things, this murky stream, and it's my favourite spot in town. Just don't ask me to put a foot in the water. Those hooked eggs we see in stool samples? *Schistosoma*—a parasite that comes second only to malaria in affecting millions of people worldwide. Itchy red bumps is all you may notice in the days after bathing, at which time the parasites, having now penetrated your skin, will migrate towards your lungs. Next stop, the heart, then the liver, where they'll pair up with a like-minded partner to mate. Herein, the real trouble: pregnant females will either stay put or migrate to the intestines, and they'll begin laying several hundred eggs each day; some of these will be shed in faeces and end up back in the river, but others will lodge where they are, leading to potential complications like bloody diarrhoea, bowel scarring, cirrhosis, even liver failure. Another brand of this parasite will do much the same, only to the bladder instead. So I marvel at the water, but don't dare touch it. And I ignore the hookworm larvae burrowing into bare feet and seated bums, the clouds of malaria-carrying mosquitos, and the million other things out here that penetrate, bite, infect, or adhere to various body parts.

'*Onde vais?*' I ask a young boy, who's filling his two yellow jerry cans from the edge—Where are you headed?

'*Lá!*' he smiles—There!—pointing to the snaking track that heads south to a group of huts, then Namibia.

'*Está longe?*'—Is it far?—but the walkie-talkie beeps before he can answer. I turn up the handset—something we're required to carry whenever outside the compounds. '*Sim?*' I ask.

It's the guard. There's an emergency in the hospital.

We run, no idea what towards. The guard won't say or doesn't know. Last call was for a broken ankle, before that it was Pascal wanting me to pick up six Castles. Could be nothing. Could be a disaster.

We leg it, past boys driving a large herd down the main street, around the corner, where the guard waves—'In here,' he points, 'it's a child'—and ushers me into the first room, where a large group of people stand back. A young girl is lying on the assessment table, the urgent heaving of her chest in violent contradistinction to the rest of her body, which is drowsy and weak. She's panting and gasping, a little sprinter who's just run a big race. I grab a stethoscope and can hear that her lungs are full of infection.

'What's the history?' I ask Carlos, who's inserting an IV cannula into her hand. 'How long has she been sick?'

The mother says nothing. She's singing quietly as she strokes the girl's cheek, oblivious to the rest of us in the room, oblivious to the rest of the world. A lone bulb casts severe shadows around the room from where it hangs above, the only light source we have to work by now, and even in this light and despite even her dark skin, the young girl looks pale and sallow.

'She's had a cough,' says Carlos. 'For a few days. Now a high fever and lots of diarrhoea. It took them most of the day to carry her here.' He runs to get a malaria test while I draw up saline and antibiotics from supplies on the shelf and give it to the *enfermeira* to inject. Carlos returns and pricks her finger, but it'll be minutes before a result comes so we give her antimalarials anyway. Next, IV glucose in case her blood sugar is low—we can't test for it—and we call for the lab worker to check her haemoglobin.

We repeat the fluid bolus but the girl remains drowsy. We set up a fluid infusion, then carry her to *Intensivo,* where mum cradles her. The girl needs oxygen but we've got none, and Carlos volunteers to stay late as the rest of the staff get on with the evening handover. We reassess her frequently and adjust her infusion. We stay beside her. We give her another bolus, double-check the handbooks, and after an hour she's still chugging away, hanging in there, but her eyes are tired. I step outside to radio Pascal about the generator because we'll need the light for hours yet, and while I'm there I hear a cry.

I run back in. The mother's up, walking in circles. She looks back in disbelief with her hand over her mouth. The four men draw closely around the bed. I squeeze past and can see the girl's stopped breathing. *Christ.* Carlos grabs a rubber bag-and-mask from the cupboard and hands it to me to ventilate her. I place the mask over her mouth and begin resuscitation but there's surely no point because it can't possibly work, not out here, so I wrestle with my conscience while the mum paces behind me: *Is it crueller to give the parents another few minutes of false hope than to just call it like it is?* The girl's chest rises with the deflation of the bag but it means nothing. There's no pulse. The family are silent. *Do they think she's breathing?*

Carlos begins chest compressions. I ask the *enfermeira* to get a vial of glucose and adrenaline and we give both. The families of the three other patients in this ward come over. There are too many people and I don't know what to do so I keep ventilating her body while Carlos continues with the chest compressions. *How or when are we going to stop this futile exercise? What do the family expect?* I whisper the questions to Carlos and he says they hope we will still save her. I say softly to him that it's over and he nods, says he knows, and I wonder if the family will sleep better for getting their child to a hospital where a foreign doctor could try to save her.

'Tell them the infection is too severe,' I say to Carlos, still inflating the bag. The bed squeaks like an old tumble dryer under the compressions of her little chest, and a conversation in a local language follows behind me. The mother looks at me and tears well in her eyes and she covers her mouth again and starts to cry into her hand. 'I'm sorry,' I say. 'I'm very sorry.' A word I'm using too often on these wards. I stop ventilating. Carlos stops the compressions. The mother starts screaming.

It's clearly not the Africa of newspaper articles and TV documentaries where people just accept tragedy.

Mum falls to the floor. She pounds it, pounds her chest, holds on to the leg of a man standing nearby. People begin wailing. Women come in from outside and see the body and go back out crying. Men cry and gather around the father. Big, powerful-looking men, and they raise their hands and yell and seem to question something, and like a deer caught in headlights I don't move. *Are they angry? Do I apologise and attempt to console this sea of waving and pounding arms?* They carry on for what feels like an eternity until Carlos wraps the body in a blanket for them and then they lift it up, a crumpled little package, and they go wailing out of the compound, into the dark. Carlos heads home and the *enfermeira* wipes the bed, and I don't know what happens now, I have no idea, so I go home to play cards with Pascal and Tim.

I don't know what else to do.

7. BARGAINING FOR BODY PARTS

But the night won't end.

I lie in bed, and for hours there's absolute silence—a sound disconcerting in its own right. No traffic, no voices; no hint of any life. Then the roosters start. Then the donkeys. And then the soldiers, performing their drills on the airstrip; but anything's better than silence, and their singing is somehow soothing. I may yet drift off. Only now the sun's rising, cleaving a shelf of bright dusty light below my wood shutters.

I get up. I search my room for a distraction, but pickings are slim. Two pairs of pants, some MSF T-shirts and a few other clothes sit on a metal rack beside the window, and my laptop gathers dirt on a plastic desk. On the cold concrete floor, underwear; on the blue-grey walls, nothing. The only other objects of note are the half-dozen books stacked beside a candle on the cardboard box I'm using for a bedside table, but they're exactly the wrong books for a day like this. References on African history and tropical medicine, a novel set in Afghanistan, and an account of the Rwandan genocide. I've got no idea what I was thinking when I packed.

Back to bed.

Andrea begins to stir in her bedroom, to the right of mine, then heads out for a jog. The others are likely still sleeping. A relative silence descends again, and in it I hear termites rustling softly, gnawing at the crudely hewn poles of the roof frame above me. An almost imperceptible mist of wood dust drifts down, creating a brown residue on the mesh of my mosquito net—the supporting structure of my shelter being chewed, milligram by milligram—and I imagine it won't take much to bring the remaining honeycomb down. A few days of rain in the wet season, perhaps, or the rumble of another cargo jet landing. Or a bird. One of those large, big-bellied, waterbirds. They'd weigh five or ten kilograms; this thing could hold maybe one. Not that there's much chance of large waterbirds flying past here, though. The war decimated wildlife populations. They say that thirty years ago one could find black rhino, elephants, lion, buffalo, giraffes, buck and zebra roaming the area, but domesticated animals and small birds are all I've seen since arriving. A cruel irony given we're in a designated wildlife reserve.

The desperate search for food during the war led to these animals being eaten out of local existence. Even the country's national animal, the black sable antelope, was hunted almost to extinction, although elephants suffered a more senseless fate: rather than for food, entire herds were slaughtered by UNITA troops (at times with machine guns, in coordinated attacks from helicopters) for ivory, which was then sold on to Asian markets to help fund the war. It's understandable then that the earlier leopard attack, as dramatic as it was, had actually been viewed as a positive sign by many: native fauna are finally returning. Hippos are known to wallow in downstream pools, and I've heard our staff mention that elephants have been spotted further south. But still, nothing in Mavinga.

A door flings open loudly to the left of my bedroom. It's Pascal's.

'We need to do something about this!' he says, uncharacteristically animated for this hour.

'What?' calls Tim, from the other end of the compound.

'THESE FUCKING DONKEYS!'

'I'M IN THE SHOWER,' Tim yells.

Pascal goes on, complaining to no one in particular. '*CAZZO!* THEY HITCH THESE ANIMALS BEHIND OUR FENCE, AWAY FROM THEIR HOMES, RIGHT NEXT TO OURS. HOW CAN WE SLEEP WITH THIS NOISE? EVERY NIGHT, RIGHT OUTSIDE MY—'

'I'M IN THE FUCKING SHOWER!' Tim calls again, but Pascal's on a roll now. '*VAFFANCULO, PEZZO DI MERDA—*' he goes on, which I find amusing because he does it so frequently, and so passionately, about the most benign of incidents.

As for Tim, he's likely to be in the shower for a while yet. He appears to actually enjoy the freezing water, singing in a rich baritone as he flirts with hypothermia in that little shed. Pascal and I do no such thing. We've deferred instead to the heat-a-pot-to-splash-yourself technique for the moment—best undertaken during the warmer afternoon hours. Andrea puts us all to shame, anyway. She showers straight after her dawn jogs, long before the rest of us have contemplated rising, then once more at night, long after even Tim's deemed it too cold.

Not that I'm taking an active interest in the living habits of my workmates. It's just the unavoidable reality of living in close confines. Proximity, squeaky doors, single-brick walls and poor insulation have long negated any illusions of privacy, and we already know well each other's personal oddities—and on a level I'd even find uncomfortable at this stage of a torrid romance. Andrea, for example, whose Germanic obsession with neatness is rivalled only by her team-mates' lack of it, wears sandals to go to the latrine during the night. I know this because my bedroom window faces the latrine, its shutters an inch smaller than the opening they're meant to cover. Pascal, however—who makes it through most of the day on Nutella and cigarettes, and whose resemblance to Che Guevara goes beyond the mere physical (had he been born thirty years earlier, I'm confident he'd have swapped his MSF T-shirt for the uniform of a freedom fighter)—wears no footwear to the latrine, and is usually the culprit for leaving the pit's lid open. In contrast, Tim closes the toilet grate. He also speaks in his sleep, snores heavily, and, since his previous breakup, no longer believes that love exists . . . which is all just the tip of the iceberg. Who knew we'd be each other's relationship counsellors, career advisors, political sounding boards, and private audience—willing or otherwise—to tales of sexual misadventures? Living on top of each other like this can't be underestimated.

As for my insomnia, the donkeys had little to do with it. The death of that young girl unnerved me. I've not seen a child die before, and I've never seen people react like that. Not to anything. I'd expected that deaths would be an inevitability out here; one in four Angolans die before their fifth birthday, probably more in places like Mavinga; and as a doctor, I've dealt with death. I've certified bodies of patients on the wards in Australia, and been called to open bags in the morgues of regional hospitals in the small hours of the morning. I've made phone calls to relatives and heard their sobbing on the end of the line, and been a part of discussions with families regarding end-of-life decisions. It's always sad. But it's never been like this. Never children. This is different. And the intimacy of it all, being there to watch that family grieve like that . . .

I heard crying early this morning as news spread around town. The family carry the body around afterwards, I'm told, and a funeral procession will snake its way towards their village today. So now I wonder: did we make a mistake with her care? Did she even have a chance at all out here, with or without our treatment? I can see no way to objectively assess this. As with so many of the patients on the ward, I'd give anything for a senior medical colleague who understands this context to come out here, just for a day, to guide me, correct me, even to reprimand me if needed. Because I've read the medical guidelines many times, and the theory I'm okay with. It's the application of it that's not so straightforward.

Patients here often present late, in advanced stages of illnesses that aren't seen back home, and that crutch of Western medicine that I normally rely on is absent: abundant tests. It's as if we're practising medicine in the nineteenth century. To determine a patient's haemo-globin level, I pull down their lower eyelid and gauge the colour (we have a lab test, but it's rudimentary), and to check a foetal heart rate, Andrea listens to the mother's belly with an empty cone-like device, a Pinard's stethoscope, as if eavesdropping on a conversation in another room. Fevers present a particular problem. The causes are infinite, the cases many and the only tests we have are kits for HIV, syphilis, malaria and hepatitis, as well as that little microscope and devices for blood grouping. So I trawl textbooks for clues I'd not ever needed in Australia. If it's typhoid, for example, the pulse will be unusually slow; in neonatal tetanus the baby won't latch onto the breast properly. If it's *Borrelia* the fever will likely recur, and in measles you'll see telltale white spots inside the mouth. Such signs can be subtle and easy to miss, though. Yet even diagnosing things as ostensibly straight-forward as broken limbs is not without difficulty. A conversation with a soldier last week, who'd fallen on his arm during training—

'How did you break it?' we asked.

'So it *is* broken?'

'Possibly. Does it feel broken?'

'What does broken feel like?'

'Good question. Is it very sore?'

'Yes.'

'Did you fall hard?'

'Yes.'

'And what if I wiggle it a little here?'

'*AIEEAH!*'

'Sorry—let's assume it's broken. We'll plaster it, and you'll need to wear this for four weeks, okay?'

Then again, even having a clear diagnosis doesn't always make things easier. Days after we saw the soldier, a young boy presented with a significantly deformed forearm—undoubtedly broken. How then to assess it? Good painkillers and a firm feel along the fracture line, pushing hard enough to feel through the swelling. Were there two fragments of bone in there, or more? Who knew. Had he suffered any damage to nearby nerves or blood vessels? Didn't seem to be the case. So we gave even stronger painkillers, took a breath, then pulled, bent and massaged the arm back into shape, all of which contradicts my every instinct as a Western doctor regarding certainty. Who would do such things in a litigious, resourced society? My experiences in Thailand had certainly been challenging, but there we had a modern hospital to refer people to.

So I've taken to contacting anyone I can for advice. The MSF surgeon in Europe graciously replies to my many emails, and I frequently query specialists in Australia. Last week I called the switch-board of Melbourne's Royal Eye and Ear Hospital from our satellite phone and spoke to the on-call ophthalmologist about a young man who'd been carried to us from the Christian mission, an hour from town, having gone suddenly blind. Their advice was excellent; people are always keen to help, the problem is that we seldom have the equipment needed. Drugs we're usually okay for—I've not yet needed a drug and not been able to find it in the pharmacy, or at least a suitable substitute—but equipment is the issue.

So yes, I need an experienced colleague. And while they're here, I'd ask them kindly to take one of the nights on call for me, because this enduring sense of dread regarding a call to the next disaster, every day for the foreseeable future, is draining in itself.

Indulging my self-piteous wallow, I called my girlfriend last night—or ex-girlfriend, or whatever we are at the moment because we've been emailing each other a lot so I wasn't really sure where we stood. *She* was. 'I can't be your support,' she said. 'You left me to go there. I need space.'

(Sofia was right: you do need someone to think about out here.)

My parents fortunately didn't need any space. They were thrilled to hear from me and encouraging of this whole experience, something I desperately needed to hear because I wonder at times whether massaging arms in one needy village out of the thousands on the continent will make any difference at all, no less if we're going to leave soon anyway . . . But parents are good at smoothing over that stuff. (And, at only four dollars a minute via satellite, I was treated to an update regarding the family dog, the latest rugby scores, and progress with the new kitchen flooring. A nice taste of home—a home that's already starting to feel strangely unfamiliar, even though it's only been weeks since I left.)

Anyway, there's no point mulling over what happened yesterday. I can't change it. And today of all days is not to be squandered with introspection: it's Sunday. Our day off.

'Hey, Damien,' calls Tim.

'Yeah?'

'You up?'

He sounds like he's in the office, next to the shower at the hospital end of our compound.

'Still in bed,' I call back.

'What?'

'IN BED.'

'YOU HAVE AN EMAIL FROM SOMEONE NAMED *ANNA* ON HERE,' he shouts.

'THANKS.' I'll read it later, I decide. She's an old university friend.

'I DON'T REMEMBER YOU TELLING US ABOUT AN *ANNA*,' he says, and now the door on the other side of my bedroom swings open again.

'*Anna*?' asks Pascal. 'You definitely did not mention *Anna*. TIM—IS HE KEEPING THINGS FROM US?'

That thing about living together? Yet again, any notions of privacy are shattered.

'AND YOU HAVE ONE FROM A NICOLLE,' calls Tim. 'JESUS, WHAT HAVE YOU BEEN DOING ON THE INTERNET, *NOVO DOCTOR*?'

'SHE'S MY SISTER!' I shout back.

'IF YOU SAY SO. PASCAL AND ANDREA, A FEW HERE FOR YOU. AND *MERDA*! DAMIEN—ANOTHER ONE FROM THE EX! DID THIS THING NOT END?'

I bury my head under the pillow.

• • •

Spending a day off in Mavinga is not without its challenges. A walk around town is the norm, and we'll make one together, although not until the daytime heat wanes this afternoon. Dominga is off, too, so one of us will have to prepare lunch and dinner—no pleasant task in that dingy kitchen. And we'll need to do some exercise; a jog on the airstrip, or maybe set up the badminton net we found in the store room. But even doing all of this, everything we can think of—twice even—will leave at least twelve hours to spend with the others. Or in the hospital. *Again*. So really, there's no rush to get out of bed.

We lounge around our bedrooms for much of the morning, taking turns catching up with correspondence from home. Reading fills in a little more time. By midday I've shaved, checked emails, cooked porridge, reviewed the handful of sicker patients and been thrashed by Pascal in a game of chess. Andrea's busy in the kitchen, where, in a fortuitous turn for the rest of us, she's embracing a personal stress-management technique benefiting us all: baking. We three meanwhile kick a football in the back yard, an activity that's cut short when the ball's thumped far over the fence—

'You go.'

'Fuck that!'

'But it's *your* turn.'

'No chance! No way am I going that far.'

—because we're not entirely sure about the ground where it's ended up. The airstrip to our left is free of mines, the collection of huts further along is fine, and we can see no *Perigro, Minas!* signs in the foreground, but our map on the office wall has this area marked as being off-limits. We think it's safe; to the north of the airstrip are the bulk of those de-mining grids I'd seen, and we're now to the south. As well, bridges, water collection points and fruit trees are more likely to have been danger areas, but there are none of these features ahead of us. And none of the donkeys grazing here seem to have any injuries, either, but before we can agree on who's going to retrieve the ball a group of young kids have run over anyway—*'CUIDADO!'* we yell, 'BE CAREFUL!'—and had a kick of it among themselves before kindly throwing it back.

By mid-afternoon we've exhausted all extracurricular activities. Paperwork is what we've defaulted to. And it's now, with the temperature rapidly dropping, that it's best to head out.

As with previous days off, the market will be our ultimate destination, even if Toyota was right: there's little of interest to buy. People-watching is the real reason we go, because the same piles of donated clothing and cheap goods (candles, batteries, soap, cigarettes, handheld radios, hair beads and Western-styled wigs) clutter the shelves of the three dozen ramshackle stalls, while the town's meagre food supplies, sold on the outskirts, are a sobering sight. Here, women and girls kneel behind paltry quantities of stock spread on cloths before them—little mounds of maize, dry biscuits, small piles of okra, a few tubers, maybe some oil or cans of fish. How the town feeds itself with this we're not sure. Ironic then that the only other goods we've come across being sold, aside from beer, are diamonds. As fanciful as that sounds, we've now been approached twice by men offering handfuls of the uncut gems, taken presumably from the large alluvial deposits to our north. The stones look merely like broken glass, but there's every chance they're genuine; the trans-border trade is still thriving in the region, although the prospect of time in an Angolan *prisão* has so far kept us from investing in it.

So the market it is. I charge my camera. Put a few Angolan *kwanzas* in my pocket, change batteries on the walkie-talkie and let the hospital guard know. We'll leave in fifteen minutes, we decide, except that Sergio's at the office door right now, describing what I suspect will be my alternative arrangements. Surgery.

• • •

For three weeks we've not taken a major case to theatre here. Potential candidates have been managed medically, albeit not always with Roberto's agreement, but Sergio now leads me to see a young woman who unequivocally needs an operation. This worries me greatly. Not so much her condition—likely appendicitis. More, the conditions under which we're about to operate.

The theatre is a small brick room attached to Maternity, where the only hints of modernity are a handheld pulse-oximeter and halogen lamp. A car battery powers the latter. Two shelves of medical supplies, a steel operating table and a curtained window account for the rest of the fittings, and a crack in the wall allows for some ventilation.

I enter and find the anaesthetist setting up in the room. Veronica's her name. She normally works with Andrea in the pharmacy, sometimes also on the wards as an *enfermeira*.

Veronica looks a little nervous.

'Have you done this before?' I ask her.

'A few times,' she says, meekly.

'What training have you had?'

'One of the other doctors showed me,' she says. 'And I use this chart on the wall.'

'What anaesthetic do you use, Veronica?'

'Ketamine.'

'And what else?'

'Just ketamine,' she says. 'We only have ketamine.'

This is a problem. I've given the drug in emergency departments as a sedative and painkiller for minor procedures, and vets use it widely for surgery on animals. It's an illicit party drug, too; Special-K, it's called, taken for its dissociative and hallucinatory effects. But for use as the sole anaesthetic, in open abdominal surgery? I'm not convinced.

Roberto's here. Sergio had called him earlier and now takes me to see him. He's squatting in the doorway of a small shed behind the adults' wards, watching something simmering over coals at the centre of the space. He looks up.

'*Novo Doctor*,' he notes unenthusiastically. He returns his attention to the coals.

'How are you, Roberto?'

'*Bom*.'—Good.

'Good. Have you seen this woman?'

He nods, watching the coals.

'And?'

He thinks it's appendicitis, he tells me. I tell him I agree. He says nothing.

'So what now?' I ask.

'We will take it out.'

'Okay.'

He stares quietly at the coals.

'When?' I ask.

'Soon.'

'Okay.'

Another awkward pause. Sergio walks off.

'Uh, have you done many of these appendicectomies before, Roberto?'

He stares at me, saying nothing.

'Is that a yes?'

He continues staring. I take it as a yes.

'Good,' I say. 'So, do we do it now?'

'As soon as the steriliser has finished,' he says.

'*Sim*. Okay. But what steriliser, by the way?'

'This one.'

'Which one?'

He nods towards the large pot simmering above the fire.

'That's the steriliser?'

'An autoclave, *Novo Doctor*,' he corrects me. '*Sim*. This is an autoclave.'

Jesus Christ! Our steriliser is a pot on top of a fire?

My anxiety levels ramp up as he asks me how I thought we'd cleaned the instruments, but I really hadn't considered it at all, hadn't needed to until now. But that's the least of the issues, just the start of it, because an hour later we're standing in theatre, scrubbed and gowned, only an iodine-bronze square island of the young woman's belly visible below us and the rest of her covered by a sea of sterile green drapes, when Roberto turns to the woman's husband—*the husband's in theatre, too!*—to ask him for permission to proceed.

'Sir,' Roberto says. 'We are going to start cutting now, okay?'

Sofia had forewarned me about this, although seeing it is no less surreal. The patient's husband is sitting not far from us, on a wooden stool; a farmer, dressed awkwardly in green surgical scrubs, about to watch us open his wife's belly. 'It's a security thing,' Sofia had explained. 'It's important the family know exactly what's going on in theatre, in case something goes wrong. They won't operate without the relatives there.'

Four others are crowded into this room, too. Veronica and her *enfermeira* assistant; Agostinho, the surgical assistant; and Andrea, who's kindly offered to help me.

The husband smiles, nodding his permission to begin.

Roberto lifts a scalpel from the tray of steel instruments to his side, then re-examines her belly and feels the anatomical landmarks. Satisfied, he makes a firm, straight, midline incision below her navel. The layers of her abdominal wall cleave neatly under the pass of his blade; black skin, yellow globules of fat, beef-red muscle, each in turn. Roberto pauses briefly to allow Agostinho to tie off oozing blood vessels, then opens the abdominal cavity itself with a pair of scissors. I feel a little easier about my decision. He seems to know what he's doing. Gently, he slips the gloved fingers of his right hand into her abdomen and feels around for a moment. He removes his hand and extends the incision slightly, then re-explores the cavity and retrieves a loop of bowel.

'Her appendix,' he states, pointing out the finger-like diverticulum. He reinserts his hand. Kissing noises fill the air as moist organs slide against each other, sloshing and slurping while he probes. 'Her ovaries,' he declares next, pointing to the relevant structures.

I nod in agreement.

'Which ones do you want us to take out?' he asks, voice somewhat muffled by his surgical mask.

'*Sorry?*'

'Which of these, *Novo Doctor,* do you want us to take out?'

'Say what, Roberto?'

'Her appendix, *Novo Doctor,* or her ovaries? Which would you like me to remove?'

Did I just hear wrong? I look to Andrea, who's standing beside Veronica, but she's equally wide-eyed, which only confirms it.

'You serious, Roberto?'

He is.

My low-grade sweat of background unease shifts gear into a full-scale tropical deluge. 'You're the surgeon,' I stammer. 'This is your decision, no?'

It traditionally is.

'I'm not a surgeon,' he says. 'You know this.'

'Are you kidding me?'

'I'm a surgical *clinico*. I do the cutting. *You* are the doctor, so you must decide what her diagnosis is, and what is normal or not normal in her belly. Now, are you happy with her appendix and ovaries?'

The words resonate in my head like a guilty verdict being delivered in a bad courtroom drama. Roberto drops a clamp back onto the tray; it clangs, bounces, echoes like a judge's gavel and I can't believe what we're doing in here. *Christ, it's hot in here—Andrea, is it hot?* This surgical garb is killing me. I want to adjust my mask, I need a little air. *My God, Andrea, what the hell are we doing in this town!* I glance around the room and try to gather my thoughts as I look to the husband, his face one of simple humility as he stares back, implicit in his expression the enormous trust he's placed in us. Beside me is Agostinho, comfortable, relaxed, adeptly tying off oozing vessels; watching me from across this open belly is Roberto, wearing the confidence of a man relieved of the burden of decision-making for the time being. To my right, Veronica's sweating as she corrects the position of the simple plastic Guedel device in the patient's mouth to help her breathing—like a big plastic straw, really—but the patient begins to gurgle so Veronica tries again, then introduces a suction catheter to the patient's mouth to clear the airway secretion, and now she's hopping—*Andrea, she's fucking hopping!*—and a loud *clank* commences beneath the table so I drop my head to look below and see her stomping energetically on a small metal foot-pump to generate suction for the tube. *This is utter insanity! I want out,* we need to close this woman up as soon as possible but gleaming ahead of me on a bronzed belly is the soft whiteness of her two ovaries . . .

'Uh, my God, Roberto,' I stutter. 'Her ovaries look completely normal. Let's leave them in.' I've assisted and watched enough operations to know what normal looks like, and her ovaries look fine.

Roberto agrees. 'Then we will just remove the appendix,' he states.

What—we're bargaining for body parts now?

'Hang on, Roberto. Let's look at it again.'

He gently returns the ovaries via the incision and isolates the appendix. Although rupture is not imminent, it's definitely inflamed. I agree with Roberto—we should remove it. He nods and turns to address the patient's husband, who's still sitting on the stool against the back wall. 'Come here, sir,' he says. 'But do not touch anything.'

The man approaches and peers over Roberto's right shoulder. Roberto lifts the small, finger-like structure as the husband regards the tissue with a detached fascination, not in the least bit squeamish. I've seen medical students faint over far less—*and this is his wife!* The husband nods his approval.

'Good. You can take your seat again, sir,' Roberto tells him, and that's where the man stays: on his stool, quietly, in his scrubs, watching two strangers debate the fate of his wife's organs over her open abdomen.

Roberto then performs an appendicectomy—not the fastest, but more importantly a competent one. I'm immensely relieved. The three of us assist with closing each layer of the abdominal wall, then dress the wound and carry the woman to *Intensivo*. The ketamine wears off quickly.

The husband's thrilled with our work.

'You did the right thing, *Novo Doctor*,' says Roberto, as we head to the side room to get changed.

I nod, still rattled by what I've seen.

'You did,' he repeats.

I sincerely hope so. More, I hope that the young woman recovers. And that we never, ever, have to operate on someone again.

8. FIGHTING CUBANS

The low sun ignites the first clouds I've seen in the five weeks since I arrived, colouring them deep reds and hot pinks: a pair of woolly lips, pouting as they kiss a cool sky. It's the first hint of rain. A promise that the world here may not be brown and dusty forever, and that this town may soon be able to feed itself properly. We're now entering the ominously titled *hunger gap*—the period between the exhaustion of the last harvest and the arrival of the next—and the spread at the market is looking more worrying each day, the land even drier.

Pascal's busy with Toyota as I enter the hospital, working on the awning above the waiting area. They've been checking the compound roofing lately, but this area appears to get more than its share of attention. My suspicion is it has something to do with the triage clerk beneath it.

'Why are you up there again?' I ask Pascal.

'What?'

'Weren't you up there last week?'

'Maybe,' he smiles.

'She's far too busy to flirt with you guys,' I stir, nodding towards the attractive young clerk. The first of the day's hundred outpatients

110

are queuing in front of her desk, an unimpressed child crying beneath the weighing tree to her right.

Pascal shakes his head. 'Just fixing the canvas.'

'This canvas gets very loose, *Novo Doctor*,' laughs Toyota. 'The wind can make it very loose.'

I'm not convinced. But either way, whether they're flirting or not, I still envy Pascal his job. I'm not sure how to manage the hospital. Of the three thousand volunteers MSF sends out annually, around half won't undertake a second stint. The reasons are varied and include, among others, family and career commitments, volunteering with a different organisation, disillusionment, or simply having been over-whelmed. And as I now enter the assessment room to join the team for the Monday handover, the start of my second month here, I empathise fully with this latter group. I'm in over my head.

Twenty of us squeeze onto the wood benches, uncomfortably cold. Woollen hats are pulled low and lab coats cinched tightly, and everyone has a cough—dry air and smoky huts ensure this. The light in the room is gloomy, the mood equally so. And the smell: burned flesh. It's inescapable. Both doors are wide open and our twenty bodies huddled together, but still we smell it. Still we *breathe* it. And still my stomach churns from it. The source of this is a man lying in *Intensivo* behind us, who'd arrived two days ago with charred expanses of skin after having fallen into a fire. These black *eschars* cover most of his lower body, and they're crisp and hard, like bark on a human tree, and they all need to be removed. Without doubt we should fly this man out. His chances of survival here are minimal and we've spoken with him about it, but he lives on the Christian mission just outside town and has no money for treatment in the city. No way to get back, either. He wants to be with his family, he says, even if we could find a way to send him and arrange for treatment. Here, people from the mission can visit him, and his wife and young daughter can stay beside him. He wants that more than any treatment.

Carrying through the rank air this morning is the sound of moaning, although not from the man with burns. It's from the next bed, where the patient I'd performed the lumbar puncture on two weeks ago is becoming increasingly delirious. Just yesterday I found him tied to his bed with gauze bandages; the staff had done this to stop him lashing out, although by evening he'd become too drowsy to do anything of the sort. When I last checked on him during the night, two other patients shared that tiny room as well; one, the young woman with the ulcerated breast cancer, recovering from her severe infection; the other, an infant boy who's no longer here. Literally. He was carried home hours ago, wrapped in blankets by a distraught family.

'*Bom dia*,' begins Senhor Kassoma, drawing my attention away from *Intensivo*. He's standing at the front, dressed immaculately as always, this morning in neat blue shirt, grey trousers, old business shoes, and a floppy denim beach hat—his solution for a cold bald head. He nods to the attendees and opens his black journal, then begins recounting last Friday's supervisor meeting. First up, last month's statistics. He goes through all of them—admissions, deaths and deliveries—and delves next into the minutiae: numbers of chickenpox cases, and what exactly was stolen from our big delivery. People soon nod off. I try not to—Roberto's directly across from me—although the five health workers huddled to my right are long gone, rocking back and forth like white-breasted budgies about to fall off their perches as they succumb to the *Snooze-Jerk-Wake* cycle. I smile, but not for long.

To my immediate left, wedged between myself and Sergio, is Adolfo. Adolfo's a soft-spoken, competent *clinico* in his late thirties, and uncle to that boy who'd mysteriously gone blind. The two of us spent much time with the boy but despite advice from the specialist in Melbourne we still couldn't diagnose him (I suspect it was a brain tumour), so last week Adolfo made the decision to take the boy home. This week, Adolfo's staring at his shoes. The boy died a few days ago.

Behind Adolfo, propping himself against a wall, is Manuel, another of the *clinicos*. Although genial, Manuel is jittery and nervous, flitting confusedly around the wards like a jumpy butterfly as he makes repeated mistakes with patients. He's by far the least capable of the health workers so I've made it my goal to coach him. We've started meeting twice a week in private to revise the basics, but only yesterday—my fourth Sunday, and ostensibly a day off—I came past and found him about to administer unprescribed, frankly dangerous quantities of IV fluids to two children. He'd read the wrong protocol—the one for someone a mere sixty kilograms heavier than the children were—yet next week Manuel's supposedly running this place at night.

And then of course there's Sergio. Belligerent, moody, at times unpredictable, although I'm beginning to suspect he's all bluster. He's without doubt a capable health worker, and for the moment anyway we're getting along well enough.

And really, as I sit here and look around, it strikes me what a disparate group we are. Ten *enfermeiras*, seven *clinicos*, four midwives, myself and the dispensary clerk—just this morning's shift. Together we range in age from late twenties to early sixties, and possess work habits varying from remarkably competent to frankly dangerous, motivated to profoundly lazy, compassionate to disinterested, and irreproachably virtuous to almost certainly alcoholic. (The dispensary clerk is looking a little too red-eyed these mornings.) Hard to tell at times whether treating patients or managing the staff is the more challenging aspect of work.

Kassoma continues. Half the room is by now snoozing but like an experienced school teacher he knows how to get his audience back; '*Então!*' he calls—So!—and bangs his diary on the desk. A dozen bodies jolt suddenly and he smiles dryly. 'Enough statistics, *colegas*! Let us change the topic.'

Throats clear and bums shuffle.

'*Finalmente,* our *Coordenador* told me of MSF activities this last month. If I may share this with you.' He stands tall and turns the page of his journal, his shirt pocket sagging under the weight of a half-dozen pens. 'Last week, *colegas,* the cholera outbreak along our coast came to an end. This is good news for Angolans, you will agree. Twenty-six thousand people were treated—'

'*Eh's!*' fill the room,

'—but MSF are now closing treatment centres.'

Nods of approval circulate. The outbreak was the largest in recent years, with an estimated five hundred new cases occurring each day during the peak. Two thousand people had died.

'Next,' says Kassoma, '*Coordenador* informed us that MSF are increasing their response in *Ha* . . .' He stops. He apologises and squints at the page, adjusts his too-big glasses. 'H. A. I. T. I.,' he spells out. '*Novo Doctor?*'

I nod. 'Sim, Senhor. *Haiti.*'

'*Obrigado.*'—Thank you. 'In Haiti, MSF have treated thousands this past month. They were victims of violence. MSF hope that—'

'Because of what?' interrupts Therese, the slim, stern-faced head nurse. 'Why the fighting? Is there a war?'

Kassoma's not sure. He looks to me and I try to explain what little I know, adding that there's a UN mission in the country. The Angolans know well of the UN—a peacekeeping force had monitored the failed elections here following a short-lived ceasefire agreement during the 1990s.

'*Obrigado, Novo Doctor,*' says Kassoma. He tells us next of a malnutrition crisis in Niger where MSF have admitted two thousand children for treatment in the past week, but he's not sure the figure's right. '*Verdade?*' he asks me. True?

I nod. I've been following the field reports via email.

'*Two thousand!*' he exclaims, shaking his head. Others around the room express their disbelief, too, clicking tongues and muttering softly. 'Please,' says Kassoma, 'we must all pray for the people in Niger. This is a sad thing. Too sad.'

He pauses for a moment and turns the page. 'Next, MSF are worried about casualties in *Leb* . . . L. E. B. A. N. O. N. *Novo Doctor?*'

I pronounce the name for him, and he goes on to list the half-dozen countries in which projects are scaling up this month, his demeanour that of a pastor delivering an important sermon. He's the oldest of our staff, clearly the patriarch of the hospital, and people listen intently. But I find this surprising given the topic—could they even know where any of these countries are? Surely not. Kassoma, by far one of the more educated in town, can't even pronounce most of them! Yet everyone seems genuinely interested, far more than with the housekeeping issues regarding our own hospital—some are now even taking notes! Like Senhor Calvino, to my right, the jovial, obese *clinico* from Outpatients—he's actually writing this down! So too is Roberto, and Nene, the regal head of Maternity—both are jotting this in their journals! But for whom? For what conceivable reason? Why should they care about these unpronounceable countries? Yet they genuinely seem to. They express their collective disapproval, shake their heads empathetically . . . which, as I sit in this bitter cold, bathed in the smell of body odour and burned skin, I find quietly touching. Do they not know that others are reading about Angolans and their difficulties, shaking *their* heads? That when I send my group emails home, watered down as they are, they prompt a flood of pity and disbelief aimed *their* way? Or that MSF have serious concerns regarding their pulling out of here?

I'm not so sure that they do. And I may be mistaken, but what I suspect is this: they don't perceive themselves as victims. Before, there was a war. Now the war is over. To whom or what else can they compare themselves? No travellers pass through, and no TVs project images of Hollywood lifestyles into their crumbling huts. No one here receives phone calls from overseas relatives (there are no phones) and the only accessible media is Angolan radio. Many haven't seen a city since before the war, if ever, and we volunteers are their only regular contact with an outside world. And if MSF are confident enough to soon leave them, yet are rushing headlong into these other countries, then surely things here must be okay?

I'm making assumptions. Although really, whatever their reasons may be, I'm not sure if any group could empathise more with people in need than those I see huddled around me. Because more than anyone, they must know true hardship. The kind it takes to make a child stoop to eat sand.

Kassoma comes to the final item on his agenda, the antifungal trial. Today is just over two weeks since we started. Decision time. So now I brace myself, because if the results don't go my way, then I may well be forced to browse Kassoma's list for another posting.

Kassoma calls Carlos to the front. He's the younger of the health workers, a good-looking, charismatic man with an affinity for aftershave, and he's been charged with keeping the results. He pulls crumpled sheets from his pocket and reaches for a calculator. 'Wait!' he calls over chatter. 'Okay, in total, eighty-two children were watched.' He goes through the numbers slowly, then raises his eyebrows. '*Eh!* Okay, in the end it looks like the children were the same! Almost all were good in three days. So I cannot say I saw a difference.'

Murmurs ripple through the room. Sergio jumps up to fetch the calculator from the desk, scrutinising the papers as Kassoma watches keenly over his shoulder.

'I am not so sure,' says Kassoma. 'Maybe *Novo Doctor* did not record his numbers clearly?'

'Carlos recorded everything,' I say. 'Not me,' although I had kept a close eye on the patients as well, and it's been obvious no one was worsening.

'But two weeks is not enough, *Novo Doctor*,' protests Sergio. 'And we have been treating our patients like this for a while in Mavinga. For some it *may* be helping.'

'Fair enough, Sergio. If someone gets worse we can consider it,' I say, 'but otherwise we're just wasting money. These bottles are flown from France.'

Sergio's not happy. Andrea's sitting just behind me and offering to help translate, but—*for the first time since I arrived!*—I seem to be understanding most of the conversation. Sergio argues the point until Kassoma finally cuts him off, unable to find a mistake with Carlos's maths. 'A deal is a deal,' says the older man, looking more resigned than convinced. '*Novo Doctor* has made his point. Let us agree to stop using it, and we will watch closely what happens. But if things begin to change, *Novo Doctor*,' (out comes the pointed finger again), 'or if any of our children get sicker, we will talk about this again.'

'I'm happy with that, Senhor,' I reply.

'Because we will not tolerate our people getting worse,' he cautions.

'Of course not, Senhor.'

'In that case we have an agreement,' he declares. And with that, Mavinga General Hospital—where surgical instruments are boiled on the fire, and kids with swollen bellies and no shoes want high fives; and where staff worry more about the Haitians than the drugs stolen from our last major delivery—reaches out and hugs me. Not necessarily a big hug, but a hug nonetheless. And I relish it. And as the morning sun beams through the doorway, the world outside ablaze in warm orange light, I bask in the first small promise that I may actually last the months here.

• • •

Carlos is the man to stay beside on the rounds. His cologne creates a haze of impenetrable scent as we enter the kids' ward, although we're running late and people are already up, the windows open and fresh air flowing, and it's quite the sight, too—part breastfeeding centre, part hairdressing salon, it seems. Mothers and older sisters have gathered on beds to work on each other's hairstyles, fashioning cornrows, plaits, braids, tufts, dreadlocks, and twists from thick hair, with bright plastic beads often tied in for added effect. The breast-feeding continues as an aside. The mood is buoyant and almost all children improving, so we move quickly through the ward.

The adults present more difficulties in terms of medical treat-ment. The infections that dominate younger patients' admissions (gastroenteritis, malaria and pneumonia) are less common, and the consequences of war more evident, both physically and psychologi-cally. Many bear the scars of old injuries, often only incidental to their current presentations, or else symptoms that I suspect are related to stress. The variety of conditions seen is far larger, too.

We enter the women's ward. Eight patients lie in here this morning: seven women, and a man who's snuck in because the men's ward is too crowded, he says. As we begin, an interesting distraction is provided by the husband of the woman in bed six.

'*Desculpa!*' he says. Excuse me.

'How is your wife?' we ask. She's currently being treated for abdominal pain.

'Very good,' he replies. '*Muito melhor.*' Much better. 'But my knee is the problem. It is hurting too much.'

Sergio points him out the door. 'You can see Outpatients. We only see hospital patients here. *Female* hospital patients. And you too, my friend,' he adds, pointing to the man who'd snuck in.

The man with the knee pain asks again. He is too old, he says, and he cannot wait on those benches all day. He rolls his trouser leg up and climbs up beside his wife. 'Come. Please, you are already here. Just look quickly for me.'

Sabino obliges and asks him when the pain started, although before the man answers I know that we're already talking years here, maybe even decades, because intricate patterns of fine cuts form a tapestry of scars around his knee. He's been visiting traditional healers. 'It began a while ago,' he shrugs.

'When, more or less?'

'During the war—since the Cubans shelled us!' he replies, which catches me off guard. I'm more conditioned to hearing things like 'since I slipped in the supermarket'.

'In Cuito,' he adds. 'Cuito Cuanavale,' which sparks immediate interest across the room.

'You were in Cuito?' asks the man who snuck in, who himself is suffering back pain as a consequence of a shrapnel injury. 'I was there too,' he says, sitting up. 'When were you there? Were you with the South Africans?'—and suddenly knees and backs and requests for consultations are forgotten entirely as the two swap stories across the room. I've read about Cuito—it was reportedly the largest tank battle on the continent since World War II—and their comments are loaded with history. Why indeed were the Cubans fighting, and in such large numbers, on the opposite side of the Atlantic? Or the South Africans, for that matter?

I try to get my head around it as they chat. So I tune out from the wards, suspend disbelief, and visualise this little corner of earth on an online map. Then scroll out, hover high over the Atlantic and veer just a little to the left, pausing when Angola is on my right, South America on the left and Europe above, and go back in time a little while . . .

Sometime between two to three thousand years ago, these men's *Bantu* ancestors began a series of migrations across the continent, fanning out from our north to populate much of sub-Saharan Africa. Not until the late 1400s was there any contact between Europeans and Africans this far south, but that changed when a Portuguese *caravel* chanced upon the Congo River at what is now the north of the country. At around the same time, directly west across the Atlantic, the Portuguese landed in Brazil, and by the end of the century had colonised both regions. Trade grew, and in particular large sugarcane plantations were set up in Brazil and the Caribbean, requiring intense labour to maintain: the trans-Atlantic slave trade was born. And it boomed; by the early nineteenth century, between three and four *million* Africans had been taken from what's now Angola and shipped west, many of them ending up in Cuba—a fact that becomes relevant to the Angolan war, when heritage, not just the socialist ideologies shared with Angola's MPLA forces, is a large part of the reason Castro sends his troops here.

But what then of South Africans? What was a white apartheid government doing here, at The Edge of the World, fighting alongside black people for this dusty outpost?

Back to the map. Angola's long southern border is shared with Namibia, where the South Africans were involved in a separate war in the 1970s. By this time most colonial powers had divested themselves of their African interests, but the South Africans, who'd taken Namibia from the Germans, refused to grant the protectorate independence. A Namibian resistance movement sprang up and the South Africans fought back hard, chasing them north into Angola, where the group received support from the MPLA. This, and the prospect of Angola becoming a Marxist country, was unacceptable to the South African government, who consequently invaded Angola. In aid of this they also provided support to UNITA, who were already fighting the MPLA from bases in the south-eastern regions—which is where our little town comes in.

For over a decade the fighting drew on, and by the late 1980s UNITA were pinned down in Mavinga, on the brink of defeat. A huge battle ensued. South Africa sent more troops to help them (landings were made at night on the town's airstrip, alongside which UNITA soldiers would stand with kerosene lamps and candles to guide the pilots), and together they chased the MPLA north along our dusty road to the town of Cuito Cuanavale, a couple of hundred kilometres away. There, both sides dug in. Cuba sent fifteen thousand extra troops to help their MPLA comrades, and Russian jets bombed UNITA. For months the city was battered, and after all of this the battle was a stalemate. There were no clear victors, but there were consequences. South Africa and Cuba began withdrawing from Angola, and peace talks led to a ceasefire and elections in 1993. But UNITA lost; their increasingly belligerent leader, Savimbi, refused to accept this; and another decade of war followed until his death.

'So what can you do for my knee?' asks the old man, smiling a mostly toothless smile. 'Can you fix this pain?'

And from across the room: 'What about my back? What can you do about this shrapnel?'

Probably not much, although someone's gone to call Roberto. For now, *funge* and *feijão*, the Angolan staple of maize and beans, is being ladled into tin lunch bowls from the kitchen window, so we need to finish up. And there could be no better place than our last stop, the nutrition ward.

The twelve-bed unit has come to epitomise the value of our presence in Mavinga for me. I'm still wary of it, but I've now witnessed the recovery of the first cohort of children admitted since my arrival. Their physical transformation is impressive, the change in their disposition simply mesmerising; within weeks, once gaunt, lethargic children roam excitedly around the compound, chasing each other and livening up the hospital atmosphere. Rehabilitating them is like adding water to wilted flowers, then watching them bloom back to life.

We enter, and a young girl in a bright pink dress makes a beeline for us. She'd please like a hug. Valeriano's her name, and the little beard of high energy biscuit crumbs around her mouth suggests that her appetite is very much back to normal. It's an extremely good sign;

a cruel irony of malnutrition is that a loss of appetite occurs in late stages, necessitating the use of nasogastric tubes in some children to facilitate the gentle process of initial re-feeding—as is currently the case with Alberto Kakuhi, this morning's new admission.

'One year old,' says Sabino, who saw him earlier.

'Any recent illnesses?' I ask.

'Just a little diarrhoea for the last two weeks,' he says. 'But otherwise okay.'

'What's their food situation?'

He chats with mum in Nganguela. What follows is a common story in here; she fishes out a thin, leathery bag of a breast and squeezes it (no milk), then points to her three other children and says that she has all of them to feed as well. I'd ask why she doesn't just buy milk from the market, but I know the answer—usually there is none, and when there is it's too expensive.

So they'll all stay with us for a few weeks. Alberto will be given antibiotics, vitamins and de-worming tablets. He'll mewl irritatedly when the *enfermeira* syringes the low-calorie milk into his tube, but he'll receive this every three hours anyway, nights included. In a couple of days we'll likely remove the tube and wean him slowly to richer milk, then solids, and within two weeks he should be playing with his siblings. In three to four weeks he'll go home, returning for weekly follow-up and a ration of food to get the family through the next three months. It's an immensely satisfying process, albeit a time-consuming one for staff. Imagine then when MSF first arrived here: forty-four emergency feeding centres needed to be set up across Angola, requiring almost two hundred expat volunteers and two thousand Angolans to run them. In Mavinga, over three hundred patients were being treated for severe malnutrition in the one centre, with seven thousand others receiving emergency food rations in town. All of which makes our little unit, poignant as the sight of skinny children is, a comparatively reassuring picture.

But right now we need to leave. Lunch has been served and the healthier patients are sitting on mothers' laps, spooning fortified maize everywhere—onto hair, blankets, mum, the floor, and occasionally into their mouths—and Sergio's getting cranky. 'We also need to eat,' he complains, as Alberto's brother listens to the wrong end of his stethoscope. 'These ward rounds always take too long,' he sighs. 'Before, the other doctors were much quicker, *Novo Doctor*, and we get very hungry . . .' so Carlos offers him a high energy biscuit. Meanwhile, the girl in the pink dress asks for another hug, Sabino's got two kids pulling his lab coat, and Manuel's just been dealt a spoonful of red beans across his lab coat by Alberto's sister, whose white string earrings flutter as she giggles delightedly.

Seems all is not bad in Mavinga General, after all.

· · ·

All is not bad in the compound, either. A Friday night in mid-July, and the four of us gather around a fire in our back yard. We're doing this a couple of times a week now, buying wood from the kids who sell it from their donkey carts and building these fires to create a little variety. And what *wonderful* variety; Tim sits forward to stoke the embers, and a hundred little fireflies of glowing ash dance their way upwards, into a sky unlike any I've seen. The night is moonless, and as we recline on the sand and gaze up I find it easy to understand why so many ancient cultures were so enthralled with the stars. Unlike the few dozen pinpricks of light visible in cities back home it's a dense and detailed landscape here, the Milky Way not some nebulous concept you think you can maybe see, rather a luminescent veil spread out above us, a glowing silky cloth of light so real that it beckons you to reach up and try to grab it.

And far below it, the faint rhythms of *Kisamba* music crackles from handheld radios in huts near to us, and the conversation still flows around this little fire—somewhat improbably given that we share every evening, meeting and meal together, but there's no shortage of topics to cover. How Toyota got his name, for example, or plans for a wooden seat over the latrine. So I'm fast coming to the conclusion that I've been lucky with this team. Conflict is reputedly common in the field, but we've so far had only one disagreement (regarding breakfast cereals, of all things). Not bad for six weeks, four first languages and only three other faces. That said, visitors would be good, just *some* social variety, although Tim tells us that we're in luck. A group of Brits will be visiting the Christian mission near town in the coming month, and they may stop here. I look forward to it. And what then of any intimate relationships among the four of us? It seems fate has dealt us an interesting hand there, because Andrea, who turns heads as she leaves the shower, and who could have her pick of the men out here, just happens to be a born-again Christian. Of the strictly No-Flings type.

Earlier this evening we walked down to the river. On the way back I stopped at the hospital, watched the sunset with the families gathered along the fence line as they stirred maize into their tin pots over cooking fires. We made small talk (mostly asked each other 'Quê?' and laughed), and in the background we could all hear the choir practising in the mud-walled church off Main Road, singing Portuguese gospels in the most beautiful acapella. The kids from the Nutrition ward came out, too—they didn't dare want to be excluded from any gatherings; and as Tim now stirs up another shower of fireflies, and Pascal sings the Italian football anthem for the umpteenth time since their World Cup victory last week, I remind myself that money can't buy this.

Whatever *this* turns out to be.

9. WHAT APPENDIX?

In the whirling, dusty wind that blows through town these mornings, hundreds of people gather at our compound entrance.

'I want to make sure we are clear,' states Pascal, addressing the log team assembled near the gate. 'We need to keep this line moving. There are far more here than we planned for, so remember—each person gets one blanket, one bucket, one piece of soap, and a packet of high energy biscuits. And only the widows, elderly, and disabled. Okay? No one else receives anything. *No* exceptions. There won't be enough to go around otherwise.'

We'd only recently planned this handout. An excess of certain items had been found during a stock-take by Pascal, and we'd decided to arrange a free distribution rather than give it to the local Administration when we leave. And so it begins. The gate opens and barefoot elderly people, those with old injuries, and single mothers with children wrapped to their backs like surprised little starfish begin filtering through, taking away the packages one at a time. The poorest of the poor, in a country where more than half the population live on less than a dollar a day. The first wheelchair I've seen in Mavinga passes by, too—a man with no legs being pulled backwards in it by his friend, the wheels long since having shed their tyres—and by late morning the heat is oppressive, the crowd no smaller, yet still they stand quietly. Still they trickle past the front of our storage tent, one at a time, and carry off their packages.

'The people thank you!' says the King of Mavinga, who's seated in a plastic chair at the end of the table. I'd not met him before (I didn't even know Mavinga had a King!) and the man couldn't be further from the stereotypical image of an African leader. Not to my mind, at least. Dressed in off-white sports jacket and grey pants, he's a diminutive, grey-haired elderly man, speaking softly and smiling to all as they pass him. Toyota says he's a genuinely respected leader, democratically elected to the role by the *sobas*, the traditional heads of all local villages, and is empowered to deal with traditional issues like land and livestock disputes. The appointed Administration, on the other hand, representing the MPLA government in this UNITA town, are nowhere to be seen.

But the King, affable as he is, is unwittingly adding to some sense of guilt I'm feeling about this. 'I thank you, too,' he says, 'for what you are doing in Mavinga. The people are very grateful'—which frankly embarrasses me. Because please: *a bucket? A scratchy blanket?* There's little doubt that our gesture is token, we know this, but what worries me is the faint whiff of neo-colonialism: wealthy white people handing out freebies to impoverished Africans.

Our living conditions have previously prompted discussion of this issue among us expats. Ours is a relative island of wealth out here, a bastion of laptops, generators and imported food, and Pascal believes strongly that we should eat only what locals do. Tim doesn't. He's spent enough time on these missions, he says, having turned his back on a lucrative career in business, to accept that a little luxury is small recompense considering what we've given up to be here. Andrea and I are inclined to agree with him—if frozen chicken, South African porridge and a few chocolate bars are what it takes to keep us happy, so be it.

As for this distribution, we'd all rather be teaching or providing health care than giving handouts, but I've seen inside the local huts. A pot, water container, several blankets and straw baskets are the sum total of most people's assets, and few here have the capacity to earn money. The hundred Angolans employed by this project are almost the only group of salaried workers in town, so far be it for me to scoff at these packages.

The crowd gets no smaller. For every one person who comes through, two more gather in the distance. By midday, young men begin to force their way in. 'Why do we get nothing?' they shout. 'Why do you ignore us?'

Our outreach nurse is at the gate, allowing entry only to those on the lists made by each *soba*. He grabs the megaphone and re-explains the criteria as the organisation's obsession with strict impartiality becomes clear to me. A few of the men arc up.

'This old man is not even Ovimbundu!' yells one. 'Why are you letting him through? He is Nganguela! Is this not an Ovimbundu area? What of us?'

'It is based on necessity,' repeats our outreach nurse. 'Not tribe. We are here for those that need it most.'

But the criteria are largely redundant. Everyone here needs it most.

'My mother is too sick to walk to your compound!' declares a muscled young man, 'so why can I not take one for her?' Another pushes his way to the front, shows the long scar on his chest. 'This is an injury from the war! I too have an injury, so why can I not come through? Just because I am not missing a leg like that man, I cannot get help?'

The prospect of fighting seems possible. Ethnic tensions exist in the region, though this is the first time I've seen direct evidence of it. (Only months before I arrived, a person had been killed here when riots broke out over political differences.) For now, younger men become more agitated, and faces of those who've clearly already received goods begin to reappear. The team at the registrations table shuffle confusedly through their loose sheets of paper, but no one has any identification—

'Are you Joseph Lumumba, from *bairro* Seixta-Feira?'

'Yes, I am him!'

—so people say what they want anyway. Verifying it is impossible. Those most in need are getting pushed to the back, while those most aggressive will get their goods, one way or another. The logs soon abandon the criteria and hurriedly give out everything, and I wonder now what will happen when we shut this hospital, retrench a hundred staff, and try to fly out equipment when all these people watching it have nothing left to lose . . .

A fortuitous time for me to have to return to the hospital.

• • •

A complete change of scene over the road. The front hospital yard is unusually tranquil (most are at the distribution), but I hear moaning from the small room that Roberto and Agostinho use as Surgical Outpatients. It can mean only one thing. The Mavinga Dental Clinic is open.

'Morning, Agostinho,' I say, stepping past a handful of anxious-looking patients near the door. 'Everything okay?'

He looks up. He's standing behind a young man, leaning over him with one hand gripping firmly across the patient's forehead, the other prying out a tooth with dental pliers. Hard to tell who's sweating more.

'*Sim*,' he replies, stopping. 'Why would it not be?'

The patient looks immensely relieved by this sudden reprieve. Somewhat dazed, he explores his mouth with a finger; disappointment washes over his face as he discovers the offending tooth still in place.

'No reason,' I say. 'Just taking out the one tooth?'

'No,' he replies, and continues pulling, forearm trembling with effort. 'A few,' he groans.

'Has he had local anaesthetic?'

'*Novo Doctor,*' laughs Agostinho, stopping again. 'I do all of the dental work in Mavinga. What do you think?'

A half-empty vial and clean syringe sit on the nearby tray, so I presume so. I only hope it was an adequate dose because Agostinho now ups his effort, straining hard, and something's going to give— pliers, tooth or Agostinho's shoulder, I can't yet tell—and I wonder what the group of patients sitting outside are thinking. I've seen none running into the distance on any of these Dental Clinic days, so I suppose they've accepted this as the price of free treatment.

'You seen Roberto this morning?' I ask.

'*Sim.*'

'Where?'

'At the steriliser. Preparing for surgery.'

My stomach knots.

'Why do you look so worried, *Novo Doctor*?' chuckles Agostinho, and I only smile, shake my head unconvincingly, and lie that I'm not. But really I am, because I recall the roosters wandering out of theatre this morning, the car battery, that suction pump, the anaesthetic, the—

'Why do you look so worried, *Novo Doctor*?' chuckles Roberto, standing before the iodine-bronze belly of the young woman in the theatre only an hour later, and I only smile, shake my head unconvincingly and lie that I'm not. But really, I am, because—

'Sir, you will need to take that hat off,' Roberto tells the woman's husband, who's sitting in the far corner. (*Which is a part of the worry, Roberto.*)

The man shuffles outside, returns a moment later.

'We ready?' asks Roberto, clinking his surgical instruments into arrangement.

The husband nods.

'Veronica?'

Veronica nods, nudging her foot-pump into position.

'*Novo Doctor?*'

I grimace.

Roberto then grasps his scalpel and neatly divides the layers of her abdominal wall; skin, fat, muscle; then gently snips the pearly-blue peritoneal lining of her abdominal cavity with scissors. Air gushes into her belly as he stretches the opening. 'We should train you to be a surgeon, *Novo Doctor*,' he says, reaching for retractors.

'That would be good,' I say, rivulets of sweat already tracking their way down my back. A surgical gown over thick cotton scrubs make this small room unbearably stuffy.

'Tell me something,' he says, peering over his mask. 'We have been wondering about this. What kind of doctor does not know how to operate?' He pauses as Agostinho ties off a bleeding vessel—a time-consuming process, with each oozing vein or spurting arteriole having to be carefully closed with dissolvable sutures. A diathermy machine would cauterise the same within seconds back home.

'The others sent here could operate?' I ask.

'The good ones,' he says. 'Not all. But the good ones could.'

'Most doctors in my country can't operate, Roberto.'

'No?'

'Not at all. Only surgeons. Most of us use only medicines.'

Roberto chuckles. 'And how then is a doctor to cure his patients if he cannot operate?' he muses.

'We see different diseases, Roberto,' I say, explaining that we'd have used scans and blood tests to diagnose this woman's condition well before surgery, and that we're usually able to treat patients adequately with medications or less invasive procedures.

He opens her abdominal cavity further, sliding his right hand into the incision.

'We've also never had a war,' I go on, hoping that the Portuguese coming out of my mouth correlates with what I intend to say. I frequently have to stop and try to find a different way of explaining something. 'In our hospitals we see mainly older people with problems like heart attacks, diabetes, or emphysema,' I tell Roberto, and as we talk it strikes me that I've not seen a single person here with these conditions. My medical background would have to be the complete opposite to Roberto's. His, an education during the war by South African military surgeons, dealing largely with severe, acute problems in fit young patients, a large proportion of whom would urgently have needed surgery; mine, an education in the context of chronic illnesses associated with affluent lifestyles and an ageing population. For all that I'm learning here, there's little I'll be able to apply to an urban Australian hospital. I'm going to be wholly out of touch when I return.

'So, *O Novo Doctor* works in emergency centres?' Roberto asks.

'I do. Emergency departments.'

He looks again at Agostinho as he fishes around the patient's pelvis. 'An *emergency* doctor,' he notes in a playful tone. 'Imagine that: a doctor for emergencies, but one that can't *operate* in emergencies!' He ponders this as he shakes his head again. 'Never mind, *Novo Doctor*,' he says, sifting through loops of bowel. 'You do work well with the children here, this is true. And the adults' ward is doing fine. Sabino tells me too that things are changing in the malnutrition ward, that you are writing clearer protocols—and in Portuguese? I like the idea of this. You know that I was not a big supporter of this antifungal business you pulled—*Eh! To experiment on our people!*— but the children are doing okay. This is a good thing, *Novo Doctor*. And this chest tube you put in the other night? This I don't do.'

It was another dramatic night call. A man had arrived with a punctured lung and dislocated ankle following the first road traffic accident I'd heard of here: a cart rollover at the riverbank. The ankle was easy enough to clunk back into position, but his chest was the bigger issue. To allow leaking air around the injured lung to drain (necessary for it to re-inflate) I inserted a plastic tube via a small incision between two ribs at the side of his chest wall. This I've done in Australia—although not without an X-ray, and never without familiar equipment. So we improvised. As per instructions in an old textbook, I cut the finger of a surgical glove at both ends, then fixed one end over the end of the chest tube, the other hanging free. The collapsible lumen of the free end of the finger has the effect of a one-way valve, allowing air to escape but not re-enter his chest, and had worked perfectly well. At least until we found a better solution in the pharmacy the following day.

Roberto looks to Agostinho. 'You have done them?' he asks.

Agostinho mumbles something, but I struggle to understand what the man says. With or without his mask.

Roberto chuckles. 'I dare say that you did it well, *Novo Doctor*,' he says. 'Like a doctor should. But still, we are going to need to train you to be a *proper* doctor before you leave—a doctor who can *operate* on his patients. One who can really treat people.'

The others nod.

'Now, Agostinho. Let *O Novo Doctor* tie the vessels. We must not delay his teaching any longer. Pass him the sutures!' Roberto locates the patient's ovaries and pulls them to the surface, ending our conversation, heightening my unease.

The issue of surgery continues to remain problematic here, particularly decisions about which patients we should operate on. Our mandate is clear—that we're to operate only for life-threatening conditions that we can realistically manage—but a significant confounder remains. Namely, how can we know whether a condition is life-threatening if we can't diagnose it? It's a classic Catch-22: the only way to be sure in many cases is to open patients up and look, yet the only reason to open them up is if we're relatively sure of what the condition is.

We've performed two operations since that appendicectomy, a below-knee amputation and an emergency Caesarean, and in both patients the need had far outweighed the risk. Often though a woman will present to the hospital with non-specific pains and actually *insist* on surgery—the Rolls Royce of medical care, by public perception. The probability is that their condition is benign, although we can't always be certain. No less when the patients say that they're getting worse, and the family insist that they're dying, and partners get upset, and the rest of the ward rally around them to say that we must operate immediately. How then to be objective? I can't reassure them with a scan. And opening them up to look, with the risk being that they then succumb to any of a thousand complications, is clearly unjustifiable. As is waiting too long—they could then deteriorate. It's immensely difficult, a balance between being cruelly hesitant versus dangerously over-zealous, so Roberto and I debate each case (albeit a little more amicably these days). That said, the issue remains the bigger difficulty on the wards.

—But right now an ovary is demanding attention, glistening under the glow of the lamp; car batteries and ketamine will not last forever.

'You see this?' Roberto asks.

I nod. Two abnormal cysts blemish the gonad's milky surface. One's about a centimetre in size and filled with blood; far from a life-threatening condition, but we at least have a likely explanation for her pain.

'You happy if I remove these cysts?' asks Roberto.

'You happy to remove them—?'

'Sir,' he calls to the husband. 'Come here, please.'

The husband gets up and peers over, the affected ovary held up for his scrutiny. *Another non-squeamish relative!*

'We will take out these two problems,' says Roberto.

The husband nods.

Roberto neatly excises the two cysts and sutures closed the raw surfaces. He leaves the rest of the ovaries untouched and carefully reintroduces them to the cavity, then demonstrates her appendix.

'We can take this out as well now, okay?' he asks me, in what sounds suspiciously like a rhetorical question.

'Uh, why?'

'We always do,' he replies.

'It looks normal, Roberto.'

He shrugs.

'Do we agree?'

He rolls his eyes towards Agostinho.

'Let's leave it in,' I say.

He sighs. '*Novo Doctor*, listen to me. We always take it out. In Mavinga, always.'

This is probably true. Surgeons routinely remove the appendix once they've opened the belly, even if it looks healthy, to avoid future confusion from the scar. But this woman's appendix is normal. More importantly, the *clunk* of the suction device has begun as the patient's saliva accumulates; Veronica's leg is working hard. Better to finish up, I tell Roberto.

He's not convinced. He mumbles irritatedly to the others, perhaps seeing this as an affront to his skill. Turning to the husband, he makes a somewhat loaded query. 'Sir, would you like us to take her appendix out? If we don't, she could get a severe infection.'

Replying that removing it seems like the best thing, the husband is sold. I'm not—and I've told them about not ambushing me in front of relatives.

'Roberto, the husband is not the one responsible for that anaesthetic right now.' I dig my heels in. 'Explain to him that the appendix looks completely healthy. Let's just close her up.'

'*Novo Doctor—*'

The theatre door opens suddenly. A *clinico* puts their head into the room. It's Sabino, and he's looking flustered. 'We need you in Nutrition, Doctor,' he says. 'Quickly.'

'Now?'

'Yes.'

I pull off my gown and follow him out, turning back to Roberto as I leave. 'Close her up please, Roberto. Leave that appendix!'

Sabino leads me to the Nutrition ward, where a new admission is battling away. We insert a drip and initiate treatment, stabilising her before moving her to *Intensivo*. The surgical patient should already be in here as well, starting to wake up, but she's not. No one has seen her.

There's a problem.

I run back to theatre. She's still on the table, unconscious. The team are around her.

'*What happened?*' I call.

Roberto looks up suddenly.

'*Novo Doctor,*' he says, looking startled.

'What's the problem? *Is she all right?*'

He holds my gaze with a surprised look. There's no movement for a few seconds.

'Roberto?'

I step closer. I can see the oximeter. It's still beeping, and her chest is rising.

'Roberto?' I ask again.

There's dead silence. Veronica shuffles awkwardly but Roberto says nothing. And really, as I look around, it's clear he doesn't need to. A pink object dangles from the surgical clamp he's holding.

'That an appendix?' I ask.

The slow, acknowledging nod of the indisputably guilty.

'I presume it's *her* appendix?'

The nod continues.

'Probably not much point in asking you to put it back, is there?'

Only a shake this time, as they ponder whether I'm serious.

• • •

Tim takes holidays in early August. Pascal covers his job, soon discovering the trials of dispensing monthly salaries in a region with no banks. Most of our hundred staff are paid different amounts (a hundred and eighty dollars per month for a junior guard, up to three hundred and fifty dollars for the older *clinicos*) so cash requirements must be anticipated, flown in, and securely stored beforehand. Small-denomination US dollar bills are insisted upon, although certain years of production won't be accepted due to high rates of counterfeiting. For two days Pascal sits surrounded by stacks of bills, checking each one, re-counting, then paying the workers one at a time in the office.

'But this dollar bill is 1982, *Chefe*,' says one of the guards, opening his envelope onto the table. 'And here. This five-dollar bill is 1997. I cannot take it.'

Another re-enters the office. 'All my ten-dollar bills are from 1996,' he says. 'They will not accept this in the market. And this, look—this dollar bill is a little torn. This also I cannot use.'

So Pascal, who's dealing as well with a faulty water pump and lack of spare parts for it, is worn. Andrea and I also have a difficult run—two stillbirths and the death of two children from malaria within ten days—and with only two others to look at during mealtimes, cabin fever sets in. In a telling indictment, a light-hearted debate turns into a days-long argument between Pascal and me over whether glass is structurally a solid or a liquid. Meanwhile, Andrea, whose experience in Brazil was nothing like this, and who can still neither manage to get Dominga to use less oil nor the midwives to check on the newborns regularly, wonders aloud what she's signed up for. Conversations grow old. So too the food. Someone's going to crack. I see Pascal sprinting back from the airstrip one afternoon, breathless, ranting in half-sentences as I leave the hospital. Seems he's the first.

'YOU OKAY?' I yell.

He shouts back, waving his arms.

'WHAT?'

He yells something about a flight.

'PASCAL?'

'THE MISSION!' he screams. 'FOR THE MISSION . . .!'

He arrives at the gate, babbling about a plane.

'What plane? Our delivery's not due until next Tuesday, no?'

He's ragged and wide-eyed, now gushing about Europeans.

'What do you mean, *Europeans*?'

'That group—visiting the mission,' he pants back. He says a plane landed while I was in the hospital.

'What—when?'

'Before. The far end. They've gone to town. But they're coming here soon. We need to change! *Fuck*—we must clean!'

I laugh at his suggestion and steer him towards the dining room, reminding him that Tim said this would happen. It's been over two months since any of us have kissed anyone—hell, hugged anyone—and it's adding to the strain. There's no end to it in sight either, because relationships with local women are out of the question. Other than being of dubious ethics given that we're the largest employers, and perhaps also seen as the only prospect of a ticket out of here, cultural idiosyncrasies make it difficult—and dangerous: unwittingly inviting an ex-soldier's love interest back for coffee presents a security risk to the entire project.

Pascal's insistent. He says there were four blondes on the planes. A few others, maybe, and some guys, too, but definitely four blondes. I laugh and tell him we'll take the night off—he's clearly been working too hard—but he's anxious, pacing restlessly, and before I can say anything more the guard leads them in, four blondes, *My God, late twenties, fair-skinned and—*

I can't speak. Connections between brain and mouth dissolve as high concentrations of disbelief and hormone flood through me. Pascal and I try to find chairs, to straighten our T-shirts, to not—

I stand. Then sit. Then stand again. I shake their hands—*is that what you do these days?*—but they're European so I opt for a kiss on the cheeks instead. No–they're English. *I shouldn't have done that! The English aren't like that!* They introduce themselves one at a time but the names fail to register, their lips move in slow-motion as my eyes zoom in tightly, their Vaseline Lip-Care SPF30 looking like Max Factor's sexiest lipstick ever and now the lights of our dining area dim as one embraces me, and we embark on a dizzying whirlwind of passionate dancing, laughing, carefree, just a couple of crazy kids in the night . . .

Get a grip.

Pascal talks. Accommodation is offered for indefinite periods of time. Tours around the compound are insisted upon, countered by better offers of a ride in the mine-proof car. *Wait—the river! Jesus, Pascal—wait until they see a sunset down there!* They'll melt when they see that sky, those ox carts and the kids playing, and we can show them what we call Oxford Street, that short stretch of road where the stalls sell chewing gum and biscuits and batteries— they'll love it! And my mind darts back to that European poll I'd heard of years ago in which being an MSF doctor had been ranked as the sexiest role on earth, and admittedly it may just be a myth propagated to recruit volunteers *but this could be my chance to live it!* Right now though Pascal and I are all over the place, two sixteen-year-old boys at a first high school dance, deliriously excited but far too nervous to do anything about—

Andrea walks in. Composed. A little surprised, but sane. She plays the attentive hostess and offers them drinks and invites them to stay for dinner. Pascal and I excuse ourselves to find Vasco, our guard, and ask him to build a bonfire and kill a goat for dinner, which he obligingly does, and I ransack my bedroom for a T-shirt that's remotely presentable, but the search is futile—everything hints of some or other incident at the hospital. We beg Dominga to stay late and make some salad and rice, and not long afterwards we all gather at the fire, carry our dining set-up outside and place it under that veil of stars. It couldn't possibly get more romantic.

'How long are you guys around for?' I ask, as we fill our plates with goat. The girl across from me smiles coyly (*coyly!*), runs a hand through her hair as she tilts her head and smiles. *Is she flirting?* A thousand shudders run down my spine.

'For a few days,' she says. 'Actually, for four days near Mavinga, but we have two weeks in Angola.'

Four days of this! Pascal and I can't stop beaming as we try to make small talk with them. Tim will never hear the end of this—what a time to have taken his holidays! We go on, delving a little more into each other's backgrounds.

'And exactly which organisation are you here with?' asks Andrea.

'A Christian aid organisation,' replies one.

Pascal looks up sharply.

'Uh . . . and what do you do with them?'

'Oh, we're spending some time with the mission we support near Mavinga,' says the girl opposite me. 'Documenting their work, interviewing people, that sort of thing.'

'You're not staying *in* Mavinga, then?' I ask. The mission is where our burns patient, José, came from, and is about an hour's walk from town.

'No. Just with the mission.'

It's not ideal, but things are still salvageable. We're not permitted by MSF to use the road that heads towards that mission, but our guest's organisation allows them to use their project's four-wheel drive. They can visit us.

We talk a little more of their work. I ask how they got into this field, and finally drop the burning question—burning for Pascal and me, at least: 'Do you have to be a, uh . . . a Christian to do this sort of work? I mean, to work for your organisation?'

Pascal's stopped chewing. His eyebrows hover somewhere near his hairline.

'You do!' comes the answer. 'I mean, it's not a written rule, but all of us here are committed to the Church,' says the girl who'd been flirting. 'We're Born Again, actually.'

Andrea kicks me under the table. The irony of three men being stuck for months with only one woman, who's both attractive and highly dateable yet far more interested in the Church than any of us, is not lost on the team. Nor the fact that the issue has just repeated itself.

'My fiancé is actually working for this organisation too,' adds the one beside Pascal.

Andrea suppresses a laugh.

'And my husband used to work for MSF as well,' adds a third. 'In fact, that's how we met.'

Andrea's lost it. Pascal takes a renewed interest in his food. 'Fascinating,' he lies, and we instead go on to spend the night chatting of approaches to development, the weather in London, and various other things. Not an unpleasant night by any means, although not how we'd have scripted it. And in fairness to the women, I'd also have professed to be both engaged and born again if I'd found myself in the company of Pascal and me in our present state. Our deodorant ran out weeks ago, razors not long afterwards.

So it seems then that fabled stories of passionate love affairs in the field are to remain just that: fabled stories. Unlike others in town, my mosquito net is to witness no romance beneath it, but some respite is ahead. In two weeks I fly out for my holidays, so the prospect of at least *some* change in this routine looms large. It's not a moment too soon, either. The tensions born of living on top of each other are building, and I need to not be on call, to not talk about MSF, and to sleep through just one night without waking at least once, worried by the prospect of being summoned to watch yet another child taking its last breaths.

I need a break.

10. SLEEPING EASY

The roar of the plane, and Andrea's suddenly looking worried. Not without reason. I'm off for holidays, which leaves her as the sole medical expat for ten days.

'And that woman with the breast cancer?' she asks, as we race to finish an early ward round.

'We'll have to put a bed in the tent for her,' I say. 'Or move her to *Intensivo*.' The other patients on Maria's ward have been complaining about the smell of her ulcerated breast tumour, and she wants to get away from them.

'And Manuel? What am I going to do about him?'

A good question. Manuel's on a roll this morning; he gave two litres of IV fluid to a young child for reasons unknown, and hasn't written any legible notes. He's all over the place lately, despite the extra time we're spending together.

'Keep him off nights,' I say. 'And out of *Intensivo*. And the kids' ward. Don't let him start treatment on anyone without calling you. Wait—maybe you should keep him out of the hospital altogether. Get Sergio to adjust the roster and give him time off.'

'And the guy with the burns—?' she asks.

The pilot's waiting. I need to go. I feel bad leaving Andrea as the only medical expat here; she's in for a week and a half of sleep deprivation covering this place alone, but there's no alternative. Of some consolation, she'll take holidays right after me.

I run home to grab my bag and say goodbye to Dominga. Tim and Pascal are already unloading food and mail on the airstrip, the paediatric ground crew buzzing excitedly around the plane. 'Don't let the team down,' warns Tim, who only recently got back from holidays in Cape Town. 'Make sure you do us proud. Did you email the Red Cross girl?'

I nod.

'Don't you dare come back without stories,' he says.

'Yes,' says Pascal. 'We need stories. *Good* stories.'

I promise nothing as I farewell them, joining the handful of de-mining technicians in the cabin of the twenty-seater World Food Program plane that's passing through town today. The propellers soon roar, high fives are exchanged and a warm Castle lager passed around, and everyone's thrilled to be taking a break from Mavinga. No matter the destination.

• • •

Luanda is mine. The Angolan capital, sprawling along a picturesque stretch of foreshore in the north-west of the country, that strikes me as a poor, rundown version of Havana: a steamy tropical city with a distinctly Latin flavour, its waterfront *Marginal* lined with coconut palms on one side and tired colonial-era buildings on the other. Spared much of the fighting during the war, the old buildings of this once-beautiful colonial outpost, dubbed The Paris of Africa in its heyday, crumble from neglect rather than mortar damage these days, while new ones are hoisted skywards by the cranes of Chinese construction companies.

It's a huge city, and as big a paradox. Hemmed in by vast, crime-ridden shanty-towns into which half of Angola's twelve to sixteen million people are crammed, and through which street kids and stray dogs pick at decomposing mounds of rubbish, it's an impoverished, dilapidated metropolis; yet at the same time it's ranked as the world's single most expensive city for expats. Rent is around ten thousand US dollars per month for an average house in a reasonably central suburb, and all but the most basic foods need to be imported. Trendy nightclubs exist, too. Plenty of them, not far from the slums, situated along white sand beaches that overlook a horizon sparkling with deep-sea oilrigs, behind which those show-stopping tropical sunsets glow. Inside, sheer hedonism: well-heeled oil-workers and foreign advisors rub shoulders with attractive *mulatto* prostitutes over fifteen-dollar cocktails; outside, the larger reality: a rabble of scruffy kids will watch your car for a few cents, while *os mutilados*—Angola's disabled, known literally as 'the mutilated' and estimated to be about ten per cent of the population—pass by with their crutches, prosthetic limbs, or various other injuries. Two days is enough for me.

Unable to leave Angola due to visa issues, I take a commercial flight to Lubango, a smaller city in the central highland region where MSF recently ran a cholera treatment centre. Granted, that's not a traditional selling point for holiday spots, but the town is tranquil and picturesque, nestled among the first hills I've seen in months and possessing as well two supermarkets, a dozen restaurants—and *grass*! Lush, green lawns—something I'd entirely forgotten could exist. This was once the heart of Angola's lucrative agricultural region, and in the early 1970s more Portuguese migrants lived in town than Africans. However, along with the rest of Angola's half-million European residents at that time, almost all fled at the outbreak of war, mostly for Portugal, Brazil or South Africa.

I drop my bags at the MSF guesthouse and head immediately to find Stephanie, a Red Cross delegate I'd met on my way to Mavinga. Her house is on the outskirts of town and is a paradise compared with the MSF offering, possessing a satellite TV, hot shower, and a toilet that goes *whoosh*—all the persuasion I need to wander no further. Not that Stephanie herself isn't reason enough. She's a brown-haired Austrian woman who heads a team working to reunite Angolan families separated during the war, travelling the country to create databases to help match people with their families, then arranging transport when confirmation is made. *And* she's beautiful. And great company. She shows me around, swaps books and cooks wonderfully, and for my last weekend arranges a camping trip.

In two LandCruisers we head off with a group of de-mining friends of hers, driving down the steep face of the Serra de Leba, where the high plateau of Angola's centre drops to kneel suddenly at the strip of coastal desert that runs the length of the country. Driving south-west across flat gravel plains, we pass heavily eroded sandstone cliffs and rocky bridges, and arrive finally on a long, desolate honey-coloured beach that merges further to the south with Namibia's famous Skeleton Coast. Our accommodation for the weekend is three tents on the sand, and our nearest neighbours are the residents of a small fishing village, where salted fish are laid to dry on wooden racks, and where the features of the children, who're noticeably whiter than their landlocked compatriots, hint at past stops by foreign sailors.

It's a blissful couple of days. We do little; stroll along the beach, make a fire, sip wine under the night sky. Not surprisingly, the de-miners make for interesting company. Two are middle-aged Italians who'd done time in the military, and the third, a younger Brit, is a professional opera singer who'd once read an article on de-mining. 'Never even touched a gun before,' he says, but he'd thought that this would be a great way to contribute. It sounds like it. They tell me of the thousand known minefields still awaiting clearance, and of the hundreds of suspect roads. After another bottle of wine they begin talking of backfiring detonators, of individuals who'll re-mine a strip and extort money from drivers before revealing the location of the device, and I find it hard to believe that three months ago I was in

Melbourne discussing interest rates. How to explain all this when I get back? Or any of it, for that matter.

Andrea contacted me via Stephanie's phone last week. I took the call with some trepidation (sprawled on the couch at the time, an entire box set of DVDs to still get through), no less when she told me they'd had a rough few days in the hospital. She needed advice, she said—there were big problems with the man with burns, and now a premature infant as well—and as she spoke, reminding me of it all, I actually found myself missing the place. I've now had the sleep-ins and hot showers I wanted, and spoken to other people. I'm ready to return.

Which is just as well: two days after the beach trip, the little Cessna bumps me back towards the airstrip again; and this time, as I regard the somnolent bustle of this dusty little town from above, three months since the first time and my Portuguese now at the vastly improved level of a six-year-old native speaker's, I feel none of the fear I'd known previously.

Just contentment.

· · ·

'Hey *Novo Doctor*,' exclaims Sabino. 'You are back!'

Seems then that this *Novo Doctor* tag is here to stay. Three months, no signs of its waning popularity.

'Where did you go for your holidays?' asks Senhor Kassoma, who's passing by as I join the ward round. Everyone's keen to know how things are going in the cities—many have relatives in Luanda.

'So you didn't visit your family?' asks Sabino as I describe my trip, and I tell them that Australia is too far. I'd likely spend a week just flying there and back.

'Impossible, *Novo Doctor*,' laughs Kassoma. 'Nowhere is that far!'

I sketch a rough map on the back of a patient's chart, explaining the six flights via three continents it took to get me here. They laugh. 'I do not understand,' chuckles Kassoma, drawing a straight line between Mavinga and Melbourne, 'why you would not just do this.'

So it goes. A pleasant digression as we stand outside *Intensivo* barely an hour after I landed, covering house prices in Australia ('*Eh!*—they don't believe it), the beach I'd camped on ('*Fascinante!*'—they've never seen the ocean), and the dolphins I'd seen off their coast ('*Quê?*'— they're not sure what I'm talking about).

And the good feelings continue as we begin the round when Marco, a young boy on the kids' ward, waddles clumsily to us in the yard. He's now two months into his six-month course of treatment for TB, and clearly no longer malnourished. In fact he's almost a little *over*nourished. His face is different, almost unrecognisably so, his hair even thicker and darker than when he'd arrived. He'd been another late-night call when his mum first bundled him in, his eyes half-closed in that frightening pre-terminal state of fatigue, so I decide that from now on Marco will be my poster-boy for why this can be the best job at times. It'll be sad to finally discharge him. Not that there's been any shortage of discharges lately; 'Where's that other patient,' I ask the team, as we continue. 'You know, the man in bed four?'

'Oh, we sent him home,' the reply. 'We sent a few patients home while you were away,' say the *clinicos*. 'We did a little clean-out, because you sometimes keep people here too long, *Novo Doctor*, no offence, and people will just stay here forever if it is up to them. So if we didn't know what was wrong, and they were not very sick, we sent them. But do not worry—they will come back to Outpatients.'

No discharge for Toto, though. He's still here, still sitting beneath the floppy canvas door of his tent, not far from a patient who should *definitely* have been discharged: a man who thinks he may be in his eighties, who's not sure but who definitely looks it, and who's waving to us from the edge of the concrete steps. We'd inserted a suprapubic catheter—a rubber tube to drain his bladder, via a small incision into his abdominal wall—in order to bypass his blocked prostate, but that was well before I left. 'Why's he still here?' I ask the *clinicos*, who reply that Our Old Father (a respectful title for the oldest person seen here these months) would like to stay a little while. He likes the food and the company, they say, and he's not ready to walk home. So can he stay? And when we go over to say of course—hell, Toto's been here for four years!—he proudly straightens his brown suit, holds up his bag of urine and smiles a toothless grin.

'Look!' he says, his face crumpling into a thousand little stories. 'Look at this! The stuff just keeps coming!'—which is great because it's both funny and touching, yet a little disgusting at the same time. And behind him the kids' wards are running well, the protocols we've worked on for common conditions still on the wall, clear, being followed for the most part (I'm really getting a buzz on these rounds) and soon Senhor Kassoma calls me to see some patients he'd asked to return today.

Kassoma leads me past the two dozen people waiting for malaria tests near Outpatients (at least half of whom will likely test positive for *falciparum*, the more severe of the four strains of malaria), and into his office. We squeeze around the small plastic desk, alongside the first patient.

'He has had this rash for many years,' begins Kassoma, who two months ago rarely called me. He opens our dermatology atlas to a photograph. 'I think it is this one here: onchocerciasis,' he says. 'This man lived in The Congo during the war. We do not see this in Mavinga, but maybe he got it there?'

The patient's amused by the fact that we're comparing him to photographs, which is great—I'd be frankly worried were I in his place. But we find a match. I agree with Kassoma that it's the likely diagnosis, so we send the patient to our dispensary with a script.

Kassoma brings several other patients through over the following hour, a young infant being the last. The diagnosis is unmistakeable: hydrocephalus. An excess of fluid in and around the child's brain has caused significant enlargement of his head, so much so that he can no longer hold it up. Mum cradles him gently. There's nothing we can do for the condition; neurosurgery is the only option, and his mum looks devastated when we say as much. I ask Kassoma to explain that in Luanda or Namibia they may find treatment, but that they'd have to pay for it.

'Not possible,' he replies. 'These *campesinos* could never afford that. No way.'

So, yet another patient passes through who would've been okay if they were born elsewhere, or with more money. But I've long had to accept that we're in the business of providing the greatest good for the greatest number. This hospital already costs a million dollars each year to run; flying out specific cases for expensive treatments is not within our scope. A justifiable decision in principle, but a hard one to swallow at times.

I return to the wards, where a man with HIV/AIDS is our next patient. Paradoxically, as devastating as the war had been, the isolation imposed on this region has partly protected it from HIV. Fifteen per cent of neighbouring Namibians and Zambians are HIV positive, twice that number again in Swaziland, yet Angola has an estimated prevalence of only two per cent. This man is the first case I've seen here, but the relatively low rate means that there's no treatment available in our region.

'There are charities in Luanda that can help you,' I tell him, in private.

'This is too far.'

'Can you get to Namibia?'

'I have a card for Zambia,' he says. 'I lived there for years.'

'Then you'll have to go there.'

I apologise and write him a letter—a referral to no particular clinic in an unknown town, somewhere in another country. We give him antibiotics to treat opportunistic infections, and a box of condoms. I explain the importance of using them.

'They are uncomfortable!' he laughs. 'I do not like these things.'

'Do you understand what will happen if you don't use them?'

He shrugs.

'Listen: you'll infect your wife. She will get this illness, and she will be sick too.'

He looks away sheepishly.

'I'm telling you—you need to understand this. And if your wife gets ill, she may pass it to your children. Is that enough reason to use them?'

'But having sex with these things is not good,' he laughs. 'It is like eating a sweet that is wrapped in plastic! It is not fun.'

'*Fun* sex is not your priority at the moment. Their health is. Yours too.'

'But she will know something is strange if I use them.'

'Then tell her you can't afford to have another child. Make up a story. But listen to me—use them! You have an obligation to protect your family.'

He takes the box, reluctantly, and wanders off to another country. Things come unstuck after this.

. . .

Mid-morning, and we stand in the small side room that comes off *Intensivo*: previously a storage area, now the hospital's only private room. I swallow the smell; José, the man with the severe burns, is lying naked on his back. His injuries are the result of a seizure that flung him into a cooking fire weeks ago (he's an epileptic and has no treatment), and we've since removed the charred skin, exposing instead large patches of red-raw flesh. What he must have thought when he regained consciousness on that fire, I can't imagine.

His wife is crouching in the far corner, and smiles solemnly at us. (They're a strikingly handsome couple: she, big eyes, luminous coffee skin and fine, sculpted features; he, a young, bearded Denzel Washington). Roberto and Agostinho are changing his dressings. They pull gently at a piece of gauze, and José grimaces.

'What are we giving him for pain?' I ask.

'Paracetamol.'

'And?'

'Sometimes ibuprofen.'

'Nothing else?' I ask. I'd use the same for a mild headache.

'We tried the Tramadol when you were away,' says Roberto, 'but he had more seizures from it. And here—look—he scraped all of this open and was in more pain. So now we give a little diazepam as well.'

The combination would make him mildly sleepy at best. 'What about the pethidine?'

'We have ten doses left,' says Sergio. 'Andrea says to keep it for emergencies. She said he would use it too quickly.'

She's right.

Roberto pulls at another piece of gauze. It's stuck. He wets it with saline, tugs gently at it with forceps and it finally comes free. The pain relief isn't cutting it, though. A quiet tear runs down José's cheek. He never does ask for anything, just lies naked in this stifling cell of a room, smiling warmly whenever we come past. I usually put my head in a few times during the day to say hi, and no matter my protestations he'll always insist on sitting up—no easy task with raw thighs and buttocks, and weeping genitalia that stick to the sheets. To help, Toyota rigged a wood frame at the foot of his bed with a rope attached so that José can pull himself up, but it still requires Herculean effort. Once upright (he refuses help), José lifts each leg in turn, below the knee, swinging it cautiously over the bed, and sits on the edge (naked, because he can't tolerate clothing over the wounds), and only *then* will he shake our hands and talk with us. I gave him a handful of the news and gossip magazines that my parents occasionally send, so that he'd have something new to look at, but that was a month ago. They're still here. Still beside his bed, wrapped neatly in a square of old cloth—the only items, aside from a candle, on the wooden stand that Toyota had also made for him.

'We need more dressings,' Roberto says to me. 'We are using boxes of it. Look how much it takes to cover all this.'

I tell him I'll email Luanda.

José's fortunately beaten the infection that Andrea had phoned me about, although another one is an inevitability in these conditions. I'm not sure if he'll survive all this. Meanwhile, Roberto pulls at another sheet of gauze on José's groin. José winces. He'll need to endure these dressing changes every forty-eight hours, though, and for weeks to come.

'Thank you,' he says softly, as we turn to walk out.

Intensivo is no more uplifting. Kidje, the young man who'd become progressively more delirious before my holidays, is now completely unconscious.

'He still getting the same medications?' I ask.

'We've changed nothing,' says Sergio. 'We give him the TB tablets and a little milk twice a day by this tube. Andrea crushes them. And now we have started the IV fluids.'

All I can suggest is to turn him regularly, and to pad the bed with cushions. I apologise to his brother. The boy's not ever left his side since he carried Kidje here, except to cook himself a meal near the fence.

Our last stop is the tents, where we share a happy, semi-imaginary dialogue with Toto. He seems well. As do the blind albino woman and her demented mother, although they now have room-mates—Maria, the young mother with the ulcerated breast cancer, and her husband and daughter.

'Is she showering?' I ask the team. Maria's not here, but her young daughter's sitting alone on their bedding. She's maybe ten, and smiles meekly when I greet her.

'Sorry, *Novo Doctor*,' says Sabino, pulling me aside. 'There was a problem. Maria died last week. For now, the little girl is still sleeping here. The father is at home. They are from another village, a day or two away, and the father does not know yet that Maria died. But we have sent word for him. Is it okay if the girl sleeps here until then?'

. . .

A lengthy staff meeting fills the afternoon. The weather's noticeably muggier, and through the fibreglass window of our dining room this evening I see a handful of woolly clouds, their bellies seared orange by the setting sun. Still no rain, though. Just three men, an attempt at cheese fondue in an old coffee can on coals, and the predictable grilling.

'You didn't get laid?' cries Tim. 'But you stayed with her!'

'Wait, it wasn't—'

'And you know you've got more than two months out here—two more months without sex,' Pascal reminds me, confident in the knowledge that he'll soon meet his girlfriend on holidays. 'You will go crazy.'

'How did you manage this?' asks Tim. 'This is unheard of on a mission!'

'It wasn't like that,' I defend. 'We got on great. She's really nice, just not that kind of—'

They laugh. 'Everyone's *that* kind when they're on mission. We're all stuck in these places for months. *Everyone* is in the same boat.'

'That's the problem,' I say. 'We got on really well, but she said she's tired of all these guys from the field hitting on her. She says it's a cliché, that she's tired of—'

'*Tired of it?*'

I attempt to shift the focus of the conversation, but with little success. It's a pleasant enough change following the afternoon meeting, anyway, time spent mostly discussing the looming handover of the project—a topic that's becoming a sore point for all. The move is an inevitable one given that Angola is now stable. Our presence as an emergency humanitarian organisation is no longer justifiable, not now that the emergency is over. If we were to stay here indefinitely, why not then open projects in the thousands of other African towns with equal needs? I agree with the decision. Handing over health care to the government is the right thing to do. In principle, that is.

In reality, Tim can't get the Administrator to meet with him. The town's new hospital was built a year ago by Namibian contractors but still sits empty, with no water supply, beds, or medical equipment. We've offered to complete it for them—the log team will do it for free, no strings attached—but we get no answer. We've also offered to donate a three-month supply of drugs and move our own staff and equipment there, but again, no answer. Tim meanwhile struggles in the middle of all this, caught between being necessarily diplomatic yet appropriately pushy, and dealing as well with our team's growing frustration. We've asked MSF coordination to push for action at a higher level, but for the moment dozens of emails just fly backwards and forwards within the organisation, CCed to everyone who's remotely involved with Angola. Seems that being strictly *apolitical* can be a highly political process in itself.

'What else did she say?' asks Tim.

'Just that she's tired of guys passing—'

'Stop! I can't believe this. *You* are single. *She* is single. You are both staying together—end of story!'

'And tell me this,' says Pascal, with an air of contemplation, as he dips bread into the can of lukewarm cheese. 'What are you going to do with all those condoms they gave you in the briefing? That entire box, *Novo Doctor*—what will you do with them?'

I excuse myself after dinner to check on a patient in *Intensivo*. I cross the yard and step into the assessment room, stopping suddenly. The scene is frightening. A *clinico* is standing beside the bed, swaggering as he tries to guide a syringe into the buttock of a young child lying prone. The brown plaid shirt is unmistakeable.

'*Manuel?*'

He swings around unsteadily. '*Ohhhh! Boa noite!*' he slurs. 'You are back? *Eh*, I did not think you were back!'

'What are you doing?'

'Just treating this child, *Novo Doctor.*'

To a near-death experience, perhaps. I can't believe it. The real cause of his increasing ineptitude and fidgety demeanour is now revealed to me, the evidently un-astute doctor and supervisor. Manuel's an alcoholic.

'Put that syringe down, Manuel.'

'Yes. I will just give the injection,' he says, pivoting to face the child again, his arm arcing wildly.

I step closer. His breath is thick with alcohol fumes. He looks over and relaxes his arm, averts his eyes in resignation. A heavy silence follows.

'Go home,' I tell him.

He can explain, he says. 'I had the day off. Okay, yes, I had a few drinks, but I was not working for hours, you see—'

I take the syringe from his hand and guide him out the door. The patient's family watch. I ask the guard to please find another *clinico* to do the night shift, but Manuel won't leave the gate. He stands. Begs. Holds my arm and cries, says that he's the only wage-earner in his entire family and he's never done this before, and I think, What a pitiful sight: a fifty-year-old survivor of war with no other job prospects, being reprimanded by a privileged white man half his age who's threatening to leave him unemployed.

I tell him to return in the morning. I'm not sure what we'll do. Tim will be obliged to fire him if he knows the extent of this, so maybe we can bend the story a little, play down the drinking and make it more of a competence issue. There's simply no way we can allow him to treat patients; maybe we can keep him on the payroll as an attendant with no clinical duties, and I'll insist that we deal with his alcohol abuse.

Was it really only this morning that I landed back here?

I head home, help finish the cheese and climb into bed. But how does one fall asleep after all this . . .?

Surprisingly easily. I refuse to keep going in circles. For months my mood has ebbed and flowed according to our failures or successes, but not anymore. I can't keep wondering whether what we do makes any difference, whether any of this is actually worth it, so I don't. I light a candle. I grab a book, tuck my mosquito net in and ignore the termites, and remind myself of our successes—and there are *many*.

The reality is that work here is boring at times, although it's taken me a while to work out why: most of what we do is easy, and most of the health workers do it well. While I'm distracted by the minority of cases with serious conditions—the Kidjes with encephalitis, the Josés with burns—the *clinicos* quietly manage the majority of inpatients, and almost all of the two to three thousand outpatients, each month. Cases of malaria that are treated in time, cured with three days of tablets; children with mild coughs who are given antibiotics, long before they become the three o'clock night call with pneumonia; and many hundreds with simple gastro, brought into the hospital hours after it begins, and managed adequately with advice and a few cheap sachets of oral solution.

Even our water system quietly prevents untold cases of illness. I'd go so far as to say that by running it, Pascal and the logs save far more lives than we health workers ever have. And from what I've seen, this is the reality of medicine in developing countries: people die of preventable conditions that are easy to treat, or even prevent. Of the millions of children who won't survive the year, most will succumb to one of six things: poor nutrition, pneumonia, diarrhoea, malaria, measles, or a lack of basic neonatal and maternal health care. All of these are easily managed or prevented. None of it is rocket science—or expensive. Here, the death rate in our little hospital is remarkably low (four or five of the three hundred inpatients a month), not because of the occasional operation or clever diagnosis we make, but because the *clinicos* plug along every day, treating easy-to-manage conditions, with cheap drugs, over and over again. A fact that I find immensely empowering, yet equally heartbreaking that such a situation exists.

And for me, this is the thing about Mavinga overall. These powerful contrasts, these glaring dichotomies, that make working and living out here what it is: a confusing, intoxicating, frustrating, heartbreaking, inspiring, disillusioning and life-affirming blend of all the best and worst things. Every day, all at once. I don't think I've really started to make sense of it, but I'm not sure one could.

So for now I don't even try. I blow out the candle, shut my eyes, and do what I do each night: try to picture something good. Like Marco, that young boy admitted with malnutrition and who's now almost overweight, except that another image keeps appearing ... *What's this?* ... An old man, I think, and he's sitting on concrete steps, his deep-brown suit soaking up the morning sun as he grins a toothless grin, triumphantly waving ... *Is that—?*

It is. A golden bag of pee.

Hardly the image I'd hoped for, but it'll do nicely under the circumstances.

II. MEMORABLE LINES

Late August, and Pascal's coaxed a small vegetable garden to life outside the bedrooms. Basil, ailing tomatoes, zucchini, and sunflowers that are yet to bloom, with cow manure for fertiliser and tap water to keep it going. He also bought a guinea fowl and set up a large enclosure for it in our yard; a beautiful but noisy addition to the family. So for now, between the roosters, cats, donkeys, soldiers, generator and this new bird, gone are any moments of silence, although the place is feeling wonderfully homely.

I get up, shoo a rooster from the veggie patch and step past to the bathroom. First order of business, to locate the spider. I hold the door open and look around. Wait for my eyes to adjust, open the door a little more, and scan the room. *Got it.* Back left corner, as usual. The thing's getting bigger by the day. A small dinner plate now. A small, *hairy* dinner plate. I prop the door open with my foot and wash with one eye on my towel, the other on it, but it saunters towards my towel. I shift the towel. I wash quickly but it gets closer again, scuttles then disapp—

I'll brush my teeth later.

Over to the kitchen, where Andrea's making breakfast. She returned from holidays late last week looking like a new woman—tanned, relaxed, happy she was back (as was I, I'd had to cover Maternity for ten days)—and now carrying a black baby on her hip.

'Yours?' I ask, and she flicks me a dry smile. But Dominga jiggles.

'Mum's the one with the high fever in *Intensivo*,' she says. 'I'm just minding her for a few hours. Isn't she gorgeous?'

She is. We coo and dote on her, all three of us, then Dominga goes back to rubbing this morning's meat across the uncovered wood bench—the same uncovered surface we've been massaging pizza dough onto these recent Sundays.

Andrea fills Dominga in on her holidays. Like me, she'd also spent them in Lubango, and Dominga likes that we saw a little more of her country. '*É lindo, não?*' she says—It's beautiful, no?—which we all agree on. Andrea then asks Dominga about her holiday, but Dominga laughs and casts her eyes heavenward. I stick around. I've heard the story before but still can't believe it.

Dominga took her annual leave two weeks ago, paying for passage on the back of an old truck to take her the four hundred kilometres to Menongue, the provincial capital. The trucks rumble through here a couple of times a week in both directions, though timetables are haphazard. They come when they come. From Menongue, she'd hoped to catch a bus to the northern city of Kuito (around fifty dollars more) to meet her new grandchildren for the first time.

The first day went fine. Dominga sat on the open back as they bounced along sandy roads, but she at least had food and others to talk with.

The following morning the truck broke down. No phones and no towing service out there, so for two days the driver toyed with the engine and at nights they slept on the back of the flatbed. A minor logjam of other vehicles meanwhile built up behind them, because brave is the driver who mounts the shoulder of a rural road in these parts of Angola. (Initial mine clearance doesn't include the road verge. Unlike the heavily time-consuming process of de-mining by hand, roads are cleared using a more rapid but less definitive technique in which metal detectors make a first sweep. A heavily weighted trailer is then towed to detonate any non-metal mines.)

By day three the truck remained stuck. Dominga realised she'd no longer make it to her family and back in time, so she began walking towards Mavinga. That took another couple of days. And where did she sleep? *'Eh! On the road!'* she jiggles. But you wouldn't know it to look at her this week. Her shoes have been scrubbed back to a gleaming white, no trace of the dirt that caked her when she'd walked into the compound and asked someone to please look at her foot.

Andrea's speechless, but Dominga just shrugs. *'Aqui é assim,'* she smiles. Here, it is like this.

She's not as nonchalant about the food situation in town, though. We're now well into the hunger gap, and the soils couldn't possibly be drier. It's a precarious state for a population that relies almost entirely on subsistence farming. Toyota says it's as bad a season as they've had since the war, and that we may need to consider a general food distribution; some families are eating their seed stocks. For the moment we're screening all under-fives who pass through Outpatients for signs of malnutrition, and hoping for rain. The weather is definitely changing—nights are sticky, the wards stifling in the afternoons and increasing tufts of clouds are lingering nearby—but September arrives, and still there's no rain. Temperatures begin to flare. So too the tempers in staff meetings.

'We'll pay three months' salary,' says Tim, 'and a bonus for every year of employment,' as he explains the retrenchment packages to the staff gathered in the gazebo one afternoon.

'But this is not enough! How will I support my whole family on this?'

'And if we will not have jobs here,' says one of the guards, 'we must leave Mavinga. How are we to live in the city with this money? Will you help us in the city?'

We can't. MSF are closing all their Angolan offices. So Tim begins running small group sessions with everyone, an orientation to the rest of the world: phone numbers and how to use them; interviewing for jobs and how to bank; what food is likely to cost; and making sense of a rough map of Luanda. He asks staff to bring in any certificates they have (UNITA ran schools and courses at certain stages) and begins typing up resumés for all staff. Some are fascinated, others frightened, but a few are plainly angry.

At around the same time, Pascal takes his leave. Toyota looks after most of the logistical issues, but Tim and I ponder the generator one evening when the guard calls us—'It coughed then just stopped,' he says—although it seems all is okay, just that the fuel had been siphoned from the tank. It's part of a growing trend in theft as this closure looms, necessitating even more locks, keys, spreadsheets and vigilance to keep track of everything.

But Mavinga's more pressing problem is at least solved one September afternoon, when the rains arrive—in dramatic fashion. Brooding anvils of clouds hurl improbable quantities of water at the town for hours on end, and every afternoon following that, and within days the town becomes green. *That* quickly. A stubble of grass shoots colours the earth (who knew their seeds would've survived such a drought?) and farmers hurry to sow crops. Soon, maize and other necessities begin their much-awaited growth towards a cloudy sky, and an impending nutrition crisis appears to have been averted. And all it took was a little rain.

Mavinga changes for another reason this month, too. The deployment of over one thousand policemen takes place in the region—a costly and remarkably efficient government exercise, and one that becomes a shameless testimony to the adage *Where there's a will, there's a way.*

• • •

Sunday morning in mid-September, and the four of us stand on the airstrip. In awe. Whether we're watching a festival, celebration, or an impending riot, I'm not yet sure.

Large numbers of police line the edges. They've been arriving on frequent flights these past two weeks, staying in the large sheds in the centre of town that have been hastily converted to barracks by a Namibian work crew, and here they now are: heavily armed, hot, young, and bored. And watching the gathering crowd ahead.

The crowd, so far at least, is not overly large—a couple of hundred at most, although growing quickly. Two distinct groups have formed. The first is just metres from our compound, dancing passionately, singing pro-government songs and wearing pro-government T-shirts, and waving the pro-government posters they've just been handed— the first things I've seen given to the town's people by Administration since my arrival.

The second group is much the same size. Twenty metres to the left, they're dancing every bit as energetically in front of the four supply aircraft parked nearby, although there's no pro-government paraphernalia among them. Quite the opposite. The colours of the UNITA flag (red and green, with a black cockerel in the centre) adorn their banners and T-shirts, and they're displaying them in proud protest. These are the two political parties who'd fought each other so bitterly during the war, but for now the mood seems buoyant. Plenty of women and children dance among both groups, and our staff and patients gather nearby at the compound fence. Even the King is here, watching with an entourage of elderly *sobas*. So it's not the crowd that concerns me. It's the police.

The sun climbs and the crowd continues to grow. Excitement builds. Drummers lead their respective groups in song, pounding *batas* made of dark wood and animal skin, while tall women blow percussively on referees' whistles at the front, stomping and dancing feverishly as the rest of the group mirrors their movements. It's spectacular. Bright colours and beautiful songs; deep drums, and the smell of sweat. Utterly mesmerising. We'd been told there would be a celebration—today is National Heroes Day, the birthday of Agostinho Neto, the late Angolan doctor and poet who'd led the MPLA at the time of independence—we just had no idea it would be like *this*.

It's mid-morning when the third of the day's flights, another Russian military transport, makes a low pass. It lands and taxis closer, and the crowd becomes even more frenzied as the cargo door lowers, but the excitement subdues when only police exit the plane. It's not who we're waiting for: the Vice-President of Angola, who, unbelievably, is said to be coming to inaugurate this large police deployment. Here, on our football pitch with no goalposts.

Minutes later a fourth flight arrives. The excitement again grows. The door opens and men in sharp suits descend the air stairs, followed by a TV crew with cameras, generators, a transmission dish and dozens of rolls of cable, all unloaded onto the sand. But it's nothing on the absurdity of what follows. As if direct from Zurich, a gleaming private jet bears down on our little town, blasting dust over the skinny kids and mud huts along the edges. Police surround it as it rolls to a stop near us; men in even sharper suits exit the jet; and *now* the crowd erupts. Two groups, trying to outdo each other in song and dance. MPLA supporters celebrate as UNITA supporters protest. Call and response anthems ring out, a lone voice followed by an impassioned chorus that's harmonised perfectly, and a warm sense of nostalgia comes over me as I recall the first time I'd heard such music being sung, sitting in a primary school hall in Cape Town when a group of black children were led onto our stage. A township choir, they were the first black Africans I'd seen in the school, and they'd looked terribly uncertain about the whole idea as they took their position in front of five hundred white boys—until the moment they sang, that is, filling the hall with the most heartfelt, beautiful music in languages I knew nothing of.

Pascal nudges me. He points out a lean man draped in a UNITA flag who's walking defiantly through the centre of the pro-government group. The singing crescendos as the man heads deeper, and I wonder if he's about to get beaten or cause a riot, and so I forget all about township choirs and think instead of the township anti-apartheid protests I'd seen on South African TV at around the same time, many of which had turned violent, and I wonder how much, or how little, it'd take to ignite this crowd.

The ministers exit. Police stay close. We're ushered by the police chief to join a row at the front, alongside the King and ever-elusive Administrator. Various other seniors are here, too—old men in military khakis with cowboy hats, hanging on to their posters of Neto—and the group of ministers make their way towards us to shake our hands. The TV crew film it all, moving around us, and I'm completely seduced by the thrill of this whole event although not entirely sure we should be standing here. These were the men in power during at least the latter years of the war. Pascal sums it up for me when he nods towards the hands of one of the nearby ministers, quipping that he wonders how much blood is on them.

Police jeeps arrive, whisking the VIPs to the soccer field. The crowd is now maybe a thousand people strong and follows on foot, heading past our compound, left onto the main street and a half-kilometre further to the grounds, where they gather in front of the specially built stage. The first in a series of long speeches is given by the dignitaries (we're told that the Vice-President didn't make it, but the Defence Minister and other MPs did), and the mood ebbs as the afternoon drags under a scorching sun. The probability of any unrest now appears unlikely. Armed police watch closely, and people look utterly bored.

So, why then is all this happening in Mavinga? We're not exactly clear. The T-shirts and posters just handed out bear the slogan, *With the thought of Neto, we rebuild Angola*, and I can see no reason the government wouldn't be trying. The economy is now growing at almost twenty per cent per year. Oil exports are second only to Nigeria's in all of Africa, with the state having a monopoly on the industry, controlling as well the billion-dollar-a-year diamond sector. And Neto's mausoleum in Luanda would suggest money to burn: the outlandish concrete 'rocket' towers over nearby slums, and is rumoured to have cost up to one hundred million dollars.

And things do seem to be changing. When I'd returned from holidays two weeks ago, Mavinga had only a handful of cars, a dozen police, and no electricity. Today, fifteen hundred police reside in the new barracks, and hastily erected street lights, powered by the large diesel generator flown in, cast a glow over the main street. Two dozen jeeps have been airlifted in as well, along with other supplies on the frequent cargo flights. It's all a part of the effort to rehabilitate this region, according to the Administrator, and also to tighten border security and stem the illegal diamond trade. But the first national elections in more than a decade are scheduled within two years, and the words of the Defence Minister leave little doubt that this is at least part of it. 'Make no mistake,' he'd said, an MPLA man addressing this UNITA town, 'that we will shoot troublemakers.'

The speeches continue past sunset, hosted by an Angolan anchorman behind a spotlit desk on the football field. At the end of the formalities, the ministers move to the purpose-built gazebo behind the stage, where things take a more telling turn. In full view of all, a gourmet meal is served—seafood and beef, washed down with wine—just metres from skinny kids and barefoot adults, who stare more with wonderment than any outrage. And then, as quickly as it all began, it's over. The TV crew pack up their equipment and fly out with the ministers. The meeting arranged by our Luanda office regarding the hospital handover never takes place, and within a week the new generator runs dry. Flights stop arriving, and construction ceases. But the police remain. All of them. Armed, cashed up, bored and young—and supplied with alcohol. A sure recipe for trouble.

• • •

Our last weekend together comes suddenly. Tim's done, flying out next week, and I'll follow in a month (briefings and flights reduce my field time to only five months rather than six). The others will leave shortly after me. So for old time's sake we're spending the day together, doing what we've done much of these months. Mooching in the dining room.

'Tim's in love,' says Pascal, ashing his cigarette onto a plate.

'What?'

'Tell them,' he stirs. 'Tim, why are you being so shy?'

Tim laughs and draws another card, then wipes the sweat from his chest. It's now mid-morning and already too hot to sit with shirts on in here, although Andrea's prepared to endure it.

'We're just friends,' he smiles.

'Ha! Please,' says Pascal. 'I have seen those sat-phone records, my friend. You are going to need a loan to pay for this. You spend hours on that thing with her—do you know how much that will cost you?'

He does. Four dollars a minute. He'll be invoiced when he returns. The issue though is not costs, nor the time he spends talking with her. It's that for months we've been listening to him grumble that he doesn't believe in love, yet he's evidently rescinded this after only a week spent with the colleague of the Red Cross woman I'd stayed with in Lubango, an Italian aid worker who'd visited here during my holidays.

'We're just planning a trip,' he smiles. 'Nothing else. We both finish next week, so we'll travel a bit. It's nothing serious.'

The amorous titles in the 'subject' column of her emails would suggest otherwise. It's good to see him distracted, though. The handover's weighing heavily on all; the four of us had our first full-blown fight (flying plates, overturned lunches) last week during a discussion about it, so we're all now pushing for more action. Andrea and I fired off an emotional email to MSF to articulate the urgency from the medical side of things, and Pascal's casting a wider net. As a proponent of sustainable development he finds the handling of this closure unprofessional, so he's taken it on himself to find an Angolan organisation able to at least run the water system for the coming years. I'm not sure if he'll work with MSF again.

'What do you mean "nothing serious"?' laughs Pascal. 'You are full of shit. I have never seen you change your clothes so often. Tell Damien. Tell him that when she was here, you put on a new shirt every day.'

'*Every day?*'

Pascal nods sincerely.

'He even wore contact lenses,' laughs Andrea, nudging me.

'Yes! *Contact lenses!* Do you believe this? Have you ever seen him wear this? And what about the hair gel? Tell me, Tim—who the fuck wears hair gel in *Mavinga!*'

Definitely not Pascal. He's not cut his hair since we arrived, though he may have trimmed his beard—once. Other than Andrea, who still runs every morning, we're all a little wilder and woollier-looking now. Thinner, too.

'Listen,' says Tim, 'you two can both think what you want, but—'

A shout.

A lapse of time—

(seconds?)

—and I'm standing in maternity with Andrea, breathless, this woman is unconscious, midwives anxious, family screaming . . . *how did I even get here? . . . Jesus she's pale*, what's her blood pressure, wasn't I just talking to Tim, someone—*anyone got a blood pressure?*

'Seventy,' says Andrea, struggling to get a reading. 'No. Sixty-five.'

The two other midwives look anxious but I've never seen them look remotely worried, not these African women—they pull out twins and breeches and deliver stillbirths without their colourful headscarves so much as budging, rarely calling me for anything. I ask what happened and they say that the patient had a big fall, then complained of pain and became drowsy.

Andrea's on her knees. She manages to put in an IV line and we start pouring in fluids and insert a second drip.

'Did she fall onto her stomach?' I ask.

Nene is here. She speaks with relatives. 'They think so. She fell from the back of a cart.'

'What's the blood pressure now?'

'Seventy.'

We squeeze bags of fluid into her IV. Her belly is rigid and I can feel the baby's arms and legs right beneath the abdominal wall, far too close to the surface. *A ruptured uterus?* I've read about it although never seen one, but it would explain her signs and symptoms. Mum's surely got a belly full of blood. Andrea examines her and agrees. The baby's chances of surviving this are minimal but if we don't stop the mother's internal bleeding she'll die soon herself.

'Sixty-five,' says Andrea. 'Blood pressure's sixty-five.'

Serious trouble. We squeeze another bag of fluids into her. I ask someone to find the guards and tell them to round up people to donate blood urgently. A church service is in progress just down the road, so we send someone running and within minutes people are lining up in the yard to have their blood group tested—

'Wait! Where's the transfusion *clinico*?'

—and the guard goes back out to find staff. We try to track down Roberto on the walkie-talkies but he doesn't reply. Agostinho answers instead and runs here within minutes. 'Where's Roberto?' I ask him. He's panting, dressed in a Hawaiian shirt and sandals.

'Visiting family in a nearby village,' says the guard. 'A few hours' walk away.'

Fuck it! Agostinho's not nearly as experienced and I can hardly understand what the guy says because he mumbles incessantly. 'We need to find Roberto too. Send the other guards—they can use the anti-mine car.'

The guard says they can't go there.

'You can. Get Pascal. He'll give you the keys.'

'The driver's not here today.'

'Never mind the driver! You drive! Anyone can drive!'

'*Novo Doctor,* only Jamba can drive. He is the only one with a licence.'

'Fuck the licence! Pascal or Tim will drive. Get them.'

'The road is not safe there. There is a small track, but it is only for walking. No cars will get up it.'

Fuck it! No choice. It's going to be Agostinho and me. Andrea will do anaesthetic.

Back to Maternity. The patient's family are pacing, distraught, the woman's now received over four litres of intravenous fluid and her blood pressure barely registers an improvement. In what must be a new record for the region we have her on the operating table and ready for surgery within half an hour. Everyone pulls together, but for the first time Agostinho's actually *reluctant* to operate. 'I think it is better to wait for Roberto,' he says. 'Her blood pressure is very low. This is too dangerous.'

'That's exactly why we *cannot* wait,' I tell him. 'Agostinho, she'll be dead in half an hour. There's no doubt.' I push him hard. 'It's you or nothing. The baby's probably dead. We just need to tie up that uterus and save the mother, okay? No debating this one. If the mother dies on the table then she dies, but this we cannot sit out and watch. You can do this. I've seen you work. You *have* to do it.'

What a position to put someone in.

He stares at the ground for a long moment. The line of people has grown near the small lab and our tech is here, taking samples.

'*Sim*,' he says. 'Okay. *Vamos*.'

I think that's what he says.

He sets up the instruments fast. He's on his game. I hook the lighting cables to the car battery and Andrea gives the anaesthetic by referring to the chart on the wall and keeps a close eye on the patient's blood pressure. Agostinho washes her belly and lays green drapes around, and someone runs in to tell us that the *clinico* in the lab has found a blood match. 'One unit,' he says. 'Ready in half an hour.'

'Thanks—but we need more. Keep looking. Get someone else to help. Screen everyone, get as many units as you can get.'

Agostinho opens the patient's belly. A single midline incision with scalpel, then dissects with scissors and inserts retractors. She's got an abdomen full of blood. We each grab a side of the wound and pull hard to tear it wider and make more space to work in. The suction machine isn't working properly despite frantic stomping and blood wells up like an overflowing basin, pools to the wound edge, up and over, spilling to the floor and around everyone's feet, and the baby's right there outside the uterus. No pulse, it's already dead, and we take it out and hand it to Nene, who runs back to Maternity with it to assess it properly. We need to worry about mum.

More blood wells up. I put in handfuls of gauze to soak it up but within seconds they're drenched. We see the uterus only fleetingly between fresh gauze and make out the torn edges. More gauze. Agostinho looks up at me. He feels around her pelvis, orients himself and begins tying thick sutures through the uterine walls mostly by touch because we can't see properly. The suction pump is useless. Andrea squeezes in more IV fluids and I try to clamp bleeding vessels with forceps. Her blood pressure remains dangerously low but still out comes more blood. We need to stop this flow, I didn't realise a person had so much blood inside them, but she still has a pulse and it must be forty degrees in the operating room, *Jesus it's hot* and her husband and a handful of nurses crowd around the table and *for Christ's sake—still more blood! How much can there be?*

Agostinho begins working smoothly. More sutures, more gauze, more blood, and my shoes are sticky wet with red. He keeps tying. Over and over, slowly bringing the ragged edges of her uterus together, and the flow ebbs. But her blood pressure's still seventy and there's a worryingly large pile of drenched gauze on the floor.

Steadily, Agostinho brings the last of the edges together. There's now only a slight ooze. We dab the surface and watch to make sure. There's a little more bleeding, so he puts in another suture. We dab. Then wait. Mild ooze, another suture. We do this a few more times until finally there's no bleeding. He's controlled it. We wash her belly out by pouring saline into the wound, then close her abdominal wall in layers. The lab *clinico* sends someone in with the first unit and says that they're collecting more, and the first of the many transfusions she'll get this afternoon starts running as we carry her to *Intensivo*.

Agostinho and I step back into theatre to get changed.

'You did well, Agostinho,' I say, my heart still pounding. He looks remarkably unruffled. He just mumbles something back to me, smiling his understated smile. Pascal's always joked that Agostinho could've been Angola's biggest film star, the way he swaggers around the compound in gaudy shirts, his chiselled face delivering what may be memorable lines—if we could understand them.

'Seriously,' I say, 'I was sure she was going to die.'

He says something back.

'Sorry?'

He repeats himself, but I swear it's not Portuguese he's speaking.

'You saved her life, Agostinho. She had no chance otherwise.'

He shrugs, puts his Hawaiian shirt back on and swaggers out. And I can't help but marvel at him, the less experienced of the two surgical *clinicos* here. Like Roberto, he too acquired his skills with only a year of training in military hospitals set up during the war, having had no formal medical education beforehand. And I also can't help feeling that I've misjudged them. More than a dozen major surgical cases carried out by the pair since I arrived, and not a single complication. Two emergency Caesareans, an obstructed hernia, two limb amputations, appendicectomies and a repair of a bowel perforation—not to mention the dozens of dental extractions, wound debridements, and abscess drainages—and not a single patient has suffered an adverse outcome. What are the odds of that—*out here?*

I go home to shower. By the time I return to the hospital a crowd of dozens have gathered outside *Intensivo*, mostly the church congregation, because it turns out she's the pastor's daughter, and— *unbelievably*—Roberto's niece! She's now receiving her second bag of blood and slowly waking up from the ketamine, and her wound is good and blood pressure stable and the bleeding's stopped entirely. I'm confident she'll be fine. *No—she'll be great.* And everyone's thrilled and grateful and it's a joyous moment, and her family and congregation begin singing for her outside *Intensivo* as patients gather around to listen. Even Toto leaves his canvas sanctuary, I can see José with the burns watching from the window of his little room, and the woman's family come to thank me and I say cheers but Agostinho is the man, and he says that no, I am the man, although who really gives a shit who the man is at that moment; and Roberto and his brother the pastor are ecstatic and we all laugh and pat each other on the back, and instead of being a tough-guy doctor my voice breaks and I fight back tears. At least until I get back to the compound. And then, for the first time since my arrival, I cry. Big, dirty, get-all-that-stuff-out sobs, though I'm not sure why. Pent-up frustration? What-might- have-been? Relief? Joy? Who knows. *Who cares!* But I need it, and it feels good.

And I don't want to leave this place.

12. WATCHING STORMS

This rain just gets heavier. It sheets off the eaves like a thousand water-falls, the sound utterly deafening. Even the roar of thunder is hard to discern over the howl of metal roofing. From where I'm sitting, here on the bench outside the Surgical Outpatients room, a grey soup accounts for the rest of the world; sky and puddles unite. A meteorological *blitzkrieg*, it seems—the type of storm where one is compelled to ponder just how much water could possibly still be in the air; and, just as puzzlingly, how it all got up there in the first place.

We walked to the river yesterday, no longer the struggling stream it used to be. Crossings now need to be made a little more cautiously across the large boulders at the laundry section, although decent-sized *tilapia* can be seen dangling from the ends of homemade rods, and thick grass along its banks. The rest of the town is benefiting from the weather, too. Worn-out huts have had their long-awaited makeovers, fresh mud clinging defiantly to old walls and patchy roofs re-thatched, and the food market boasts plump okra pods and leafy greens as fruit swells slowly on orange trees near the centre of town—the same trees around which landmines were once laid, and below which children now shelter.

'*É SEMPRE ASSIM?*' I shout to Roberto. Is it always like this? He's sitting beside me on the bench.

'*AS VEZES*,' he calls. Sometimes. '*INCRIVEL, NÃO?*'—Incredible, no?

I agree.

We're not alone under the eaves. A few others have pressed themselves against the walls of his Outpatients building with us—women and children waiting to get back to the wards; Manuel, who's now working as an assistant; and a few policemen, whose colleagues are unfortunately taking up much of the men's ward, mostly with injuries after having drunkenly assaulted each other at night. One of them I recognise well. His wife is currently recovering from a stab wound to her cheek—something he'd inflicted, he told us matter-of-factly, because he'd been drinking and she wasn't listening, so you know how it is. As for the force's presence in general, I can't help thinking we were better off without them. I recall a fitting saying I'd once heard from a friend in Indonesia: *If you lose a chicken and report it to the police, you'll end up losing a cow.* Better to just stay out of their way.

The rain's now even heavier. Toyota's standing beneath the opposite wall but Kassoma's caught beneath the leaking awning of the waiting area. He puts on his floppy denim hat and dashes over, the rain pummelling it flat like a swimming cap. When he gets to us he peels it off, wrings it out and laughs, then wipes his glasses.

'*MALUCO!*' he shouts—Crazy!

I shift across. He takes a seat on the other side of me.

'*NOVO DOCTOR*,' he says, his voice as gravelly as the day I arrived. 'YOU WILL STILL FLY HOME, EVEN IF IT IS LIKE THIS?'

I shake my head vehemently. I'm supposed to fly out in the next week, but a herd of wild horses couldn't drag me onto a light plane in weather half as bad as this. I try to explain this but the phrase doesn't seem to translate well; Kassoma chuckles anyway. I'm generally trying to avoid the topic of my departure, though. Roberto and Kassoma still have no jobs, nor do most of our staff; only Sergio and a dozen others have so far been given government contracts to work in the new hospital. On the upside, the Administration has kindly agreed to let us finish their hospital for them, and MSF have since sent a French construction log to oversee it all. Pascal managed to find an agency to maintain the water project for another two years, as well—a significant load off our minds—but the closure nevertheless remains a touchy subject.

The storm's worsening. Still early afternoon but it's already dark as dusk, bolts of lightning periodically slashing the grey. Another flash; I count aloud, making it to six seconds before thunder rumbles the bench again. 'TWO KILOMETRES AWAY,' I shout, and they ask how I know. I explain that for every three seconds between flash and rumble the source is another kilometre away. Kassoma quite likes this.

'*VERDADE?*' he asks—True?

'*VERDADE, SENHOR.*'

The sky lights up again. The thunder follows almost instantly this time. '*MERDA!*' shouts Kassoma, and Roberto exaggeratedly shoots his feet from the ground as if avoiding hot coals—'*EH!*' he yells—and the three of us laugh. He does it again a moment later, an image I'll cherish for a long time: three men, several decades and many melanin granules apart, with little in common other than this hospital, all laughing on a log bench. We'd not ever have met otherwise. I'd not even have known such people existed. *Who would?* I mean, a *clinico*, who's neither doctor nor nurse, who removes teeth, opens bellies, saws off infected legs, or quietly sorts through two dozen outpatients each day, in a rickety hospital somewhere in the Land at the Edge of the World? *As if!* Yet here we sit. Improbably. Laughing as Roberto pulls his legs up again, shitting ourselves as lightning thumps a clutch of trees near the airstrip.

And this is how days have been for much of this last month. Busy mornings with long ward rounds (increased malaria cases and the thousand policemen ensure this), and quieter afternoons when storms tend to keep all but the sickest patients away. So I chat. I sit with the staff outside, start to actually get to know them, and ignore the mounting paperwork. Something I'd like to have done months ago.

'*É ASSIM NA AUSTRALIA?*' shouts Roberto, gesturing to the rain. Is it like this in Australia?

Not where I live, I tell him. In the tropical north it is, but I'm from the south.

'*QUÊ?*' shouts Kassoma on my other side, so I turn to repeat my answer to him.

'*VERDADE?*' he asks.

'*VERADE, SENHOR,*' but now Kassoma asks if I'm talking about the rain or the hospital, because he didn't hear the question. The rain, I say.

'*QUÊ?*'

Another flash—

'*EH!*'

—and the legs go up again.

It's like sitting on a veranda with two old grandfathers.

Was I honestly scared of them when I arrived?

Funny; I'd had such vivid notions of befriending staff when I applied to volunteer, of being invited to their homes and getting to know their families, but the divide between expat and local staff here is rigid: exclusive employer versus employee with few options. And I can't invite Roberto to dinner, for example, because what then of the other health workers? It puts us all in awkward positions. So I regret to say that after five months I know little about them. What I know of Toyota, for example (that he was a mechanic with UNITA, saw much battle first-hand, has three kids and recently asked Pascal to formally ban him from entering the storage sites—his own work-place—because people in town are pressuring him to steal what he can, and he'd rather not) is through Pascal's stories. As a fluent Portuguese speaker who spends his days with a small crew, he's become exceptionally close to them. In contrast, Roberto, who I see six days a week, hadn't ever mentioned his wife to me until a few weeks ago, when he finally introduced us. (He called me 'the *Novo Doctor* who'd operated on their niece', which I quite liked.) He's since brought his wife back a few times, too, and asked if I could suggest good treatment for her high blood pressure. A nice gesture, I think. Like sitting here these latter afternoons. No less considering how we started out all those months back.

The rain eases a little. Toyota dashes over from across the yard.

'*Novo Doctor*,' he says, his blue overalls soaked. 'The women's ward is also leaking. For now, I have put more buckets inside. I will get on the roof later. But for now, just buckets. Everywhere, more buckets,' he smiles.

Kassoma wags his finger. 'We need these leaks to be fixed,' he says. 'It is very difficult to work like this.'

Toyota nods and apologises, says they'll get straight onto it after the storm. He jogs off but promptly turns back. '*Novo Doctor*,' he says. 'I forgot to tell you—I finished that wooden frame. It is ready.'

'What frame?' asks Roberto, and I explain that it's for the young patient we'd admitted earlier. A three-year-old, the boy had arrived with a fractured femur after falling from a tree, a severe break that plaster alone won't fix. Searching through an old surgical manual in our office, I found a sketch for a simple traction device called a 'gallows', a wood frame from which we'll vertically 'hang' the boy's leg from the ankle, using tape and cord, with just enough tension to lift his buttocks slightly off the bed. The weight of his body will stabilise the nearer bone end, the traction device 'pulling' the distant one to counter the force of his leg muscles. Within weeks the bone ends should knit together in a straight position.

Roberto likes this. We thank Toyota and ask him to bring it as soon as he can.

'I will bring it now,' he says, bounding off again. But he turns straight back.

'Also, I forgot, *Novo Doctor*, about Nene. She asked if you could bring the coffee. For the babies. Andrea and her are busy with a delivery, and she said the baby is late for coffee. Nene said you would know what that means. Do you know what that means?'

I nod. Roberto and Kassoma's ears prick up again. *'Café?'* asks Kassoma, and I suspect that this is going to need careful explanation. If they thought the antifungal trial was pushing things, I'm not sure what they'll make of this. (Not that Roberto is any stranger to improvisation out here—he's been making sterile burns dressings for José for weeks now by mixing Vaseline with standard gauze in the autoclave, boiling it over the fire, and has quietly been treating two babies with club foot using a series of carefully graduated plaster casts.) I tell them that two premature babies born recently have been having frequent apnoeic attacks—brief periods where their breathing stops—and that an option back home is to administer caffeine infusions to reduce these, albeit accurately and scientifically, as well as keeping the baby on a monitor. Here we can do neither. Given that a prolonged apnoeic episode can cause death, I feel we're compelled to try something; what we do have is plenty of coffee, rich in caffeine, so theoretically it should help. So we're trialling it. Cool coffee via nasogastric tube, several times a day, titrated to effect: espresso shots for neonates. And for the moment at least the babies are well, although whether it's because of the treatment, or in spite of it, I'm not sure.

'Eh!' exclaims Roberto.

Kassoma's silent. He stares at me from behind his too-big glasses, the soft haze of an early cataract visible in his right eye. *'Verdade?'* he asks, regarding me with a look of mild suspicion.

'Verdade, Senhor.'

But he's still not sure what to make of it.

Within minutes the rain eases to soft drizzle. Kids wander out to play in puddles and patients slowly begin arriving again, so we get back to work. I head off to make the coffee, but the guard calls me to talk with a man at the gate. The man jogged here, he says, and would like us to please follow him back with a car. He says that a woman is sick.

'Very sick?' I ask. 'Is it urgent?'

Not extremely, he says, but it's better we get there soon.

I find Jamba, our driver, who's more than happy to take the mine-proof car. I jump in with the pair—it may well be my last drive around town—and we lumber out the gate, and by the end of the street we're doing thirty, close to top speed, so it's just as well that this isn't an emergency.

Jamba steers us around the bigger potholes as the man who ran here sits between us, directing. 'Go right,' he says, and the building supplies slide around the back as we do. 'Okay, down here. Yes, left. Behind this hut. And past those children. Yes—okay, down that little bank.'

I ask Jamba if these roads are safe and he nods confidently, then honks at goats, shouts to kids, avoids one of the town's few bicycles, reverses to turn down the track he missed, and shifts into second for the first time, soon stopping where we're told to near a large group of people. The man who called us gets out and leads me by my arm—'In here, Doctor, they're in here,'—to God knows what because he still hasn't said, and we push politely through a crowd and arrive at a clearing where a group of men have buried a young girl in mud. She's lying on her side with only her head and neck exposed. People are packing more wet earth over her, and as I kneel beside her I can see she's still breathing.

'What on earth are you doing to her?' I ask.

'This is our treatment, Doctor,' says an older man in a reassuring tone. 'She was hit by lightning. This mud will cool her body. It will help her. You can take her to the hospital, but when we are finished.'

Behind us a group of women are wailing, and someone points me inside a nearby hut. I step in. The room is almost empty. No furniture but for some rough bedding on the mud floors, and huddled together on the floor are two women, motionless. I crouch to take their pulses, but they have none. Their eyes are open. There's a scorch mark on the ground and a hole in the straw roof where I imagine the lightning struck, and one of the victims has a large belly. She was heavily pregnant.

Outside, the men pull the girl from the mud. She's the daughter of one of the dead women. She's conscious and glassy-eyed and she won't speak, but her vital signs are good. We lift her into the back of the vehicle and I sit there with two other men who help support her, and Jamba bounces us slowly back to the hospital, pausing for cattle, detouring for goats, and by the time we get to the hospital a dozen kids are running gleefully alongside the car.

We carry the daughter to *Intensivo*. The smell of José's wounds still fills the air from the next room. The new girl won't talk, but there are no tears, just a stunned look. We ask the cook to make a warm sugary drink for her because there's not much else we can do, and Therese sits with her arm around her and wraps her in blankets and coaxes her to drink. She's got no major burns, we've got no ECG to monitor her with, but if she's survived this long she'll probably be fine.

'You okay with her?' I ask Therese.

Therese nods.

I step outside. Across the yard, stopping to look back at the compound.

Less than a week to go now.

I breathe . . .

There's a break in the clouds. An orangewarm sun, slanting through it. Toyota's on the roof, trying to patch a leak. Jamba climbs a ladder to help. Nearer the front fence, José's wife squats on her haunches and empties the water from her battered pot. Her daughter carries some wood over and they set it down, stack it neatly, strike a match and blow gently but it doesn't light. They try again. Patiently, like two graceful yogis, drying the wood on the hem of their dresses, then stacking it to try once more, no hint of frustration.

I head to the back yard. Maybe Andrea will be keen for a walk to the river, I think, but a group of policemen call to me as I pass. '*Oi! Branco!*' says one, slouching outside the men's ward. 'When will you fly us to Luanda? This hospital is no good. It is not a proper hospital! And this food—it is shit!'

I nod politely though I'd like to tell them to fuck off, that they have no idea what this hospital does or what the staff accomplish, but I bite my tongue and tell them only that they're more than welcome to try the food elsewhere. And I think: five months here, and I'm no closer to making sense of this place. *Could anyone?* Last week, two young boys found an unexploded grenade washed out by the rains and pounded the shiny toy until it did explode, killing them instantly; hours later we performed an emergency Caesarean, saving two lives. Ten days ago a woman walked here, mute with fear, having been raped in the police barracks; that same day, José beat another severe infection. It goes on. Needless tragedies and improbable recoveries; thuggish policemen, and inspirational staff.

But what I'll remember most is this: that Toto, the albino woman and her demented mother, for whom we do little other than provide pills, dressings, and three bowls of maize and beans a day, don't ever ask for anything else. Nor does José with the burns, who still wraps up those magazines I gave him months ago, or the old man with the bag of pee, who came back to Outpatients yesterday for review (and was quite thrilled with his new urine bag, thanks very much). Nor do any of our other patients, police aside. And for me, *this* is the thing. No one mopes, or says Poor us.

They just get on with it.

• • •

The three of us have never got drunk in Mavinga, but Saturday night puts an end to that—in *grand* fashion. We buy a cow and two goats, and Vasco roasts them on a large fire at the back of our compound. All staff are invited. There's plenty of beer, and Dominga's in oil heaven, deep-frying pastry balls by the bucketload. We even secure the emcee who'd hosted the wedding, albeit with the proviso that he not play Michael Bolton. It's a Thank You to the staff, I tell myself, more than a going-away party. The idea of the latter is inappropriate.

On Monday morning we make a final ward round together. Last-minute plans, final adjustments, scribbled suggestions, and I can't help but picture the new doctor doing the same in the coming days, looking at the protocols we're using and asking herself what the hell I'd done these past months. But midway through the round the kids run off to meet the plane as it bumps to a halt on the runway.

Time to go.

I farewell patients.

Cheers to Toto, all the best to José.

Who'll look after them? How will they pay for health care next year?

I don't know.

I grab my bags and head to the airstrip. The doctor replacing me hasn't arrived because of delays in her paperwork, but MSF have sent an experienced nurse. Andrea will follow me out in a week, although Pascal's extended his contract until the closure. He really shouldn't have—he's utterly exhausted and misses his girlfriend—but he wants to make sure that the new hospital is finished.

I load my bags and chat with the staff on the airstrip, not really sure how to feel. I'm thrilled about not being on call, sad about leaving, delighted at the prospect of restaurants and deeply regretful about abandoning what feels like a sinking ship, so I just make small talk. But thunderheads are rolling in from the south and when I point them out to the Canadian pilot he says, Yeah, we'd better get a move on because those things will rip the wings right off his little Cessna, and he says it with no hint of sarcasm so I do get a move on.

Hurried goodbyes.

Fuck, I forgot to write a plan in the chart for the kid with—

No time.

A last group photo. A shake of hands, best wishes for the future, and halfway through I get to Roberto, who gives me a firm embrace, which is awkward because he's a good four inches taller than me, so there we stand, a short, pale *Branco* reaching up to hug the frame of a not-so-pale, not-so-short Angolan man in the middle of a muddy airfield; *oh well, fuck it*, now handshakes switch to hugs for all and I start again, teeter on tiptoes to reach up to Kassoma, back down to soles to reach Nene, stay down for Dominga although my arms don't reach all the way around her, and then a long, touching, slightly malodorous embrace with Pascal and Andrea, who I'd consider as close as family after these shared months.

And that's it. Wave the kids away. A quick take-off, then it's gone, just a blur at The Edge of the World.

13. GUIDELINES FOR ABDUCTION

Experienced volunteers warn that coming home is more difficult than going to the field, but I disagree. For the first few weeks, that is.

It's like being shot from a giant catapult. I soar past Angolan beaches, bars, restaurants and the debriefing rooms in Geneva within days; then shops, more airports, a week of holidays and another debriefing in Sydney; and slide finally into Melbourne, where friends, the urgent need for a date and the search for a mobile phone plan occupy my days. It's an earth-shatteringly fast journey from the unpredictability of life in Mavinga to a zero-G life at home, disorienting though not unpleasant, but there's little time to think about it. I start my new job in an Intensive Care unit this morning.

'Mr Feldman,' says my colleague. 'Eighty-two years old. Type-two diabetic, day one post-elective revision of coronary artery bypass grafts. He arrived from theatre last night. Three grafts: L.I.M.A. to L.A.D., S.F.A. to O.M. one, radial to R.C.A.'

We look at Mr Feldman. Mr Feldman beeps but says nothing. He lies still, bathed in the sterile white of fluorescent tubes as twenty-one degrees of climate-controlled air falls with a gentle *shush* from vents above.

My colleague continues. 'No intraoperative issues. He's been stable overnight. Inotrope requirements are coming down—milrinone off at six this morning, noradrenaline still weaning—and he remains fully sedated. There's a fair bit of ooze from his chest drains though. We checked his coags and gave some F.F.P. earlier, but there's still ooze.'

'I.N.R.?' asks the senior, an Intensive Care specialist.

'One point one.'

'A.P.T.T.?'

'Normal.'

'Have we given any factor seven?'

'No,' replies my colleague. 'We thought we'd wait until you saw him.'

The specialist logs into the laptop on the table beside the patient's bed, enters two passwords and swipes an ID card, then scrolls through lab results. Pages of them. He turns next to read through the nursing charts, then examines Mr Feldman—or at least the things going into or out of Mr Feldman, that is, because there's little to be gained from examining Mr Feldman himself: he's still unconscious, heavily sedated and on a ventilator. Instead, a bank of monitors behind him displays the waveforms and acronyms of his essential parameters, while the chest X-ray taken of him an hour ago shows his lung fields and cardiac outline, confirming as well the position of the many tubes that spaghetti their way into and out of him—endotracheal and nasogastric tubes, a four-lumen central venous catheter, and two chest drains. (Three peripheral catheters are not shown.) A row of steel sutures is also visible on the radiograph, the discrete loops and knots arranged in a vertical row that hold the divided edges of his sternum together. Small metal bows, it seems, on Mr Feldman's new gift: another lease of life at eighty-two years of age.

The specialist kneels down. He regards one of the drainage bags leading from the chest, and looks up. 'This all collected since midnight?'

My colleague nods.

'We should give it then,' he says. 'Let's give the factor seven.'

He nods my way.

I nod his way.

'Yeah, let's give it,' he says.

'Now?' I ask.

'Yes.'

'One vial?'

He nods again.

I ruffle papers. Lift them up, check the back, but I've got no idea where I'm supposed to write. There's a mountain of charts clipped to the desk. As I flick through the paperwork the others watch me, and I wonder if this is what Manuel felt like when I questioned him on the rounds about quinine and saline infusions. 'Sorry, but where?'

'Here,' says my colleague. 'Infusions go here, stat doses there.'

'Cheers.'

'Got it?'

'Think so. How much are we giving again?' I ask.

'One vial.'

I write it up. Mr Feldman's designated nurse for the next twelve hours goes to the drug room to fetch it, and I quietly ask my colleague what factor seven is. It's been eighteen months since I last worked in a large Australian hospital—time spent doing that Tropical Medicine course, then the stints in Thailand and Angola—so as suspected, I'm well out of touch. And this drug is one I've not used before, either.

'It's a pro-coagulant,' explains my colleague. 'We give it a fair bit to these post-graft guys here. Great for persistent ooze but it's a couple of thousand bucks a vial, so better to check before you give it. And don't drop any!'

I nod. The specialist meanwhile fiddles with the ventilator and suggests other numbers to an appreciative audience, but he lost me minutes ago. So I look around, take stock of our surroundings and tune out for a moment, because the room we're standing in is the very epitome of modern medicine. Near us, eleven other Mr

Feldmans rise and fall in their neighbouring beds to the demands of their ventilators, and it's clear that no expense is to be spared in the management of any of them—the consultant just asked for a second vial of factor seven, and I'd spent enough time in these departments as a student to know that we'll hang on to patients for weeks, months if necessary, scanning, medicating, operating, dialysing, weaning, intubating, haemo-filtering, catheterising, transfusing and referring them, stopping only when, should they unfortunately not recover, a very clear point of no return has been crossed. Decisions will not ever be based primarily on finances or a lack of resources. No credit card details will be sought, nor insurance plans relied upon, and no young mothers will be palliated for breast cancer in a tent. It's the opposite in nearly every respect to Mavinga; a comparatively bottomless pit of resources, but it's not at all a system I resent. On the contrary, it's a level of care I would want for my family, and that I believe everyone should have the right to access. The problem now is that working here, after being in Mavinga, is a glaring, uncomfortable reminder of the disparities between here and *there*.

What a cliché, though, this difficulty in readjusting! And how thoroughly I begin to fulfil it. No less when the predictability of the years ahead dawns on me. I'd taken this job before going to Mavinga, the intention having been to complete my specialty training in Emergency Medicine as soon as I got back here (the Intensive Care job is part of that), but the program is five more years. Five very structured, very limiting years, all of which will need to be spent in Western hospitals.

A few months later I rotate to the Emergency department. It's an interesting job, a role that certainly can't be described as boring, and one that I enjoy for the most part. But while MSF are again in Angola helping with another cholera outbreak, I'm dealing mostly with paperwork, referrals and nursing home transfers, and that reliable

staple of the many night shifts: drunks. Some of whom are delightfully entertaining. Others, not quite so.

'We picked him up fighting in the laneway, doc,' a police officer
tells me one typical Saturday night. I stand in the ambulance bay with
security, contemplating how to deal with the hundred kilograms of
intoxicated fury behind the door of the wagon. 'He's goin' nuts in
there. We used the spray a couple of times, but he just went crazier.
Amphetamines, I reckon. He didn't even blink. Cut his head during
the scuffle, so now he's bleeding.'

I sigh. 'How many guards we got?'

'Three.'

'Okay. Cindy, can you draw up some midazolam? Full vial. We'll
give it to him as he comes out the door,' I say. A routine I know well.

'No way,' says the policeman. 'You'll need to give it to him in there.
We gotta sedate him *before* he comes out. We can't have him loose
out here.'

Great news. There's no way we can send a female nurse in there, so
it'll have to be me along with the officers and security guards (who, it
must be said, have the more difficult job in the department on nights
like these). I try reasoning with the man first, for what it's worth. You
never know your luck. 'We're just here to help you, mate,' I say. 'We
need to stop that bleeding, that's all, then we'll leave you in peace. You
can sleep when we're done and we won't bother you again. Promise.
We'll bring you something to eat if you want. You hungr—?'

'Fuuuuuuck yooooouuu!' the roar from the back of the van.

'Mate, either way we need to have a look. There are two ways we
can go about this. It's your choice. Seriously, it'll be much easier if—'

'This is police brutalidy! I know my . . . my fucken . . . my . . .'

'Your rights?'

'Yeeaah.'

I'd laugh, if only I wasn't responsible for this man's care. I turn to
one of the two officers. 'Is his head bleeding badly?' I ask.

He nods.

'Cindy? We good to go?'

She nods.

'Security?'

They nod.

'Officers?'

They nod. We don gloves and goggles and get the door, and I think: I'd rather deal with malaria for free than this for a decent salary.

Obviously not all is like this in the department. Most patients are great to deal with and there are plenty of seniors around to help. I'm just not sure how much more of what I'm learning here I can apply to the field.

· · ·

By mid-year I'm trawling the aid worker websites—just browsing, I assure myself—and hoping for someone to talk sense into me. I have coffee with a specialist in the hospital who's spent years in the field, and ask for his advice: should I finish the training program or return to the field?

'Go back to the field,' he says. 'It doesn't get any easier to do it. You'll climb the ladder here and set yourself up nicely, but in five years you'll have a hundred more reasons why you can't leave. You've got broad, generalist skills. If you really want to do that work again, go.'

I contact MSF to see what jobs are on the horizon—just browsing, I continue to assure myself—but they have plenty. We correspond increasingly over the following months, and the possibility of a one-year contract with their emergency response team comes up. It's extremely tempting. More so when I receive an email from Andrea, who's thoroughly enjoying the new volunteer position she's taken in west Africa.

Meanwhile, things at home begin to make even less sense at times than in Mavinga. Mum calls to tell me that she's just taken the family dog to the vet and that he wants to prescribe a new medication—

'Anxiety pills,' she says. 'Apparently he's got an anxiety disorder of sorts.'

'The *dog*?'

'*Ja*. Some sort of nervous tremor.'

—and after another weekend of Emergency department night shifts I stand red-eyed at the supermarket checkout, drunk with fatigue and my scrubs soiled, watching an overweight kid have a tantrum because his mum bought him *that* chocolate bar, not the other of the twenty varieties he wanted, and I wonder how he'd feel about therapeutic milk up his nose instead.

But such comparisons are futile. Naïve at best, self-righteous at worst.

Nothing more annoying than the person at the dinner table who notes how many kids could have been vaccinated in lieu of your latte—I've long since realised things aren't quite that simple—yet here I sit, later in the year, tuning out when colleagues speak of new cars and property renovations, recalling instead images of re-thatched roofs and re-mudded walls, and I wonder what happened to our staff, or José with the burns . . .

Bugger it. I'm in. No point agonising over the inevitable.

'Two years,' I tell MSF. 'I'd like to commit for two years, maybe longer depending on how things go.'

Almost immediately I'm offered my first choice for a posting, a project for malnourished children. They forward details of the large feeding centre where a hundred severe cases are currently being treated as inpatients, several thousand more as outpatients. Various documents arrive: nutrition guidelines, job descriptions, vaccination requirements, and then this: *Survival Guidelines During Abduction.*

The job's in Somalia. It's my dream position, in my nightmare destination. The security situation there is dire, with ongoing clan warfare, no effective government for over a decade, and now a fundamentalist Muslim insurgency as well. It's not a project I'd have dreamed of considering in the past, but I think of the nutrition ward in Angola, and of how rehabilitating those children seemed to me the epitome of humanitarian intervention—an imperative, even.

'You won't leave the compound at all,' explains an MSF senior via email. 'You'll be escorted in an armed convoy to the hospital compound, and you'll live and work there. Armed guards will always be present.' (An exception for MSF, who normally don't allow guns within their projects.) 'Any signs of trouble, and we'll pull you straight out. We take security very seriously, but you do need to understand that this area is unstable, and that we can neither foresee nor prevent every possibility. As a volunteer, the decision to go is entirely yours.'

I do my reading. Not lightly, I make my decision. I put my property into storage and say teary goodbyes, then head again for a briefing in Sydney. In Switzerland I sign security documents and a Proof of Life form, and for the next two weeks mull over it anxiously in an old hotel room in wintry Geneva, delayed by human resources issues. When I finally arrive in Kenya, I'm nervous, excited, outright frightened, but keen to just get there and start. The MSF driver picks me up at Nairobi airport to take me for my briefing at the regional offices, the last step before Mogadishu, but when I arrive there I see only solemn faces, not the cheery Welcome To the Project I'd known previously.

'You Damien?' they ask.

'Yes.'

They direct me to take a seat. 'We've got bad news,' says the French project coordinator. 'You won't be going to Somalia for a while.'

Jesus, after all that?

'Why?' I ask.

Three MSF workers were murdered in Somalia that morning, he says. A targeted attack, only metres from their compound.

14. NET FISHING ON THE ZAMBEZI

The service takes place on a blustery afternoon in a leafy park of Nairobi, Kenya, just days after the explosion. The hundred expats working with MSF in Somalia are hastily evacuated—my room-mate at the guesthouse has only the clothes he's wearing and a laptop, everything else still in Somalia—and all attend. It's a sad, sobering event.

Photographs of the three deceased stand on a table ahead of us, falling often as the wind buffets them. There are no coffins, though. The body of Damien Lehalle, the French logistician, has been flown home for a service; Victor Okumu, the Kenyan surgeon, will be buried in his home town in the coming days, although his family are now with us; and the body of Mohamed Bidhaan, the Somali driver of the ill-fated car, remains in his home country.

It's an outpouring of anger as much as grief, the service. An MSF senior speaks movingly of the sacrifice the three have made, of the senselessness of such an attack, and of how it's as much an assault on the Somali community, who'll consequently be deprived of this assistance as MSF reassess the feasibility of the projects. Team-mates of the deceased stand up, sobbing their way through eulogies. The teenage daughter of Victor Okumu has to be helped back to her seat when she collapses despairingly, and his widow is little more composed. But a relative of theirs confronts MSF seniors. 'How could you do this?' she cries, standing in front of them. 'How could you send this man to such a place? And when you *knew* this country was not safe?'

It's a painfully awkward moment. The MSF coordinator looks devastated as he weathers the outburst, though I suspect I'd have reacted like the relative had I been in her position. But for me, MSF made no secrets of the security issues during briefings. They'd made it exquisitely clear that the decision to go, and the attendant risk, was mine. A cursory browse of their public websites doesn't downplay such risks, either. Statements caution that volunteers have been raped, kidnapped and murdered in the past, and off the top of my head I can recall several recent tragedies: the 2004 execution of five MSF volunteers in Afghanistan, shot in their well-marked car; the fatal shooting of a French nurse in the Central African Republic last year, just weeks into her first posting; the kidnapping of two volunteers in the north of Somalia only months ago, since released unharmed; and the seven passengers who'd died near Mavinga in 2002, when the MSF car hit a landmine. If people know nothing else of MSF, in my experience, they know of its reputation for working in dangerous places. Mentioning back home that I'd worked in Angola garners mild interest; saying that it had been with MSF elicits admiration.

Since its inception, the organisation has been active in conflict areas. In many ways it was born of conflict. In the 1970s, a group of young doctors working for the Red Cross became increasingly frustrated with that organisation's strict policy of silence (specifically with regards to atrocities committed by the Nigerian military during the Biafran Civil War) and argued that to not draw the world's attention to such acts was tantamount to complicity. Along with a group of like-minded medical professionals and journalists, they formed MSF, and the idea of *témoignage*—of bearing witness, or speaking out— became central to the new organisation's principles, along with those

First glimpse of Mavinga, Angola, from above. Bone dry, and only mud huts in sight.

The laundry section of the Cubia River, Mavinga, just after the first rains.

Delivery of supplies by an old Russian transport plane, Mavinga. Goods are being loaded directly into our vehicle—a mine-proof, ex-military machine. The living compound can be seen to the right.

The Outpatient waiting area, Mavinga Hospital.

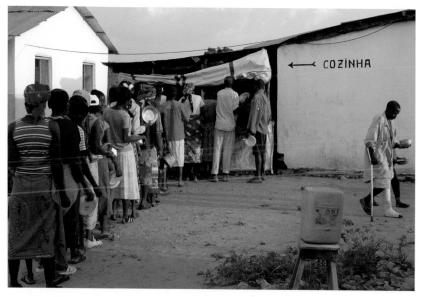

Patients queue for a lunch of maize and beans, Mavinga Hospital.

The backyard of Mavinga Hospital. The main wards are to the left, Maternity at the rear and tents for our long-term residents to the right. The town's choir was visiting on this day, singing for one of its unwell members.

One of Mavinga's many makeshift classrooms, this one in the bombed-out remains of an old building.

The girl with the beer-bottle doll. A tuft of black hair is jammed into the top of the bottle, it has no eyes, and the label is still on.

A young boy carrying water from the river, Mavinga.

With the relatives of a woman who'd just survived major surgery, Mavinga.

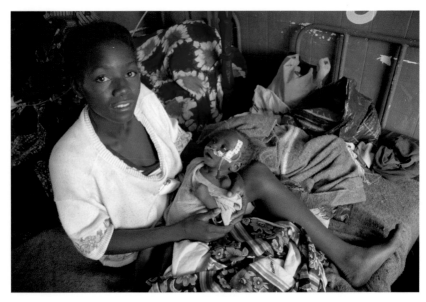

A mother cradles her severely unwell child in *Intensivo*, our 'intensive care' unit. He is malnourished, his hair is thinning and the increased effort of breathing is seen at the front of his neck.

The same child after two months of treatment.

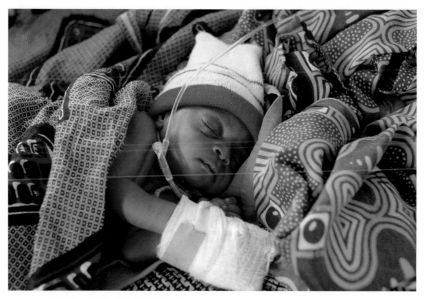

An unwell infant receiving IV antibiotics, Mavinga.

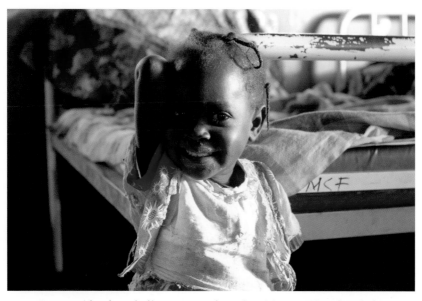

A young girl at the end of her treatment for malnutrition, sporting a beard of high-energy biscuit crumbs.

This patient was in a coma for over a month in Mavinga Hospital. He finally woke up during my last days, albeit with a degree of brain damage. His carer—a good friend, he'd told us, not the patient's brother as we'd thought—never left his side.

A group of the Angolan medical staff, Mavinga Hospital.

Waiting patiently for hours near our compound in Mavinga in the hope of receiving a free blanket, a bucket, a piece of soap and some biscuits during a one-off distribution.

A hastily-formed camp for Internally Displaced People (IDPs) in Eldoret, Kenya, providing sanctuary for those who've fled widespread post-election violence in the region.

Posing with local children, Mozambique.

Locals cross a flooded landscape, carrying their few belongings to higher ground.

Kids play on the remains of a crashed plane along the edge of the Sobat River, Nasir, South Sudan.

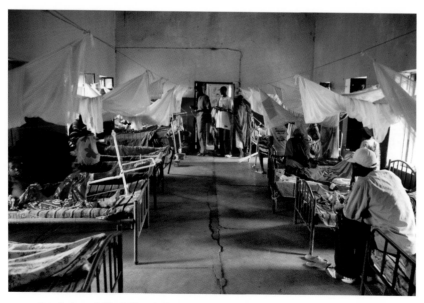

Surgical ward, Nasir Hospital.

Locals fill their water containers from one of the hospital's clean-water outlets, Nasir.

Posing in front of a hut in the town of Wudier, South Sudan.

Net fishing in the Sobat River, Nasir.

Kids from the TB treatment village make the most of a rain-soaked compound, moulding toys from abundant clay.

A blind, elderly man in Nasir, carrying the sum total of sight-aids available to him: a stick, the other end of which was pulled by a young relative.

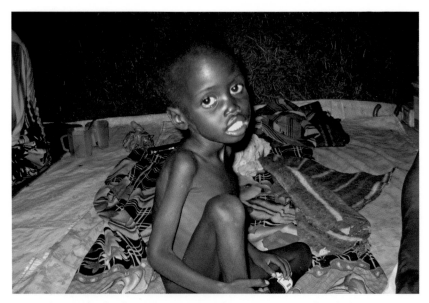

The tragedy of malnutrition. A young girl recovers in our small re-feeding unit, Nasir.

Staff and patients chatting outside the surgical ward in Nasir. The six parallel lines of scarification across the foreheads of several of the men are called *gaar*.

A sunset in Nasir, silhouetting the conical tops of a cluster of *tukuls*.

What came to be my daily exercise in Nasir: lifting and throwing the kids who'd request this—and with increasing frequency, too.

Two young siblings and one fantastic haircut, South Sudan.

of strict neutrality, impartiality, independence, and the observance of universal medical ethics.*

To allow operational decisions to be made free of external influences, the organisation relies largely on private donors rather than governments. The projects they run are varied in scope, and include, among numerous others, general hospitals and community health projects; disease-specific programs such as those for HIV/AIDS and TB; short-term, focused emergency interventions for conditions like cholera, malnutrition or meningitis; and campaigning at a political level for affordable access to essential medicines in poorer countries.

But they've always maintained a commitment to assist in conflict areas. The seventy countries they've worked in over the last decade include Iraq, Afghanistan, Chechnya, Sudan, Angola, Congo, Liberia, Sierra Leone and Rwanda—a roll call of trouble spots—and in 1999 they were awarded the Nobel Peace Prize.

All of this requires volunteers, however. A constant supply of volunteers. People from a range of professions, often with variable if any experience in such places, and who're prepared to accept the risks. And I wonder now, as I stand in this park, whether a thirty-year-old health professional from a wealthy country, who has no background in security, international politics, or conflict—me, for example—can make a truly informed decision about any of this. I read the documents. I spoke to people who'd previously been in Somalia, but I still don't understand the implications of phrases like 'increasing ethnic tensions' if I'm to be in the hospital all day, clearly assisting these people. The assumption must be that if volunteers are sent there, the

---

* The concept of *témoignage* is controversial in its interpretation. To be overly critical of groups contradicts the principle of neutrality, and can exclude the organisation from being granted access to the very populations it's trying to help. The Ethiopian government, for example, expelled MSF in 1985 after they criticised the government abuse of aid. Several founding members left MSF following disagreements related to, among other things, the application of this principle.

organisation considers it safe enough; conversely, the assumption must also be that any volunteer who'd accept such a position has seriously contemplated the risks—and accepted them. It'd be a fine line, I imagine, between being able to access these areas at all versus taking too big a chance. For me, though, the bubble bursts this afternoon. I stare at the three portraits. The risks are no longer theoretical.

And yet the recently evacuated volunteers are actually *keen* to go back! I share a guesthouse in Nairobi with a dozen of them, including a Canadian surgeon with a wife at home and a French logistician with a degree in philosophy, and all speak fondly of the Somalis. All deeply regret leaving. All of them miss the staff and patients, and all would return without hesitation if allowed back. And none strike me as ill-informed.

As to whether they will go back, the pressing issue is that of the motive behind the attack. If it's purely a local problem (a disgruntled businessman, for example) then they'll return soon, but if this represents a wider threat from fundamentalist groups, there's no chance. In the meantime, we wait. MSF send a team to investigate, and medical supplies and wages are flown to the Somali staff, who continue to provide a level of health care.

· · ·

Being on stand-by in Kenya isn't without its own problems. Normally a relative oasis of peace in this part of Africa, widespread violence has erupted following the presidential elections in December, just last month. Both parties are accused of electoral manipulation, and members of the president's Kikuyu ethnic group have become targets of violence. By late January, hundreds of Kenyans have been murdered and hundreds of thousands of others have fled their homes. Camps for these Internally Displaced Persons (IDPs) spring up across the country.

I'm sent to join an existing team in Eldoret, a town in the Rift Valley region further west, to help make a rapid evaluation of the health situation. The scale of the main camp exceeds anything I'd imagined. A vast plain of rudimentary plastic shelters sprawls over a muddy sports ground on which twenty thousand people now live, all sleeping on the dirt or on plastic throw-downs as rain worsens conditions further. These families all fled here to seek protection from their former neighbours, and everywhere in town we see evidence of the unrest: the charred remnants of selectively torched homes and businesses; broken windows and threatening graffiti; and makeshift roadblocks of logs or loose piles of rocks, at which people were dragged from vehicles to an unimaginable fate. The men from these opposing ethnic groups seem pleasant enough, though. They stand around in town as if it were all just a quiet week, and I can't help but wonder which of them had been responsible for all the violence and destruction. Could they really feel so strongly about an *election*?

It's soon apparent that I'm not going to be needed in Eldoret as a doctor, however. The aid response has been huge. The Kenyan government, along with UN agencies and dozens of other aid groups, appear to be meeting immediate needs (our hotel's car park is packed with white four-wheel drives bearing the logos and acronyms of every aid agency I have and haven't heard of), and in the larger camps school classes are even being provided for over two thousand children in a series of tents set up by UNICEF.

As for Somalia, security has deteriorated further. No one will be heading there soon. I'm instead offered a position in Mozambique, a country on the south-east African coast, which I promptly accept; and, just two days, three commercial flights and one boat ride after receiving the email, I arrive in my new project.

• • •

Being in Mozambique is like meeting Angola's happy cousin. The country has the same national language, a mostly Bantu population and those enticing Afro-Latin rhythms blaring from beachfront bars, although this is arguably the sexier of the two nations. Positioned at a similar latitude to Angola, albeit on the opposite side of the continent, its long coastline is dotted with warm, palm-fringed Indian Ocean beaches that attract a stream of international tourists, yet the history of these former Portuguese colonies is depressingly similar: a thriving slave trade; a violent anti-colonial movement; an almost immediate post-independence civil war; and finally, after fifteen years of fighting, a peace agreement in 1992.

But my posting has little to do with conflict this time. Floods have displaced around fifty thousand villagers along the banks of the Zambezi River, and similar events eight years ago resulted in a large cholera outbreak. MSF are anticipating a repeat of this.

By the time I arrive in mid-February, a dozen volunteers have been assisting communities for weeks. I spend a day with them being shown how to set up a mobile health clinic—essentially a large tent beneath a much larger tree, where short consultations are provided at a plastic table and medicines dispensed—and then head upriver to join a second, smaller team of two expat logisticians and four Mozambicans, closer to the Malawian border.

For the first two weeks we run our own mobile clinic, seeing up to a hundred and fifty patients each day. It's busy work and none of us have done this before, so we're all learning on the job. At the same time, flood forecasts change constantly and new health information is phoned through several times a day; our plans are revised often. Then, after two weeks, we're instructed by coordination to cease the clinics, and to instead conduct a nutrition survey—something I've not ever seen, let alone supervised—so by the end of our third week there's still no semblance of a routine. Except for one thing: no matter what we try, we can't get away in the mornings.

Or find our staff.

• • •

'You seen the nurses?' asks Simon, the thirty-something Canadian log running our group. His physical resemblance to Pascal is uncanny; same woolly Guevara-esque black hair, same wispy goatee. He's poring over stock lists and a map with torch in hand, the well-worn papers spread over the bonnet of one of the three four-wheel drives we've rented.

'They're still in bed,' I reply.

'*Jesus*. We're not going to have enough time out there!'

I agree.

'And the drivers?'

No idea. We should've been on the road half an hour ago. It's already after five-thirty and the sky's begun its gentle transition from black to the pale glow of a tropical dawn, yet we're still waiting in the gravel car park of the guesthouse we're using, off a side track in our small base town of Morrumbala, to the west of the country's centre. It's a four and a half hour drive each way to today's village, and we'd made it clear: not Local Time again, please people. We have to be back here by sunset, so there's no room for *faffing*. Which is ironic, because that's exactly what our team is best at.

João, one of our three Mozambican logs, soon walks up from the gravel road. 'Oh, I am early?' he asks.

'Late.'

'But where is everybody?'

It's the million dollar question. The two MSF nurses are accounted for (in bed, the last time I'd checked), and Kevin, a logistician from New Zealand, is spending the night in another village. But our three drivers and two other assistants are still missing, as too are the Mozambican government nurses we're supposed to be working with, and it's this latter issue that's becoming a problem. The local representative for the Ministry of Health has insisted that two of his nurses accompany us on all visits—'You are guests in this country,' he reminded us, 'and you are here at our invitation, so you are not to run around doing your own thing'—but, yet again, neither of them has arrived. And if they don't arrive by the time we do finally leave, like yesterday, João will guide us along the winding tracks past nearby adobe homes to look for them. Being presumably unsuccessful in our search—again—we'll then drive to the government hospital and ask if another nurse can accompany us, because that's what we've been told to do, but the hospital is exceedingly crowded and understaffed and dealing as well with rabies cases this week, so we'll almost certainly leave without any of their nurses. Then, when we return this evening, we'll be called back into the ministry offices, *again*, to explain why we left without the ministry nurses; and when we ask the official in no way facetiously if he'd rather we didn't run the clinics at all on the occasions they don't arrive—'Because, sir, let's be honest, they never arrive, but if you would rather that we cancelled the program on such days then in all good grace I will inform my seniors that that's what we'll do'—he'll just groan, wag his finger at us, shuffle papers and remind us that we are his guests, and that it is our responsibility to find them.

But where can we find them?

'And the drivers?' asks João. 'Where are the drivers?'

Moments later, one of them makes his way towards us, shuffling from the brick bedrooms across the car park. He looks awful—no shirt, shoulders hunched, almost swaggering.

'Maurizio? You been drinking?' asks João.

Maurizio arrives and leans against the nearer car. Blisters of sweat pool on his brow. 'I think I have malaria,' he groans. 'Today, I am not good.'

I put a hand on his forehead; the man's burning up. I fish through one of the boxes of medical supplies and retrieve a Paracheck malaria test, the same type we'd used in Mavinga, and lay it out on the bonnet. With just a small drop of blood from Maurizio's finger the test is immediately positive. 'You do, mate. You had it before?'

'Not for years. Before, yes, but I have been living in the city these years.'

I hand him a three-day course of artemisinin-based pills from our boxes, good treatment, and escort him back to his bedroom. João brings him food and water, then disappears to rustle up the others. One of our two nurses soon walks over—still in her pyjamas.

Simon laughs.

'What on earth are you doing?' I ask. 'We need to go!'

'I need to find the laundry girl,' she replies. 'I have no clean clothes.'

'Could you not have done that yesterday?'

'We didn't get back until late. Anyway, Katrina's gone, so we have to wait for her.'

'Gone where?'

'Into town.'

Simon folds the map and takes a seat on a large boulder near the edge of the yard. We're clearly going to be here for a while.

'Why into town?'

'To find breakfast,' she replies; Miranda's her name.

'But did you guys not remember? Five! We needed to leave at five!'

'Yes, but we need breakfast.'

'We have rolls and drinks here for the drive—like yesterday. And the days before.'

João returns to tell us that the other driver is in the shower.

'Then I am going to go have a quick breakfast with Katrina,' says Miranda. 'If we are waiting for him, I will have plenty of time.'

. . . And on it goes.

Within the hour most of the team have assembled. We decide to give up waiting for the others, and now, just two government nurses and a driver short, we begin our slow journey towards the Malawian border. The driver turns up techno on the LandCruiser's stereo but like an old man I ask him to turn it down again—six-thirty is a little early for *doof-doof*-ing our way through African villages, I suggest—but at least the two nurses are now in a great mood—laundry since dropped off, egg rolls scoffed and coffees in hand. The suspension's long since given out and our T-shirts cling to us as the humidity soars, and João's telling jokes, all of us jammed together among boxes and equipment like some kind of semi-dysfunctional, multi-racial family, and I find myself grinning broadly. Thrilled to be back in rural Africa once again, and unable to fathom a more scenic trip to work than this, the one we make each morning.

• • •

The aim of our project here has been to minimise the health impacts for those who've been displaced, using a step-wise approach that's widely applied for population movements and health emergencies. It addresses four basic but overlapping elements—food, shelter, water and sanitation, and health—and is as much a logistical exercise as a medical one. And it's what MSF reputedly excels at.

Pre-packaged kits covering most disaster contingencies are stocked at their international warehouses, ready to be flown anywhere at a moment's notice. The order sheets make fascinating reading, with options including an inflatable hospital, water purification systems, haemorrhagic fever kits, and even cars. Several of the cholera kits have already been sent to Mozambique, each one containing every-thing required to treat six hundred patients, from IV fluids and beds, to stationery and staff clothing. I'd seen them used as I'd left Angola, where large tent-based treatment centres were being rapidly set up, and it's this—a potential cholera outbreak—that's been the concern here. Cases have already occurred upstream in Malawi, and without treatment up to half of all patients will die rapidly from dehydration. With treatment (simply the administration of fluids, either oral or IV, for a day or two) the mortality rate is less than one per cent.

In terms of this Mozambique project, two logistics teams have already dug latrines and distributed non-food items (tarpaulins, soap, mosquito nets, blankets, water containers and other essentials), and a water and sanitation engineer has installed water purification systems to supply nearby villages. The World Food Program, a UN agency, has handled food distributions (they were already feeding a quarter of a million people in this region), and some basic health care has been provided by our mobile clinics. Measles vaccination would normally have been of the utmost priority, but cholera is our concern here. There's still no outbreak in our area, though, so for the moment we're watching closely and making an assessment of the nutrition situation.

• • •

For an hour we drive south-west, trampolining down a corridor of dense grasses that tower beside the dirt road, our roof a wide-open sky of glorious African sunshine. The swollen Zambezi River is not far to our south, although to me it looks more like a dam, a huge lake of brown that's swallowed farmland and now laps at low-lying villages. Mavinga's own river drains into this same waterway too, far to the west, and I wonder now if there's not a little soap bubble from that distant riverbank floating near us. (I wonder as well how people are faring there; there's no way to contact anyone.)

We slow down, inch across a bridge of rough beams lashed together over a rickety timber frame, then speed up, heading past vast cotton plantations and the patches of maize that herald an approaching village. For hours this pattern repeats itself. The heavy rains have rendered this higher landscape so lush, so green, that it fluoresces as the sun hits it, and not a centimetre of ground hasn't been overcome by a riot of vegetation save for the laboriously cleared yards of red earth surrounding the occasional hamlets we pass.

Three hours and we're still driving—you'd think we were in the middle of nowhere—but suddenly a group of children appear in the road. They turn and freeze, mesmerised by the unusual sound of a car, then melt into the long grass as we pass: a filmstrip of blurred foliage interspersed with broad smiles is what I see from my side window. Another village nears; women in the cornfields, men clearing bush with their machetes; and we become stuck behind the local equivalent of a school bus—a one-speed bicycle being pedalled by a young boy who's far too small for it, and who's almost hurdling the main bar as he steps from side to side, stomping all his weight to each pedal as he propels himself and four mates (who're clinging to various other sections of the bike) to a classroom somewhere out here. Which is nothing on what lumbers towards us next. A man has secured a live goat to the front of his bike and is seated casually behind it, the animal's front hoofs tied to the handlebars, the back hoofs nearer the pedals so that it's almost upright—*almost cycling!* And as we pass them, both rider and cloven-hoofed passenger turn their heads to regard us, as if *we're* the more unusual sight on the road.

. . .

It's late morning when we arrive in the village of Jonasse. Sheets of blue plastic cling to hastily built straw huts like Band-Aids, but it otherwise lacks the look of a disaster zone—certainly nothing like that camp in Kenya. Kids play happily and livestock roam the area, and a few dozen small fish have been laid out to dry near the side of the track, caught most likely using the mosquito nets we've distributed. (Pairs of children can be seen up and down the re-defined edges of the Zambezi, ignoring the risk of crocodiles as they stand waist-deep trying to scoop up the day's catch in the netting.)

We park in the shaded central clearing and begin unpacking, and a crowd quickly gathers. None of them know why we're here today—we haven't told them yet—but they press around excitedly anyway. Perhaps they'll receive another water container, I imagine them thinking, or dressings for an old sore.

But today we're not giving out much. Our aim is to see as many children between six months and five years of age as we can, measuring their mid-upper arm circumference to screen their nutrition status. If their reading is above a threshold value we'll send them home with a worming tablet; a dab of purple ink on their finger marks them as having been seen. If they're below a certain level, we'll measure their weight and height, then examine them more thoroughly. Moderately malnourished children will be given a box of high energy food and followed up by the government health post. Severely malnourished children will need to come back to Morrumbala for admission to hospital.

It sounds easy. At least I thought so when it was described to me in an office, and it looked as much on paper. But it's not. The population we're working with are subsistence farmers with almost no numeracy and literacy skills. To get a local worker to read a scale and write down the number is far from straightforward, although their enthusiasm to learn is boundless. And a significant number of mothers don't have a clear idea of when their child was born—

'Before the rain season.'

'Which rain season?'

(A shrug.)

—so using age as a criterion is sketchy. Then, after measuring each child, getting our staff to interpret the charts is equally tricky. Either a few healthy kids are unnecessarily admitted, or some of the malnourished children are accidentally sent home. So everything has to be supervised, repeated, and questioned. And then re-explained (with patience, I hope) over and over again.

And it all goes on at once. Within an hour there's a line of hundreds waiting, the temperature forty degrees and humidity through the roof, and we're caked in dust. Adults get in line wanting pills for their headaches while our two nurses debate which protocol to use, and curious children sneak through the barriers everywhere. Some want to be weighed, others want more of the purple dye and a few lunge for another de-worming 'lolly', but most just want to sit quietly and watch us.

Occasionally a child will scream bloody murder when their turn comes to have their arm measured, and in true crowd mentality the whole line will then start—a kind of sympathetic show of solidarity on behalf of the group. So for fifteen minutes we'll examine distressed children, trying in vain to convince them that the tape won't do anything to their arm, but then they'll inexplicably settle and we'll go through a happy phase once more—until one starts screaming again. And that's much of how the afternoon passes. Guessing ages, measuring arms, intercepting stolen lollies, watching parents wrestle reluctant fingers into the purple dye, and trying to stop yet other kids from swigging the mixture.

By mid-afternoon we've assessed almost three hundred children, and it's a reassuring picture overall. Only nine are malnourished, although two are severe and will need to return with us.

We start to pack up, and dozens crowd around.

'Please, Doctor, I need treatment for this,' one woman tells me, showing me a deep ulcer on her leg.

'You'll need to go to the hospital,' I tell her. 'In Morrumbala, but we have no more room in our cars. I'm—'

'My husband is really sick at home,' another woman interrupts. 'You must come. He is too weak to come here. Please, he's—'

'Look at this,' says a third woman, ushering her daughter forward. The girl has a large fragment of her broken radius bone protruding from a wound on her forearm—unbelievable, and surely infected— but runs off when I mention hospital. João follows but can't find her, and now the village health workers crowd around, wearing the T-shirts and caps distributed by another agency in the past.

'We haven't been paid for months,' they say. 'And we have run out of treatment. Please give us what you can spare.'

I rummage through our boxes and dole out what I can, but more people come and ask for things. I make excuses. 'I'm sorry, we don't have time. No, I'm sorry, I can't treat that. And you, sir, you'll defi- nitely need to go to Maputo to get that tumour removed'—although I may as well tell him that there's a clinic on Mars that'll remove it. Maputo is about as accessible from here.

People ask when we're coming back.

'Well, we're—'

'Because there are other patients, Doctor. There are many people you haven't seen.'

'I know, but it's just that—'

'Will it be next week?'

'Uh, the thing is—'

'When?'

Never. This is our last day. Flood waters are receding and there's no sign of an outbreak. The few cholera cases that have occurred else- where have remained limited and there's none in this region, so MSF have donated supplies and a nurse to assist the government response there. Here, we've assessed thousands of people these past weeks and watched closely, and disease and death rates aren't any higher than normal—normal for an impoverished African country, that is. They're still atrocious by any other standards, just no more than would otherwise be expected. A health emergency, by convention, is defined as a doubling of background mortality rates, and there's no evidence of that here. Our intervention can no longer be justified.

So we're off. Development agencies are moving back in to help re-establish agricultural schemes and other programs, but we'll pack up tomorrow. A project closure here means a readiness to respond to the next crisis; such is the reality of the industry. We should be thrilled that there's no outbreak here, and I am, but I'm also having trouble with being a part of this again, this retrenching of staff, this having to apologise to people and wish them all the best of luck . . .

'I've just ordered goat meat,' says Katrina, one of our nurses.

'You've what?'

'Goat. For dinner.'

'Doctor, can you look at my son's foot?' asks a woman.

'I ordered it from a family,' says Katrina. 'They're going to cook it for me. That drive back is too long.'

'Katrina, you know we can't drive after dark. We've got to get going!'

'Sorry, Doctor, my arm has been swollen like this for many days. Can you just—'

'I've already paid for the meat!' says Katrina.

'I don't care—we need to go.'

'Excuse me, Doctor. I am one of the other health workers in town, and we—'

'Damien, you need to tell Katrina to get in the car. We're going to get stuck if this rain sets in,' says Simon.

'Sorry, Doctor,' says another woman. 'I have this thing growing—'

'Excuse me,' begins another man.

'Katrina—you need to get in the car! We're going to get caught out here.'

'No.'

'Look at this rooster!' says João.

'*Mzungu*, can I have your pen?' asks a young boy.

'Look what that lady gave us!' says João again. 'This rooster will ride in the car back to Morrumbala with us, yes? Look how big he is!'

'Hey *Mzungu*! Take our photo!'

'Doctor—'

'Leave that goat meat!'

'Please, Doctor, any more of those tablets?'

But there are now storm clouds in the distance, and if this river swells anymore we'll be stuck. We load up and flee.

'Don't forget us when you leave next week, Damien,' says João, who's sitting in the back with Katrina. Two patients and their mothers are also squeezed in, along with that rooster. 'When you get to Maputo,' he says, 'don't forget us. Tell MSF we need jobs. Tell them we are good!'

Koffi, his quieter Mozambican colleague sitting between the driver and me, laughs. 'No, tell them we are the best!'

'I will, guys. Now tell me, what are you going to do with this poor bird in the boot?'

'The chicken?'

'*Sim.*'

'Eat it!'

'But it looks so happy.'

'Ha! And *big*. Of course we will eat this—you should come when we do!'

'But please, Doctor,' says Koffi. 'When you go back, ask them for jobs for us.'

'I will.'

'Please do. Please ask MSF.'

I ask them if it's hard to find work around here.

'I worked for two months last year,' says Koffi. 'As a translator for World Vision. But then? Nothing. And now I have worked for one month this year, with MSF. But it is only March. Maybe something will still happen. It is only the aid agencies that pay well around here.

Otherwise, I will have to work in the market, but this is very hard to make money for my family. Who knows, Doctor—maybe another flood will come?'

There's no malice in Koffi's wish for another flood. As in Mavinga, aid is not only a provider of essentials to people in need, but a prolific employer of local people. One man's disaster is another's opportunity to work.

By the time we pull into town most of the team are asleep in the back. The storm has missed us and a rainbow's arcing to the east, the cloud tips glowing in the last of the day's light. We park on the main street and stumble stiffly into one of the three diners in town, an Indian-run affair where egg rolls, Coke and grilled chicken constitute the menu. We order, then settle on the concrete veranda. Ahead, kids in threadbare clothes play with mangy dogs, and a bicycle speeds downhill with no brakes, its two anxious passengers laughing as they drag their sandals. Beside the market, young boys sell clear plastic bags of cooking oil that glint like some golden magical potion as the low sun illuminates them, and when I buy a bunch of bananas from a mother for five *meticais*—about twenty cents—she insists on finding me change. Meanwhile, an endless parade of people ask Simon for work, offering to unpack the cars, to carry something, clean anything.

'No? Okay,' they reply. 'Thank you anyway, sir.'

And like in Mavinga, I'm moved by the dignity of it all. No moping, just people playing their shitty hand, getting on with the full-time career that is survival. The Mozambicans here have the most wonderful expression I've ever heard, arguably the best example of a glass-half-full outlook on life: '*Não ha Guerra.*' It translates literally as 'we don't have a war' and it's used as the colloquial equivalent of 'no worries'. Because what problem could anything else be in comparison? *There is no longer a war!*

Our food arrives. We need to eat quickly. The representative for the Ministry of Health wants to see us again (he just called Koffi's mobile), and we need to check on our driver with malaria and then pack. I need to contact Geneva about another position, too; it's been almost three months since I left home now, and I've not done much of anything productive. What I want desperately is to be busy in a hospital. Somewhere where I can settle in and stay for a while, get to know the staff and patients, and practise good medicine. I want another Mavinga.

What I get is Sudan.

15. SHOOTING DOWN THE RUNWAY

Another early morning on a runway.

Another small plane.

And another pilot, perched atop a stepladder, fuelling the aircraft himself using a rubber hose, as if this were all perfectly normal. Which I'm beginning to suspect it is. Except that this time there's a striking change in scene: against the backdrop of the World Food Program's giant canvas storage tents, the carcasses of a half-dozen crashed or abandoned planes lie rusting alongside the tarred runway here in the town of Lokichoggio, northern Kenya—the staging point for two decades of aid missions into South Sudan.

'MAURICE LIKES SUDAN A LOT,' shouts my French colleague, as our little Cessna roars down the runway minutes later.

'YEAH?' I reply.

'*OUI*. HE LOVES IT. MAURICE SAYS SOUTH SUDAN IS *WILD*,' he shouts. 'HE SAYS IT IS ONE OF THE MOST REMOTE, TRULY *TRIBAL* REGIONS ON THIS EARTH.'

'YEAH?' I ask, straining to get a little closer towards him. Only two other people are on board with us—the pilot, and an Australian midwife returning from holidays.

'*OUI*. MAURICE HAS BEEN HERE MANY TIMES. MAURICE, HE SAYS MANY PEOPLE HERE LIVE AS THEY ALWAYS HAVE—

LIKE IN THE STONE AGE. LOOK,' he gestures out the window. 'SOON YOU WILL SEE SOME VILLAGES. TINY ONES, LIKE FROM A HISTORY BOOK . . .'

For half an hour more our little plane bumps and burps slowly higher as we head due north, levelling out at just over ten thousand feet. We're now high over South Sudan, where the world's largest swamp, the Sudd, stretches in every direction below us, a tangle of innumerable black waterways looping and bending their way through an otherwise dry, flat khaki landscape, flanked by narrow corridors of rich green growth. Like veins on a giant, dying leaf, it seems. A haze of moist air hugs the ground as much of this water evaporates, and what doesn't will drain ultimately into the White Nile, which runs from Lake Victoria, to our south, to the Sudanese capital of Khartoum, further north. And yet now is only the dry season, my colleague tells me; in the coming months, rains will flood much of what's below us to create a wetland the size of England—still only a fraction of the total area of Sudan, Africa's largest country.

'THE DINKA, AND NUER,' shouts my French colleague. 'THESE ARE THE TWO MAIN GROUPS IN THE SOUTH. THE DINKA ARE THE LARGER, MAYBE TWO MILLION. BUT YOU—YOU ARE FLYING TO NASIR, *OUI*?'

'YES.'

'THAT IS A HOME OF THE NUER PEOPLE. THEY ARE THE SECOND LARGEST. MAURICE HAS WORKED WITH THEM BEFORE, THE NUER. HE SAYS THEY ARE VERY INTERESTING.'

'YEAH?'

'*OUI*. VERY TRADITIONAL PEOPLE—VERY *PROUD* PEOPLE.'

We yell at each other a little more, a not entirely unpleasant way of communicating, and a small settlement soon passes below— literally just five or ten straw huts clustered near the water's edge, some cattle grazing nearby. Nothing in the surrounding wilderness alludes to any other human activity. A more isolated group of people I can't imagine, a notion reinforced even by the name of this place—*Sudd*—that translates literally as 'barrier', and it was the impenetrability of this swamp that made it one of the last corners of Africa to be seen by Europeans. It's the stuff of the *National Geographic* magazines I'd borrowed from my dad as a child; a place of papyrus reeds, Arab slave caravans and warrior Nilotic tribes; and an area that even now seems mythical, frankly foreboding.

My parents though are having less trouble imagining the remoteness. More trouble understanding why I'd accept this job. I told them about a week ago, after I left Mozambique.

'*Sudan?*' asked Dad, via a bad payphone connection. '*Ag*, no man. Why can't these people offer you a job in Thailand or something? I mean, do you actually ask for this stuff, or do they just send you because you keep saying yes? And please tell me you're not going to Darfur. *Jislaaik*, your *Ma* will go nuts if you—'

'*Darfur?*' cried Mum on the other line. 'My God, child! Do you know what all this worrying does to the two of us? We—'

'No, not Darfur!' I cut them off. 'Darfur is entirely different. It's another part of Sudan altogether. I'm going to the south, *Ma*—the south! The south is at peace now. It's safe,' I said, making arguably the most optimistic assessment of the situation there in decades. That it had been the scene of Africa's longest-running civil war they didn't need to know, nor that skirmishes were still occurring over oil. The point to stress was that a peace agreement had been signed in 2005, now three years ago. So I reiterated this. And promised, as has been the obligation since I left school and no matter where in the world I am, to call every Sunday night.

As for why I'd take this position barely three months after the Somalia tragedy, I'll admit that frustration played a part. This was the only position available to me, and returning home wasn't an option; I'd set aside the year at least for volunteering, and so far had spent three months mostly in cars, briefings or guesthouses. The prospect of seeing this region for myself was no deterrent, either. The projects here are considered by many the quintessential MSF experience: isolated, with difficult conditions and high workloads—much of which I'd coped with in Mavinga. The downside is that clan fighting does still occur, although I was assured that expats aren't being targeted, and that my posting is well away from the volatile north–south border. So I took the job—barely a week ago. Since then I've left Africa, been debriefed in Geneva, re-briefed in Amsterdam, and flown back to the continent, transiting through Kenya once again.

Something's buzzing in the cockpit. The pilot removes his headset and retrieves a satellite phone handset from the dashboard. He listens for a moment and shouts into it, then makes a radio call.

'WE'RE GOING TO DIVERT,' he yells, turning back to face us.

'OH?'

'THERE'S A PATIENT,' he shouts, pointing to nothing in particular out the window. 'IN ANOTHER TOWN. THEY WANT US TO PICK HIM UP.'

I give him the thumbs up: a detour is just fine with me. This view is incomparable, and between my fellow passenger's commentary and the briefing documents on my lap, there's more than enough to keep me occupied.

It's now almost two hours since we left. We continue to fly north, no clouds and the visibility must be hundreds of kilometres. I scan the map in my package, and from what I can tell, Ethiopia is not far to our east, beyond which lies Somalia. To our west is the Sudanese province of Darfur, where a small, under-funded African Union deployment is currently trying to monitor the conflict that exploded three years ago, patrolling a region the size of Spain. And further west of Darfur lie Chad and the Central African Republic, also regions of conflict, as too is the Democratic Republic of Congo, to our south-west. By any measure, this is a troubled part of the world.

As for Sudan's two civil wars (and the conflict in Darfur, to a degree), the origins lie in the divide between the Muslim Arabs of the north and the animist and Christian 'Africans' of the south.

For thousands of years, African southerners were captured and sold by Arab slave traders, with clashes also occurring over access to the more fertile cattle-grazing lands of the south. For the most part, though, the two groups remained separate; even during the colonial period, the joint British–Egyptian administration managed the regions distinctly, promoting Christianity in the south but not the north, and requiring permits for travel between the two halves.

In 1956, following Sudan's independence, the country became united under a government dominated by northerners. Arabic was declared the official language, and Sharia, or Muslim law—a code that in its strictest interpretations allows for severe penalties such as amputations, stonings and lashings for violations of religious precepts—was imposed on all, causing extreme resentment in the south. A resistance movement was formed by southerners, and what followed was the first of two civil wars.

After seventeen years of fighting, a decade-long truce was called during the 1970s, but the north gradually re-exerted their control. Increasing clashes occurred over the vast oil and water reserves of the south, and by 1983 a second civil war was underway—this one lasting twenty-two years. What resulted was the largest number of deaths from any conflict since World War II—two million people— and the displacement of four million others.

In 2005, after what had been thirty-nine years of fighting over the past five decades, a peace agreement ostensibly ended the conflict. The south was granted autonomy, and a referendum has been scheduled to determine whether it will become an independent nation.*

---

* The referendum was successfully held in January 2011. Almost ninety-nine per cent of voters opted for independence, and on 9 July 2011 South Sudan formally became the world's newest nation.

In the interim, a UN peacekeeping mission is monitoring the region. But the peace is a precarious one. Large oil reserves are positioned along the disputed north–south border, and, with oil accounting for more than half of Sudan's income, create a compelling reason for neither side to concede any territory.

My colleague's yelling again. 'MAURICE—HE SAYS THAT THE NUER ARE STRONG FIGHTERS, THAT THEY HAVE ALWAYS FOUGHT OFF OUTSIDERS.'

'YEAH?'

'*OUI*. THEY ARE BEAUTIFUL PEOPLE. BUT FOR EXPATS WHO ARE NOT USED TO THEM, THEY CAN BE A LITTLE . . . *DIFFICILE*.'

'GREAT,' I yell. '*DIFFICILE* IS MY SPECIALTY'—and I think of trying to get the team into the car in Mozambique.

'AND MAURICE, HE ALWAYS SAYS THAT IF YOU GET A LITTLE, YOU KNOW, *FRUSTRÉ* WITH THEM, THAT YOU MUST REMEMBER THAT THEY HAVE ONLY EVER MET WHITE PEOPLE IN ONE *CAPACITÉ*. AS PEOPLE THAT GIVE AID. AS PEOPLE THAT ARE RICH, AND THAT HAND OUT THINGS.'

'YES?'

'*OUI*—MAURICE SAYS ALWAYS REMEMBER THIS, *OKAY*? DO NOT GET TOO *FRUSTRÉ* WITH THEM. MANY PEOPLE DO, BUT THE SUDANESE ARE JUST LOOKING OUT FOR THEIR OWN. LIKE THEY HAD TO DO IN THE WAR. THEY ARE WONDERFUL PEOPLE, BUT TOUGH. *VERY* TOUGH.'

I know a veiled warning when I hear one. I heed the advice.

We're beginning our descent. I turn my attention back out the window, where a thin cover of dry scrub and low trees has appeared below, skirting quickly closer. My colleague points out some features and tells me that Maurice had spent some time in this village.

'THIS MAURICE GUY SOUNDS REALLY FASCINATING,' I say. 'IS HE STILL WITH MSF? WILL I MEET HIM OUT HERE?'

I ask, in reply to which two furrows embed themselves deeply on the forehead of my colleague, his face now one of mild incredulity. Because Maurice, as he explains—

'*C'est moi!*'

—Is he!

Appears then that Maurice, the fountain of knowledge and experience that he is, is also a proponent of the third person as mode of self-reference. And I love this quirk. I love talking with him even more now, and I love the cultural and linguistic fruit salad that these projects invariably turn out to be. People from improbably different backgrounds just lumped together in these insane conditions, often with no common language, living on top of each other as they try to find that happy medium somewhere between sleeping together and arguing over the definition of glass. A more fascinating sociological experiment can't possibly have been contrived.

'BUCKLE UP!' yells the pilot, turning to face us. 'WE'LL TOUCH DOWN QUICKLY. WE'RE NOT GETTING OUT OF THE PLANE.'

I give him the thumbs up. Maurice thinks this is a little unusual, though—we usually get out and meet the team, he says, say hi to our neighbours—but it's soon apparent why because *WHUMP!* we hit the dirt runway and taxi to the end, fast, engine still revving and armed men blurring past my passenger window—*heavily* armed men with automatic rifles slung over their shoulders. We come to an abrupt halt at the end of the runway, and a woman in a white MSF T-shirt comes to the side door as the engine cries its decelerating whine. She opens it from the outside and doesn't introduce herself.

'GET THIS GUY ON QUICKLY,' she yells, pointing to a man lying on a stretcher below a nearby tree. 'THERE ARE OTHERS LOOKING TO GET HIM.'

But there are armed guys all over this airstrip already.

'THEY'RE POLICE, AND HIS CLAN,' she says. 'THE OTHERS AREN'T. SO LET'S HURRY UP!'

The pilot climbs over his chair and begins removing the half-dozen passenger seats anchored to the floor. He folds and stows them behind the mesh stays at the back of the small cabin. A group of black men in MSF T-shirts lift the patient onto the plane's floor, and I quickly examine him. He's young, late teens or early twenties, conscious and moaning, and a hundred flies are feeding on the blood-soaked bandages adhering to his chest and neck. The engine slows and I ask the team on the ground what happened.

'Shot,' replies the woman in the MSF T-shirt. 'But come—let's get going!'

'Does he have a pneumothorax?'

'What?'

'His lung—is it punctured?'

'I'm not a doctor.'

'Has a doctor seen him?'

'No. She's out. Sick. They flew her to Kenya for a few days.'

We can't take off with him if he's got an air leak around his lung. He could decompensate during the flight for reasons of both time and the reduced air pressure up there, although pottering around to stabilise him on the airstrip while armed clansmen mill about doesn't seem ideal.

I climb to the back of the plane and quickly rummage through my bag to retrieve my stethoscope, then peel off his bandages. The entry wound is clearly on his back near his left shoulder blade, the exit wound on the left side of his neck. Small bubbles of blood gurgle at both sites with each breath. His lung's certainly punctured. He's likely also lost a lot of blood, and he isn't breathing well. Trying to resuscitate him mid-flight would be almost impossible.

'I just need a couple of things,' I say.

'Let's go,' says the pilot, climbing back to his seat. He immediately begins resetting for take-off. 'Come, let's go.'

Debbie, an Australian midwife in this project, offers to quickly fetch what I need. She runs off and returns with a large needle and several syringes and climbs into the back of the plane with me. I ask the pilot to hang on another minute. The procedure is quick, and we can finish it during the flight.

One of the Sudanese men in an MSF T-shirt explains to the patient what's about to happen. The patient grimaces. I wipe his skin clean and inject a small amount of local anaesthetic, then insert a large-bore IV catheter between two ribs at the front upper portion of his left chest wall—a simple, relatively safe procedure that allows the leaking blood and air to drain rather than build up dangerously around his lungs. I aspirate repeated syringes of blood and air via the cannula.

The pilot revs the engine. Debbie climbs out. We'll meet one day for beers in Sydney, we agree. Maurice reboards and sits beside the pilot, and the patient's mother looks decidedly uncertain about getting in although finally does. She refuses a seat and kneels beside her son, and we promptly turn and accelerate quickly down the bumpy runway as blurred images of men with guns alternate with beautiful images of huts and African scrub through the windows.

In no time we're up, climbing—*Jesus, these flights are bumpy in these warm air currents!*—and I continue to aspirate on the syringe every few minutes and keep an eye on the patient's breathing, and I think, What a welcome to South Sudan, this flight: me, a man shot in the back, his elderly mum, and more flies than a bad Australian summer, all bundled into the back of a bumpy plane, barrelling towards God Knows What through these beautiful skies where kites and hawks ride the thermals to almost the same altitude as our plane.

And I've been in this country just three hours.

• • •

We land in the town of Nasir barely half an hour later. The team are waiting for us on the runway. The patient is loaded into the back of a LandCruiser and immediately whisked to the hospital, the surgeon at his side. Maurice, myself and the pilot meanwhile wait for the car to return, standing in the shade of a wing, the three of us saying little as we look around. The scene is telling enough.

Not far from us, at the end of the dirt airstrip, the wreckage of a crashed plane rests on its belly, partially embedded into the nearer bank of the broad, muddy river that cuts past the runway's edge. A cautionary landing beacon, I'd imagine, and now an apparent play centre: a group of kids call to us as they bounce the intact wing.

Closer to our right side, a dozen people have gathered in the shade beneath a small clutch of trees. It's sorry respite from a sun that's bearing down with malicious intensity—a sun that will burn this region to fifty-degree-afternoons and beyond in coming months, Maurice tells me, and that prompted the Nuer to name the month of February simply 'Fire'—but it's some respite, nonetheless.

Three of those under the tree are Sudanese soldiers, looking bored as they recline with shirts unbuttoned, their hands behind heads. Rifles rest beside them. There's much excited chatter among the other handful of adults nearby, though; all are missing a limb, or part thereof, and they're pointing at the small collection of prostheses that the pilot is unloading and stacking gently beside my backpack. Forget where you are and you'd almost think he was an intrepid mannequin salesman doing the rounds with his samples—samples here including a replacement foot, a lower leg, a lower leg and thigh, and a leg with a red running shoe—but I imagine that prostheses are not uncommon here. These ones were custom built by Red Cross technicians in Juba, the South Sudanese capital, and are now ready to be fitted to these patients at the MSF hospital.

As for the landscape, it's as stark as the flight in had suggested. An unrelentingly flat plain of cracked, grey-brown clay, unbroken by even the smallest of rises, merging with the sky somewhere in an indistinct, hazy horizon. The river punches a twenty-metre wide channel through it as it courses west, though I see few other natural features. Looking south across the water: four trees, some cattle, a handful of huts. To the north, the town itself arcs back from the river for a few hundred metres, then thins, dissolving into the heat haze; it's along this nearer bank that things are concentrated. At the eastern end is the market, and beyond that the high fence of the UN Peace-keepers' compound. To the west is the MSF hospital and far beyond that a military compound, though I can see neither clearly from here. For the most part there's just a loose cluster of straw homes; every-thing in browns, almost no green; no cars nearby but several bicycles; and plenty of cattle—big, lyre-horned white and brown beasts, being watched over by young men, several of whom have guns slung conspicuously over their shoulders.

The LandCruiser returns. I farewell Maurice and clamber in with our gear and the amputees. We head west, no need to stick to any tracks as we drive because the ground here is smoother than any African road I've seen anyway, and the huts are clustered in small *kraals* that are spaced well apart from each other.

After a couple of minutes we arrive at two steel gates set into a high straw fence, above which the organisation's flag flies. Two guards wave us in. Through a flourish of colourful dresses and scantily clad children we nudge slowly ahead, passing between the collection of old brick hospital buildings, stopping finally at a second straw fence in the back corner. A small gate leads through it, and into the expat compound—what's to be my new home for eight months.

• • •

For much of the afternoon I'm given a tour by Zoe, the Belgian co-ordinator of the project. She shows me my bedroom (a scorching mud

NASIR

TUKULS

NORTH

MSF (COMPOUND)

OTHER

OUT-PATIENT

LAB

OTHER

WARD

WARD

ISOLATION NUTRITION WARD

MATERNITY

OPERATING THEATRE

TB VILLAGE

OTHER (DETAILS WITHHELD)

SOBAT RIVER

TREES

SWAMP IN WET (CATTLE GRAZING IN DRY)

MILITARY COMPOUND

AIRSTRIP, MARKET, CRASHED PLANE

hut, haunted by a smell I can't quite place), and takes me through the hospital (*busy*, and crowded). She points out the two fleshy black light bulbs in our brick house (bats, sleeping for the day) and casually mentions the Safe Room (where I'm to run to if I hear gunshots). And as we cross the dusty compound to the next building, all I keep thinking is that Tim was right: Mavinga *was* a paradise. But it's always too much to take in at once, these first sights, so for the moment I don't even try. I just shake hands, ponder new faces and this utterly foreign language, and revel in the state of joyous confusion that arriving in the field is: a sensory overload of the highest order, almost as if standing on a new planet.

In the evening the expats gather at the long wooden table beside our house. It's a large group—ten of us altogether—with a forty-year age range, and representing five continents and seven first languages. Half of the group sleep in the brick house behind us, the rest in the mud huts scattered around the yard.

The sun sets although it's no cooler for it. As soon as the generator kicks in, Amos, a garrulous Kenyan water engineer, bolts for the common room to watch a DVD, while Carol, a Colombian midwife in her late fifties, heads to the kitchen to make a batch of porridge. She's done with the spaghetti and chickpeas we've been served, she says. The rest of us stay at the table: Zoe, the coordinator; Heidi, a German nurse on her first assignment, and in whom I recognise that same excited but slightly bewildered look I'd worn on arrival in Mavinga; Anwar, the gently-spoken Indonesian log; Paul, a sixty-year-old logistician from New Zealand, also on his first mission; Maya, an immaculately dressed administrator from Uganda; Steffi, the somewhat brusque Austrian doctor I'm replacing; Ben, a quiet Kenyan laboratory technician; and Marina, a talkative Italian surgeon, who requests that the next time I arrive in a project I please bring cheese and wine, rather than a man shot in the neck.

After dinner I take a cold shower, then retreat to my little hut. Not that there's much point in freshening up, though; on getting into bed I adhere immediately to the sheets in a lather of sweat, and contemplate once again the ungodly smell in here. By any standards this is a simple compound—an ugly, dusty, insect-riddled space—but here's the conclusion I've come to: none of this detracts from the experience. It *is* half of the experience. Few volunteers lament it. Nor the missed weddings at home, the lost income, or the fact that one's worldly possessions are squashed into a dozen boxes stashed in a storage unit, the stale smell of which evokes an assurance of being single for the foreseeable future. Not that I'm suggesting there aren't trade-offs to volunteering. There are. Plenty. It's just that they pale into insignificance at times like this; like when lying in bed with the river gurgling on one side, kids fooling in the hospital yard on the other and streaks of moonlight dappling the floor of the hut, and then falling asleep with the knowledge that tomorrow you'll get to work in one of the most fascinating, challenging, inaccessible environments on the planet.

A sacrifice, being out here?

I'd swap it for nothing.

16. EVACUATION

And when the sun rises just hours later, gleams through the foot-wide opening along the top of my *tukul*'s circular wall, I'm already awake, thinking too much to sleep, thumbing instead through a book on the Nuer—the tribe who make up almost all of Nasir's population. A notable paragraph:

> They strut about like lords of the earth, which, indeed, they consider themselves to be. There is no master and no servant, but only equals who regard themselves as God's noblest creation. Their respect for one another contrasts with their contempt for all other peoples.

The book was written by a British anthropologist, E.E. Evans-Pritchard, during the 1930s, and eighty years later it's still in print, considered a classic in social anthropology. The author spent a year living in South Sudan, at times in remote villages and at times here— literally *right* here, in the brick house we're using, built originally by the American Presbyterian missionaries who'd arrived a century ago via steamer down the Nile, and who'd set up the first hospital in Nasir.

What strikes me most as I thumb through the book though is not the descriptions of the Nuer's complete devotion to their cattle, their lifestyle as nomadic pastoralists or of their traditional absence of any leadership (there are no chiefs or kings, the clans being described as 'acephalous' states), but rather the comments about their temperament. Forget Maurice's subtle warnings. Phrases like 'derisive pride' come up frequently, and it's noted several times that some have a tendency to be easily roused to violence. Two other quotes that catch my eye, as my alarm clock now beeps:

> The ordered anarchy in which they live accords well with their character, for it is impossible to conceive of rulers ruling over them.

Then, a little more empathetically:

> I again emphasise the crudity and discomfort of their lives. They are very poor in goods and they are very proud in spirit. Schooled in hardship and hunger ... they accept the direst calamities with resignation and endure them with courage.

If what I saw yesterday is any indication, it doesn't seem as if any discomfort has lessened. Maybe even worsened; the civil wars hadn't begun when this book was written—and there were no guns. Today, two million firearms are scattered among South Sudan's eight million people.

. . .

I take a shower and walk the fifty metres to the surgical ward to meet Marina. It's just after seven and she's already standing with a gloved handful of soiled dressings, having begun her rounds. She gives me a quick rundown of the unit.

'A bullet,' she says, pointing at the man in the first bed. He's sitting up with a heavily bandaged head, looking a little dazed.

'What—in his head?'

'*Si.* Through his head.'

'As in, *right* through?'

'Yes. As in, in at the front, out at the back,' she says.

The man stares at us as we talk. He blinks, but says nothing.

'*Seriously?*'

'Seriously,' Marina says. 'We had a few gunshot injuries arrive that day. Here, this man—he was shot through the buttocks. Both cheeks. And this woman, in the thigh. And those two over there, in the arms and legs. But they were the last gunshot victims we've had for over a week. It's been good for a little while, at least until you brought in our friend with the neck wound yesterday.'

The new patient is sitting on his bed in the middle of the room, leaning against the back wall. His mum's at the foot of it. 'He'll be fine,' says Marina. 'He may never speak again, but he'll otherwise be okay. I put in a chest drain and cleaned this all up a little, but his larynx is quite damaged.'

I follow her down the rest of the ward, a long, narrow corridor with seven beds against each of the two longer sides, the brick walls painted a deep red. It's unfathomably humid inside. And *hot*—far more than outside. Long windows reach high into the walls, their louvred shutters opened wide as if imploring a breeze to wash through, and many patients lie partially naked, draped only in light cotton wraps. Crowds of relatives are milling about, too, seated on beds, the windowsill, the floor, the doorway—

'Thomas, we're in the middle of a ward round!' says Marina to the Sudanese health worker beside us. '*Cazzo!* Must we ask these people every day? Tell them to wait outside!'

Thomas smiles. He's around six-foot three, and like the other Nuer I've met here—our entire staff and all the patients—he looks unlike any Africans I've known before. His long, thin limbs contrast starkly with the generally thicker build of the Bantu, and his face is striking: high cheekbones, heavy-lidded, almost Asiatic eyes, deeply black skin, and six deep, horizontal lines of scar that run parallel across his forehead from temple to temple.

Thomas tells people to leave. Much clicking of tongues and rolling of eyes ensues, but it's immediately easier to see patients. And Marina would have this down to an art by now. She's been working in South Sudan for close to two years, and even her clothes have adapted: the sleeves of her MSF T-shirt cut off, the collar trimmed into a plunging v-neck, a piece of medical tape securing the spot where the fabric's most likely to tear. She runs a tight ward from what I've seen. Everything has its place, and the smell of disinfectant is strong.

We continue on. The majority of her patients have burns, soft tissue infections or limb injuries, and lying in each of the three nearer beds is a young man fixed to a traction device—traction here being created thus: a thick pin has been driven through the end of the broken leg, above the ankle, to which a metal stirrup is attached; connected to this stirrup, via a length of rope, are three bricks, all bundled together in a plastic bag and hanging over the edge of the bed, providing the counter-force to straighten the fracture. It's much like Toyota's 'gallows' frame in Mavinga, and also requires around six weeks of immobilisation.

I ask Marina how they broke their legs.

'Shot,' she says. 'Through the bone.'

'In the same gunfight?'

'No. All different.'

'Seriously? So this happens often?'

'Yes, Doctor, and you'll soon get used to it. Didn't they tell you during your briefing?' she asks playfully. 'Here, we don't do a ward round. It's a *war* round.'

I ask her about the peace agreement, or why the UN don't intervene.

'This has nothing to do with the war,' she says, 'or with the UN. They are here only to observe the north–south peace process. These injuries are all because of raids. One clan steals another's cattle, then the men avenge it, try to recover the animals.'

'Over *cattle*?'

'Almost always. Then there's the ongoing grudges, the revenge attacks, and just when you think it is quiet again, another raid. And the women and children get caught in crossfire. These people here?' She gestures to last week's arrivals, three of whom are women. 'There will be payback for what happened to this group. You watch. There's talk of escalation between the two bigger clans here. We'll soon have more fighting.'

• • •

I spend the rest of the day trying to orient myself. The other expats kindly show me around their respective units, and on the third morning I attempt my own ward round. What follows resembles nothing like the orderliness of Marina's.

Medical Inpatients is where I begin. Outpatients is where I'm called to. But the dispensary is where I end up.

'I look after this as well?' I ask the assistant, who's just intercepted me. I trail him to the small room near the front gate, where patients are lining up at an open window.

'Yes,' he says. He's one of the three Nuer staff who fills the Outpatients prescriptions. 'Always it is the doctor we call. And this morning we have run out of the worm tablets. You know these ones?

They are red. The blue tablets we have, but not the red. The red are finished.'

I head to Stores, a series of steel containers behind our offices, to find the two Sudanese logs who run it. 'You guys keep pills here?' I ask, and they say No, those are in Pharmacy.

'Thanks,' I say. But I can't remember which building is Pharmacy. The compound here is a far larger and more haphazard than Mavinga's, a collection of mud huts and single-storey brick buildings on a rectangular property alongside the river.

'And Doctor,' adds one of the logs, pointing out the pharmacy for me. 'Mr Paul was looking for you. He is sick. He went home, just before.'

Better look after the other volunteers. I head to the expat compound, at the western end of the block, where our cook is washing dishes in a shallow plastic tub on the dirt in front of the house. I ask her if she's seen Paul, and she points to the latrine.

'Paul—you in there?'

'Yeah,' he groans from the small hut near our gate.

'You okay?'

'Sort of. Got the squirts again. Big time. Third lot this month.'

'I think I'm coming down with something as well,' I say. 'I was up a few times last night.'

'Yeah, well, welcome to Nasir. Anything you can give me for it?'

Back to the dispensary.

Back to find the pharmacy.

Back to—

'Hey, Doctor! We are still waitings for you,' calls one of the Outpatients health workers. He's standing beneath the awning where several dozen patients are waiting for consultations, seated on rows of wood benches. 'Still waitings!' he says, tapping his digital watch lest I misconstrue. He's smiling, but insistent nonetheless. So I sidetrack briefly—'I'll have to be quick,' I say to him, 'because Inpatients are waiting for me as well'—and I'm shown to a small, plywood-walled cubicle, where a mother with a skin infection is lying. She's an attractive Nuer woman, short peppercorn hair and deeply black skin, wearing a long, simple, royal-blue dress that's draped from just beneath her shoulders to her ankles. She smiles when I introduce myself, although her daughter is distinctly unhappy with the idea of me approaching them.

'Ha! She is scared of white peoples, I think,' says the watch-tapping health worker. 'Very scared! *Wow*—screaming so louds. OKAY, DOCTOR, I WILL HOLD HER. YOU LOOK AT THE LADY, OKAY?'

The three of us risk industrial deafness as the daughter protests my examination of her mother—'SUCH A SMALL GIRL, HOW ABOUT THOSE LUNGS!'—and I suggest we admit the woman for IV anti-biotics to treat her foot cellulitis. She agrees, and we walk her over to Inpatients (daughter trailing at a cautious though audible distance), where I'm informed that I'm now keeping these guys waiting, too.

'We must still see the other side, Doctor,' the affable Joseph tells me. He's the senior health worker on the medical ward, and he may well be the only Nuer person shorter than me. He's been trying to get me to see this other side since seven this morning. 'You run away too much,' he smiles. 'But first, I would like you to seeing this mans. He is very sick. I think maybe he has the HIVs,' he adds quietly.

Few maybes about the man's diagnosis. He's in his mid-twenties and severely gaunt, and has profuse diarrhoea and a persistent cough. I begin examining him but I'm called suddenly by a female health worker. I quickly follow her to the vaccination tent, just near the office at the northern end of the yard, where an assistant is kneeling beside a motionless body.

'I didn't even give the injection!' he says. 'Look. Here—I only took it out of the packet. But she saw it, then: *fwap!*—she did this. On the ground.'

The patient's certainly only fainted. She'll be fine. We check her blood pressure, put her legs up and head down, then move her to Inpatients to recover for a while.

'More patients?' chuckles Joseph. 'No beds, Doctors. We are already have no beds. But now we can please see the other sides? Maybe we can send some peoples home.'

I agree. We start and review a couple of patients, but soon there's a thin giant of a Nuer man waiting quietly just beside me, dressed in a neat business shirt and trousers.

'Yes?' I ask.

'Yes.'

'Can I help you?'

'Yes. It is me, Peter,' he says, grinning broadly as he shakes my hand. 'From the TB village.'

I recognise him now. He's the supervising TB health worker—the only TB health worker, in fact—and he'd like me to please come and see a man who's causing problems. 'Because, this man is trouble,' he says. 'He is crazy. He is shouting with me all the time. He is saying that if I do not call you, he will leave the village.'

I apologise to Joseph and follow Peter, past the nutrition centre and patient latrines to the back corner of the yard, not far from my own room, where a man in his early twenties is standing in front of one of the dozen mud-walled TB huts. He doesn't look impressed. 'He says that if we do not give him more food, he will leave,' says Peter. 'He says he will take other patients with him.'

'Leave for where?' I ask.

Peter speaks with him. The patient's bare-chested and standing with arms folded, squinting at me. He's doing his best to look assertive. It works. 'His village,' says Peter.

'What about his treatment?'

'He doesn't worry about this anymore. Because, he says he is better from TB, but now he will get sick with just this food. He says he needs more food. And meat.'

'Are we giving him what the others get?' I ask.

'Yes.'

'And we've always given this amount?'

'Yes,' says Peter. 'For years. Everybody is getting the same. And they get extra for their families.'

I reiterate this information back to the patient, via Peter. He's surely calling our bluff—he wouldn't really walk away from free accommodation, free meals and free treatment for a life-threatening condition, would he? 'I'll talk to Zoe this afternoon,' I say. 'I'll let you know, Peter. It's not my decision, but it seems to me he's just trying his luck.'

Peter agrees. I shake the young man's hand and smile, and tell him I'll return later. His glare softens. He seems happy enough to have made his point, no less because he's made it in front of the others who're watching on.

Back across the yard.

Back to the medical—

'Doctor!' beckons a voice from inside the nutrition centre, just south of the main Inpatient unit. I step into the garage-sized, mud-walled structure.

'Can it wait?' I ask the health worker. 'Can I come back in an hour?'

'No,' he says. Gatwech is his name, and he's another mountain of a Nuer man, also with those six scars, or *gaar*, across his forehead. A faded red Chicago Bulls T-shirt hangs from his broad, bony shoulders. 'I would like to call Nurse Heidi,' he says, 'but she is in the operating with Doctor Marina, so I cannot call her. And this little boy will not drink. He will not touch the milk. And his mother will not give it. She is tired of fighting with him.'

I look at the mother. She shrugs, raising her upturned palms as if lifting imaginary weights; what I assume is a quiet gesture of frustration.

'But if Nurse Heidi gives the milk to him,' says Gatwech, 'he will drink it. He is very happy with Nurse Heidi to feed him. But when I try, he does not like it. Watch: I will try.'

The child definitely doesn't like this.

'You try, Doctor.'

The child *very* definitely doesn't like this.

'Maybe we should put in a nasogastric tube?' asks Gatwech, as I towel milk from my T-shirt. 'And also, he has a fever this morning.'

We assess the fever, hold off on the nasogastric tube, and prescribe instead antibiotics and an afternoon with Nurse Heidi. And *then*, ignoring the Outpatients worker who's signalling for me again, I head to Inpatients and rejoin Joseph—pending the next interruption.

The following day is much the same. The plan is for the other doctor to leave on the weekend, but by the evening of my fourth day I become unwell, following Paul's well-beaten path to the latrine with increasing frequency. Steffi returns to ward duties.

On the fifth day I'm worse, unable to work at all. Soon there's a fever and some blood involved, too, at which point I recant everything I'd said about the conditions here being part of the appeal, because between the fever and forty-something-degree temperatures my mattress has become firmly adherent to my back and my *tukul* smells much like the latrine, and I wonder how the patients survive with their even-higher fevers on those wards. For much of the night I roll around light-headed in a sweat-sodden sheet, and sometime in the afternoon of the next day Steffi comes in to tell me that the sample I gave the lab showed dysentery, and that she's arranged for a plane to take me back out to Kenya. I'd laugh. Or refuse—I've lasted not even a week in Sudan—but I'm too drained to care.

• • •

Lokichoggio is where I end up, back at the MSF base. ('A record!' quips one staffer.) Within days of starting antibiotics I'm fine, eating well and waiting for the next charter flight back to Nasir. This town is an interesting enough place to spend a few days anyway. An edgy outpost that was featured in *The Constant Gardener*, it's located not far from the site of some of the oldest known human remains, and the residents are fascinating. Traditionally dressed Turkana people, many sporting Mohawk-style haircuts, gather beneath trees or the eaves of shopfronts, the women adorned with colourful bead necklaces worn in such improbable quantities, and packed so tightly together, it's as if they're wearing a vibrant neck brace.

In my second week I'm booked on a charter back to Sudan, but Nasir won't be my next destination—not for a week or two yet. MSF have scheduled the closure of a nearby outreach project due to population movements and they'd like me to go. 'You've done this before,' says a senior, 'so it's better that you do it,' which is like being told you're good at breakups.

I argue the decision, but arguing with management is something I've been doing too much of lately. I'd had issues with the way aspects of the Mozambican mission were run and made it well known, and my new supervisor now hits a raw nerve: I'm putting personal frustrations ahead of the project's needs. It's an assertion that makes me wince. I'd throw the insult back, tell him that I've seen a handful of good, experienced field workers walk away from the organisation for no other reason than being messed around repeatedly, and significantly, by Human Resources, but there'd be no point. I'd only validate his assertions.

So I go. I fly into the small village with another nurse. I spend a few glorious days living like a camper in an old hut, see some patients, walk the village with staff and thoroughly enjoy my time. Then, give employees their last salaries, dispense medical supplies, take down the flag and pack four of the sicker patients into the plane with us, and return to Nasir. Desperate to just stay put.

• • •

'Doctor!' calls the guard, as our LandCruiser pulls up at the gates. Steffi just flew out—I saw her on the airstrip, no time for a handover. 'Come now,' he says. 'For the feeding centre.'

I leave my bags and walk across the yard, step through the low doorway of the mud-walled feeding centre. Heidi's kneeling with one of the Sudanese health workers beside a young patient near the side wall, the family watching over her shoulder.

'Look,' she says. 'Look at this. They carried her in a minute ago, like this.'

I crouch next to the young girl. I've not seen her before, but I know well those eyes. I saw them in Angola. Big, white, dinner-plate eyes, sunken in a face that's too big for such a skinny body, a face that belongs to someone seventy years older with its wrinkled skin. 'Wizened,' the textbooks call it.

'Eight kilograms,' says Heidi. '*Eight* kilograms, at three years old. She's eighty-six centimetres tall.'

The girl's too short for her age (stunted, due to chronic under-nutrition) but even accounting for this lower height she's markedly too light (wasted, due to acute malnutrition). Not that there's a need for charts in her case.

She sits up from the sheet on the floor where Heidi's started treatment and squats like a frog, her knees splayed, mewling listlessly. I haven't seen a child this ill since Mavinga. Not even close. Nothing like this ever presents back home, and my heart sinks and my head rages as I think of the audacity that this still occurs.

She won't sit still. She has none of the loss of appetite I'd expect for this late stage. She grabs the cup of rehydration solution and gulps it in one go, but it's far too much for her body; she pukes it instantly, but wants more anyway. I gently pry the cup from her and she looks accusingly at me with those big eyes. Her head bobs, it's disproportionately large on her bony frame. We quickly move her to Inpatients because Joseph and the team there are better equipped to manage her.

Joseph's worried when he sees her.

We insert an IV line and let her drink limited amounts. We give antibiotics, glucose and a small bolus of fluid, but even after six months in Angola the management of these children petrifies me. We're walking a tightrope with their treatment, with little margin for error, because three conditions interplay and overlap in this little girl right now. Each is potentially fatal, and each requires a slightly different approach. Malnutrition is one, and a severe one, but she's also got diarrhoea so is likely dehydrated. Managing these two can be contradictory. Malnutrition requires extremely cautious rehydration in order to not overfill her, which could put her weak heart into failure as it struggles to pump this sudden fluid load around. Dehydration, on the other hand, can lead to shock and cardiovascular collapse due to a *lack* of fluid, and therefore requires the opposite: appropriate filling. Add to this her high fever, cold hands and rattly sounding chest, and she's quite possibly in septic shock—a third condition, also mandating prompt fluids.

So we commence management with extreme care.

'Two monthses,' says Joseph, talking with the mother. 'She has been sick for two monthses. Now she also has diarrhoea for one week. Very much diarrhoea.'

'They from Nasir?'

'Yes. But they never come'd to Outpatients. They were seeings the traditional doctor. He gave them medicines, and they tried to buy other medicines from the markets but did not have money.'

The traditional healer should see this.

We reassess her constantly. We'll soon know if we've pushed it too hard or not hard enough. We wait for her to make urine and for her peripheries to warm up, listening carefully to her chest to make sure she doesn't fill up too quickly. I gently pinch her skin between thumb and forefinger but it remains loose, crumpled black tissue paper. Joseph mixes up a fresh batch of the ReSoMal solution, and as he opens the sachet I think, How strange that we live in a world where a product range needs to be designed, created and sold for the sole purpose of treating the starving. The packet even has its own logo.

The little girl's diarrhoea is copious. Perhaps more so now that she's drinking again. Her bowels unload an impossible amount of fluid from her body every few minutes, so we cautiously give her replacement. We add extra when she has a bowel motion, but as fast as we put fluids into her she loses them.

By late evening her diarrhoea seems to slow, as does her vomiting. Her blood sugars are okay and she looks fractionally brighter. Joseph has already worked hours overtime so heads home and is replaced by his evening colleague, Deng, and the pair of us run through the girl's management plan together. Heidi's meanwhile still in the nutrition centre because there are twenty-something other patients that need attention in there, and at some point later I quickly head back to the expat compound to grab a drink and something to eat. I still haven't unpacked.

I stop outside.

I look over the fence, at the cracked-earth plains spreading for miles beyond the river. Above it all, a thin crescent of a moon glows; a silver hammock slung lazily between two stars. There's an immense beauty in the starkness of it all, this place, and this eerie silence. I'm utterly entranced by Sudan.

And intimidated.

17. WEEK FROM HELL

The guard calls me back to the assessment room within half an hour. I run in but this time there's a young boy lying on the bed.

'Where's the girl?' I ask.

'Who?'

'The girl. Where is she?'

'Back to the Nutrition,' says Deng. 'When this boy come'd, we moved her. Gatwech is looking after her. With Heidi.'

'Is she all right?'

'What?'

'She okay?'

'Same.'

The boy's a year old and in much the same state as the girl. Fragile, wasted, desperately fatigued. Why the two severe cases in one night? Is there an outbreak of something? *Jesus—is this normal for South Sudan?*

His father and three other men sit in silence on the wooden bench along the deep-red wall when I walk in. His mum stands quietly by his side. She looks up meekly at me, says nothing. Deng gathers equipment as I examine the boy. He's worse than the girl. Not drinking at all, no appetite, and I try to insert an IV line in the back of his hand but miss the little vein and his eyes don't even flicker. Big eyes for such a little body. His face looks peaceful though his chest is heaving.

I put on a pair of gloves and prepare a nasogastric tube so we can at least start giving fluids, and Deng explains the procedure to mum who then holds her son's head still. I grasp the tube, push the tip back, through his nose and down his throat, and he cries only weakly. His disapproval is feeble. He doesn't even have the energy to fight me. It's a worrying sign.

The tube doesn't go in properly. I pull it out and his tired eyes dart between mine and his mum's as he silently sobs. *Why are you doing this?*, he must be thinking.

Sorry little man. We gotta do it again.

I hate doing this.

We try the other nostril. A dab of lubricating jelly on the tip of the tube and then insert it horizontally, all the way to the back, pushing with a little more force as it curves around the bend at the back of his nose into his nasopharynx. He gags. I push a little harder and the tube suddenly slides easily, down the length of his oesophagus. Deng hands me a large syringe and I fix it to the free end of the tube. A draw back on the plunger confirms the placement as gastric fluid refluxes into the chamber. We tape the end to his cheek and give ReSoMal down it, then a small amount of milk. Deng performs a malaria test. Passers-by are watching from the doorway. It's now pitch dark outside, and the generator's humming life into the two bulbs hanging from the roof but there's still not enough light in here, never enough light in these places.

I set up again for an IV. The little boy passes copious amounts of green diarrhoea with an effortless gurgle, and it oozes like a little green tidal wave across the plastic surface of the examination table. His mum reaches over, mops it with the hem of her blue shawl. She doesn't even blink. Only a mother would do that.

Deng holds a torch as I retry for an IV, and more green foulness oozes from the boy's body, spreads across the table but my hands are occupied and I watch as it drips onto the floor next to me. I won't wear sandals to night calls anymore.

The line goes in. We give fluids and antibiotics, but his diarrhoea keeps flowing. He becomes sleepy. We add dextrose to keep his blood sugar levels up and give extra fluid whenever he passes diarrhoea, and I lose track of time. Ten minutes, six hours—it all feels the same. Eternal moments of watching, standing, and waiting; of doing nothing, then re-examining him and adjusting his infusion, but according to the chart we did that only two minutes ago. Always feels like we're not doing enough. What we should do is rig up monitors, adjust oxygen and reset alarms, insert half as many central lines as Mr Feldman had going into him in ICU and then yell for X-ray because *this is an imminent code-blue, people, on a one-year-old—*

Deng's lamp is running flat. It's rechargeable, but it needs the sun. Not a great invention for busy nights. He excuses himself and retrieves the one from the surgical ward.

The boy's diarrhoea won't settle. We keep giving fluids but for all we give even more shit comes out. Green filth, burbling from his little body. Impossible quantities for such a small boy. I draw up more ReSoMal, and the health worker from the feeding centre comes in.

'Doctor?'

I look up.

'The little girl has died.'

I nod.

'The mother will take the body. In the morning. Is this all right?'

I nod again.

'There is no father to help bury it. Only a brother, but he is away. So can it stay here?'

Okay.

For hours the little boy stays much the same. We don't leave the room. His diarrhoea settles and we recheck his fluid status, and some time later he actually starts to sip from a cup if we prop his head up; a small but clear improvement. I re-check everything—his IV line, his tube, the quantities, my notes. What we're doing is right. I draw up a plan for Deng: what to give every fifteen minutes, what to do each time he has a bowel motion.

I head back to the compound. I'll come and check on the boy soon, but right now I need a quick bite, a drink, I need to put my head down for a bit because I didn't sleep much before that outreach closure yesterday and this morning's ward round begins in a couple of hours from now, and I'm going to have to start from scratch reviewing all those new patients again.

The guard calls me.

Jesus, I fell asleep?

I run to the assessment room.

Two dead children, lying on the table.

The little girl from the feeding centre and the new little boy, just there, right as you walk in. Like two mannequins. They don't look real. Not old enough to be dead, I think, but I'm forgetting where I am.

I walk over to them and their eyes are open. Not peaceful, not anything, just glazed and expressionless. Their bodies lie side by side on the plastic surface and the boy's mother is silent, the whole family silent and the generator off and I hear only the noisy breathing of a sick infant next door, and Deng carries over the other portable lamp which is also fading and shines it onto the bodies. I walk to where the mum of the little boy is kneeling at the foot of the table and she looks up at me pleadingly, waiting for me to say something. *Surely she knows?*

I listen to her son's chest as a formality. No heartbeat, no breath sounds. I try to shut his eyes but they don't stay closed, and I wonder why they put the two children together like this, naked, it makes no sense.

I try again to close his eyelids with a soft sweep of my fingers but they remain open. I turn to the mum with the same stupid look of resignation I've had on my face far too many times in these places, and I don't say anything, just look at her, and she grabs my hands and sobs into them. The family on the bench start crying too, so I just stand, don't move, never knowing what to do because I'm no better at these moments than that very first time this happened in Mavinga.

The mother stands up and begins pacing. Her sobs build, becoming wails. *'Ayoy ayoy ayoooooooooy . . .!'* she screams. I've not ever heard people yell like this before. Strange that cries should sound different in different places.

'Deng, please tell her I'm sorry.'

'Yes?'

'Tell her I'm sorry. Tell the family.'

'It's okay—we gave it before.'

I try again but he doesn't understand me. 'Is that what you called me for?' I ask him.

'Yes.'

'No other problems in here?'

'No.'

'I'm sorry about all of this, Deng.'

'What?'

'Nothing. But Deng, could you please cover the bodies next time?'

'Yes?'

'The bodies. Can we not leave them like this? And not just near the entrance.'

I turn to walk out but he asks me for boxes. 'For the bodies,' he says. 'We are losing many blankets. It is better we use boxes.'

'Which boxes?'

'From the pharmacy.'

'The ones for packing?'

'Yes—like for the medicines. The medicine boxes.'

I get the key to the pharmacy from the small shelf in my hut and fumble around in the room, retrieve two empty cardboard boxes.

I return to the ward with two little coffins.

And walk back to the compound.

And go to bed.

• • •

Morning, and I'm back on the ward just hours later. Self-consciousness engulfs me like a dark cloud as I walk in. The children died just around the corner, beneath this same roof. There are no doors, no privacy. Everyone here knows what happened. Everyone would've heard the crying. And I wonder now what the patients think when I come to see them: *This new doctor—two patients dead on his first day! My God, whatever you do, don't take what he prescribes . . .!*

Joseph's waiting for me. He heard about what happened. 'Very sad,' he says, 'but today I have maybe happy newses. I think maybe we should start with this ones, yes?'

I couldn't agree more. I follow him to the far corner of the ward, a free-standing brick building that's a replica of the surgical unit— same high tin roof, same white walls painted dark red along their lower half, only this is longer and houses a dozen or so extra beds. Thirty-something patients are in here—men, women, adults and children, all together, all languishing in the diabolical heat. Most will go outside shortly to lie on the dirt in the shade of the eaves.

'You have met Elizabeths?' asks Joseph, whose English, aside from a tendency towards the plural form, is excellent. 'You know, Elizabeths, with the HIVs?'

I do. She's in a bed at the back right corner of the room. She's a thin, frail woman in her mid-twenties, with a halo of short black hair.

A bright red dress drapes from her bony shoulders like the lining of a sagging, broken tent, and she sits up on her cotton throw-down as we approach. She ideally should have been started on anti-retroviral therapy for HIV when she was admitted two weeks ago, but she doesn't meet our criteria for therapy; according to the guidelines, she lives too far from town and is consequently at a high risk of defaulting.

'We have spoken withs her,' says Joseph, 'and today she is saying that her family will move. Before, she didn't wants to move, but now she does. She is getting sicker. She wants treatments.'

Elizabeth stares intently, looking from side to side at us while we discuss her future. Joseph speaks with her in Nuer, a lilting tonal language with soft-sounding consonants and none of the distinctive 'clicks' of the Xhosa I'd heard around me in Cape Town.

'She knows this will be forever?' I ask, looking at Elizabeth. 'And that she must take it daily? She knows that she'll need to see John regularly?' John's the supervisor of our small HIV unit, and one of only two members of our Sudanese staff with formal qualifications, having trained as a nurse in Juba. Joseph and the others attended only basic health courses.

'Yes,' says Joseph. 'She knows. John and me talked with her.'

'Great!' I smile. 'Then let's get the treatment started! I see no reason to wait.'

Joseph translates, and now just look at that: the widest grin you've ever seen, and a red dress. There's not much more to her, really. She'd be thirty kilograms at most. I'm really looking forward to seeing her through this treatment, too; I've not treated patients with anti-retrovirals previously, although the manual is currently top of the pile at my bedside.

Elizabeth talks with Joseph.

'What's she saying?' I ask, as he starts to giggle.

'She wants you to marry her,' he grins.

'Oh?'

'Oh yes—very muches.' The three other health workers standing with us chuckle, too. 'She says because you will save her life, she should marry you. And I think this is something for you to consider, yes?' he smiles, raising a querulous eyebrow.

'Tell her I'm very flattered,' I say, suddenly aware of the heat in the room.

'Doctor?'

'Honoured,' I clarify. 'Tell her I'm very *honoured* by her proposal,' which I really am; no less as I turn to see the next of the thirty-something unwell patients in here.

The afternoon starts well. I have lunch with the team, then spend my time flitting between the five plywood cubicles in Outpatients. At some point we hear screaming. I run outside, following the crowd heading towards our main entrance, where there's a sea of commotion. A flatbed truck has pulled up at the gates. Armed men are milling about, a throng of distressed people gathering rapidly. There are no police, and no soldiers—the guys with guns here are in jeans and T-shirts, and they're carrying semi-automatic rifles. Some of them look half my age.

An injured man is passed from the back of the truck using an old sheet for a stretcher, then another patient, and another, all laid onto the ground. Marina runs back to get proper carriers. Zoe steps into the fray with an interpreter.

'How many injured?' she calls, and the men say that there are only these three. The others are dead.

Marina returns and we load the patients and carry them through the gates. The crowd tries to follow but Zoe steps in, looking improbably calm. She's a veteran of several years in war-torn contexts, and I watch as this short Dutch woman in her mid-thirties confidently addresses armed Sudanese men who tower a foot or two above her. 'No guns in the compound!' she declares. 'For now, only one relative per patient can enter. Everyone else—please!—wait outside!'

They comply, although they really could do as they please. The guards shut the gate behind us as we carry the injured to the operating block, an old brick building on the river side, where we lie them down. Marina and I make a quick assessment of their wounds. Heidi puts in IV lines as the health workers draw up fluids, and Thomas clears three surgical beds while Ben takes blood samples to screen for transfusions. It's a polished effort, considering the circumstances. The team have obviously done this before.

Within little time Marina is scrubbed and operating. All of the patients have only limb injuries—one is relatively minor but two involve bone and significant blood loss—and Marina works for the following hours with her two Sudanese theatre assistants. Heidi and I meanwhile stay on the wards. By nightfall, the crowd has dispersed and all three patients are stable, although two of them will now be fixed to brick traction devices for the coming weeks.

And thank God there's a surgeon out here, I think, because there's no way I could have handled this as well as Marina did. A pity then that she's leaving in three weeks, no replacement found yet. A pity as well Zoe's comment at dinner. 'We should review our security procedures tomorrow,' she'd said, 'because there'll be payback for this. There's no doubt.'

• • •

Wednesday morning. The medical ward is by now even more packed, but there's a saving grace: Joseph. He's outstanding; organised, efficient, and only too happy to ask about anything he's unclear of. So too is Peter, the gregarious supervisor of the TB village, who, no less than half a dozen times a day, bounds across the compound to ask if *now* I've got time for his patients. And no less than half a dozen times a day I apologise and ask if it can wait a little—because the watch-tapping health worker and his five Outpatients colleagues deal with a hundred and fifty presentations daily and invariably ask me for second opinions, and John, the HIV nurse, calls me whenever his patients arrive, and Heidi usually likes me to see the sicker kids in Nutrition with her—yet Peter always just smiles and says, 'Okay, because, it can wait.' But now it cannot wait, he says. Not this afternoon. And he's frowning deeply.

'Young boy,' he explains, 'very sick,' leading me to the square TB hut at the north of the compound. Peter cautions me that I'm not to enter this *tukul* without a mask as the patients in here have highly infectious coughs. 'Too dangerous,' he says, then puts his on and bounds in. He emerges moments later followed by a man carrying a child over his shoulder. The man lies the boy gently on the clay earth outside the entrance. It's a tragic sight. The boy's a ghost; skeletal, unable to speak, his body without tone as the father manoeuvres him like a rag doll. His face is fixed in a grimace and he recoils from the sunlight, whimpering like a frightened animal.

I kneel beside him. '*My God*, Peter. How old is this poor child?'

'Ten years, Doctor.'

'Are there any other patients like this in these *tukuls*? Are the others this sick?' I've seen less than half the TB patients so far.

'Only him,' Peter assures me.

'But why didn't you call me earlier?'

Peter explains that there'd been a management plan before, but now the boy is worsening.

We sit the boy up. Tenacious threads of saliva hang from his mouth, pooling on his raggy T-shirt. The dad spoons them with the side of his hand and wipes it into an old metal tin he's carrying in his other. I lift up the boy's shirt to listen to his chest, but stop suddenly: extensive, deep cuts run vertically down the boy's back, some old and others new, and there's more scar than healthy skin.

'Jesus, Peter—*has this guy been whipped?*'

'Traditional medicine,' says Peter. 'Because, they did it to let the chest problems out. It is from his village.'

I've not seen anything to this extent before. Peter tells me that the boy has been ill for a year and was admitted here three weeks ago, but he's since remained frail. In the last day he's developed a fever and stopped eating.

We get a sheet and lie him on it. I examine him here, outside the TB hut, then arrange a few tests, including for HIV, haemoglobin, hepatitis, and some other local infections. Ben's lab here is better equipped than what we'd had in Mavinga. We insert an IV line and add another antibiotic, but the boy can't swallow well so we put in a nasogastric tube too. I explain to the father how to give milk down it and we watch him give the first bolus, then Peter fetches an old clock from his office to aid him. 'And sir,' we caution, 'you must call us if he vomits, or if anything changes. Okay?'

The father nods. Then bends down, picks up his crumpled boy and carries him back into the gloomy dampness, Peter trailing with the IV line.

• • •

By night-time a gentle breeze has picked up. It's a pleasant change, but with the cooler air comes the rich smoke from the fires on the far bank, where cattle herders are burning dung to ward off flies. No clouds, though, and the moon illuminates the cracked earth like a floodlight, silhouetting the hospital buildings and conical tops of distant *tukuls*. I turn my torch off as I make my way across the yard to bed later. I stop, relish the moment, gaze back over the fence, but a sharp *CRACK* rips into the sky.

I freeze.

Another *CRACK*.

Gunshots?

I've never been anywhere near a gunfight before but this sounds like guns. I can't tell how close they might be. Great currents of fear wash down my back like an electric shock, what a strange feeling and that explosion in Angola was just the warm-up, this is worse. I should run but I stand still, paralysed by fear. *So, I'm clearly not the dashing-bravely-into-battle type that I may have thought.* No fight response here, only flight, except my legs aren't moving.

Another *CRACK*.

Holy hell it's all too real. This isn't like I imagined in the briefings and I'm not willing to die for this work, not like this, not here, I should at least have been treating a patient and not just standing—

'Safe room!' yells a voice. It's Zoe. 'Get in the safe room!'

The others run over. The dry grass fence surrounding us isn't going to stop any wayward projectiles and I should follow my teammates but I'm still just standing with my heart in my throat and I'm unsure of which way I should go right now because there's a problem, a big problem. I can't just run to the safe room because I was getting ready for bed and this should be the furthest thing in the world from my mind right now but the issue is that I only just stepped out of the shower. I'm not wearing any clothes—only a small towel around my waist. Adrenaline purges my brain of rational thought and I come to the panicked conclusion that I need underwear, because who knows if we're going to be in that room for hours, days, or weeks, and if I'm going to be shot or holed up it's not going to be like this—not without underwear. Pride and misdirected terror take over and in nothing resembling an act of fearlessness I make a rapid side trip in the opposite direction to my mud hut just metres away.

I bolt. Fling open the door. Scramble inside, but my bag's still not unpacked. *Fuuuck!* I pull it apart, search frantically in the dark because I'm not stupid enough to flick the light on, so I throw things, T-shirts, textbooks, sunscreen, insect repellent, *OhMyGod OhMyGod those guns sounded seriously close*—Boxers! What about my passport? *Where's my*—fuck it, I need to hurry and join the others.

Outside again. Not even ten metres of yard between me and the house but there's another *CRACK*, more adrenaline, *OhMyGod!*, I duck nonexistent bullets as I run, weaving erratically all the time because what if now I get hit and the team find me like this in the morning, right near the latrine, and even worse than wearing just a towel, now clutching my underwear like it's some sentimental object. I wonder how they'll explain to my family that my final gesture on this planet wasn't to reach for a photograph of loved ones or to write a touching note but to fetch *this*.

Halfway there. Another weave. A dash. My bald head would be gleaming like a white flare under this moon and make for an unmissable target, but I hear no more shots and there's been probably only a dozen at most so far. I tear through the brick house and out the other side and bang on the heavy steel door of the safe room, which is locked. 'Open it!' I yell. 'Come on!

The rusty blue door swings open and I dart in, shut it behind me and join my team-mates, who are sitting on the mattresses along the wall.

'Where the fuck were you?' asks Zoe, as I scamper to the corner.

'Had to fetch something.'

'Fetch what?'

I wave my underwear. Nine blank faces stare back. Paul rolls his eyes but everyone else starts to laugh, and I turn my back to them and slide my boxers on beneath my towel, then take my place on a spare mattress. And now, instead of not being hit by a bullet, I begin praying that we won't have to be evacuated; images play out in my head of the press coverage following our flight from danger as I descend the aircraft stairs behind my colleagues, worried relatives and MSF seniors gathered below, the world's media, teary parents—and me, in an old pair of boxers.

The shots soon stop. Half an hour later we leave the safe room and I head to bed, fully clothed this time, my passport at the door, although there's little chance of getting to sleep. Not when drenched in adrenaline like this. And there's little point, either. A middle-aged patient with liver failure breathes his last just hours later, vomits blood on the cool clay sometime before sunrise. Heidi is up with him and calls me for help but I just kneel uselessly beside the family under a dramatic banner of stars, sponge him occasionally and look up at the sky in between times because there's nothing else we can do.

• • •

And this is how the week continues. A macabre pattern of sorts, a series of busy but productive days, and sleepless, tragic nights.

On the fourth night, two patients die; a child, before we can even get her to a bed, and an old woman, suffering from a fever we can't get on top of. The following morning my paranoia regarding how patients may react is validated when two mothers take their children from Nutrition and carry them home. They're scared about all these deaths, says Joseph. They're worried that we're doing this. They say we're making mistakes.

On the fifth night, it happens again. Another death—perversely, one of the children who'd been carried home by a wary mother. The remaining mothers become even more frightened. Two of them argue with Heidi. 'If we go home,' they say, 'this is what happens! But what if we stay . . .?' Meanwhile, we admit three new patients, one of whom has frequent seizures overnight.

On the sixth day, a teenage boy is carried in following a gunfight far outside town. He's suffering severe abdominal injuries, and dies while Marina's operating on him.

On the sixth night there are no deaths, but now a new problem: a woman has arrived in labour, and we've got no midwife. Carol walked out this morning. Just up and left, trudged past our breakfast table dragging her suitcase, and got onto the supply flight. Zoe said to leave it. It'd been a long time coming, apparently; there's been ongoing personality differences among some of the medical staff, and the gunshots were likely the final straw. But working without a midwife is a huge problem, and Carol in particular has three decades of experience. Big shoes to fill. As I discover tonight, shortly after ushering the labouring woman to the small room behind theatre.

'*Delivered?*' asked Deng, looking at me uncertainly.

'Yes—babies. You delivered a baby?'

'Never. But I would like to.'

'Good. Anyone else here that can help?'

'Gatwech.'

'Has he delivered before?'

'Never!'

'Who normally helps Carol then?'

Two women, says Deng, though he doesn't know how to contact them. Nor does he know where the keys to the obstetric cupboard are. I've got no idea either, so the pair of us run around and quickly try to assemble what we need from the other wards, and by midnight I'm shredded, my mind foggy and I'm desperately in need of sleep, and I'm tempted to just kick the fucking cupboard door open because this is the last thing I need; and like most first-time deliveries I've dealt with, mum lingers in labour for most of the night until sometime just before sunrise she bites her bottom lip, moans slightly, and a pushes a healthy, bald little Sudanese boy out into the world.

Which is how my seventh day begins.

How it continues is much the same. Busily, mostly with the young boy from the TB village, who's become jaundiced.

How it ends is a different story.

Heidi kindly agrees to do my on call. It's a promising enough start to the night but we end up together in the safe room after gunshots anyway, very much awake. Not long after we get out, the guard is back at my *tukul* again.

'SHAMIANE!' he yells; he can't get the 'D' right in my name.

'Heidi's on call,' I say. 'Heidi. Not me.'

'Yes?'

'HEIDI. CALL HEIDI—NEXT DOOR.'

'Shamiane?'

'HEIDI!'

'Hello?'

Fuck it. I get up and stomp across the yard to Inpatients. This had better be justified, this call. Seven nights of being repeatedly woken—I don't mind when it's for the severe cases, but too often it's been for minor things that could wait—but an unusually cheery 'Good morning!' greets me as I enter the ward. Not what I'd have expected if this were an emergency.

'What's the problem, Deng?'

'Just a little question,' he says, leading me down the ward. We step carefully between the sleeping bodies filling every available bit of floor and bedspace. A tunnel of light from my headlamp, but it's otherwise pitch dark. No one stirs. Halfway down to our right, a bag of blood is emptying its last drops into the vein of a woman with anaemia; beside her, a young infant with a respiratory condition breathes as if sucking the dregs of a thick milkshake through a straw. We pass them, stopping at the bed of a man who'd arrived yesterday with marked facial swelling—the result of a snakebite to his scalp (it happened while he was sleeping, he says). He's since had a good dose of antivenom and antibiotics.

Deng picks up his drug chart. 'It says to give this one,' he says, pointing to a medication name on it.

I agree.

'What must we do?' he asks.

'With what?

'The drug.'

'What do you mean?'

Deng looks at me uncertainly.

'Well?' I ask.

'We are just making sure you wanted this,' he says. 'And we are wanting to check the dose.'

I turn to walk out. The first cracks in my façade of calmness are going to reveal themselves if I don't get away now, but Deng follows me. I stop. I'd like to give him the benefit of the doubt and assume that his real question has been lost in translation, but I don't. I unleash all of my exasperation on the man. I pull him away from the ward and give him an earful as he stands quietly and wears it, looking down, his head a good foot above mine. When I finally stop he sheepishly asks me to confirm the drug dose before I leave.

'The normal dose, Deng.'

He's not sure what that is.

I step inside and find the MSF drug book. Copies are on all the wards. It's the standard manual for health workers in all projects, and easy enough to follow. 'You look it up, Deng. I'm not doing your job for you.'

He thumbs through the book, flicking the pages.

'Flucloxacillin, Deng. "*F*". Look it up in the index.'

He looks at me.

'The index—the back of the book.'

He stares.

I take the book and open it to the index, hand it back to him.

'Pro. Pran—' he sounds out.

'That's "P", Deng. Flucloxacillin is with an "F". Go to "F".'

He flicks the pages. Backwards, then forwards, completely randomly. He sounds out words. 'Sal. Bu. Ta—.'

'Jesus, Deng! Here. "*F*: Flucloxacillin"—page sixty. It's arranged like the alphabet. See? And here are all the doses. So now you look at this table, and *you* tell me what dose you're going to give an adult.'

For a long time he stares at the page and says nothing. He tracks the text with his finger as he sounds out each word, slowly, determined to find the dose, and I want to crawl into a hole suddenly because look at me, what a big man I am right now: berating a young, semi-literate, junior health worker who'd grown up in a war. *When did I cross this line?* I've seen behaviour like this in some others in the past. I've seen it in volunteers, even among the local staff, and I loathe it. I caught myself doing it in Mozambique, too—a large group of people kept pushing into our tent, crowding it, and I repeatedly raised my voice to tell them to stay back or we'd have to leave; in the crowd I no longer saw individuals, just a wall of demands.

I take the book from Deng. 'I've just had a bad week,' I tell him. 'I'm sorry, mate. It's not you. I'm just being an arse. I'm tired. I'm really sorry.'

His reply disarms me. 'The doctor here is like a father,' he says, graciously. 'We respect them very much. But for us, it is very hard. Sometimes the doctor will not like it if we call. Sometimes they get angry if we do not. I am sorry for calling you.'

I tell him he needn't be. Wake me whenever, I say.

And I go back to bed.

And bury myself under my mosquito net. Deeply, horribly embarrassed.

• • •

But embarrassment is the least of it by the next afternoon, now my eighth since coming back. I'm more unnerved: the TB boy has died. He's the ninth patient to die during this past week. Our catchment area is huge; one hundred and sixty thousand people, we think, making it well over five times Mavinga's, and the team here see forty thousand outpatients a year and admit five thousand others. Even so, this number of deaths is worrying.

In the afternoon, myself, Heidi, Marina, and Zoe (who's an experienced nurse, although working non-clinically in this project) all meet to talk about it. We gather at our outdoor table in the shade of a large tree, where we spread out the patients' charts and try to find a pattern to these deaths. Are we doing something wrong? Overlooking something obvious? I find myself getting defensive as we go through each of the cases: *what if the underlying problem is me?*

I tell the others that I'll tabulate the patient data, looking closely at how and when the patients died. I'll talk with Joseph and the nutrition guys, go through all the protocols they're using and make spreadsheets, and I keep talking because if I stop I'm either going to cry or fall asleep. But Marina's great. She assures me it's been a far busier week than normal, and reminds me that we've all lost patients—not just the ones under my care are dying. And the thing to do, as I'd learned well in Mavinga, is to focus at times like this on the positives. So I do. I think of the fifty-plus inpatients, the forty TB patients, the twenty-two malnourished children, the dozen HIV patients, and this week's thirteen hundred outpatients who're currently doing okay.

In aid of such reflections, Marina fetches cold Ethiopian Bedele beers. We lean back in our chairs as we sip on them, regard those smoky dung-fires and the sun that's dropping slowly behind our fence, but I see sudden movement at the gate.

I cringe.

I can't possibly deal with another emergency.

I look over hesitantly.

The guard?

It's not the guard. It's a little boy who lives in the TB village, and who I only ever see wearing beads—a white string around his waist, red around his neck and not a stitch of clothing—and he's standing with hands on hips, watching us. He waves hesitantly when I do but otherwise just stands, completely still. Regarding us. Concentrating and contemplating, his podgy belly out and little eyes squinting, and his head tilted just slightly.

I'd give anything to know what he's thinking.

18. AIRBORNE REMINDERS

Like highways, these dawn skies. I stand at our fence watching thousands of bats return from their nocturnal food hunts to settle into the few trees on the far riverbank. They chirp noisily as if swapping stories from last night, jostling and crowding upside-down in dense clusters where they'll hang like fat black plums from the broad branches and sleep the day away. Then it's the water birds—herons, we think; hundreds of them flying in almost perfect arrowhead formations, off to some mysterious swamp somewhere. They'll return this evening in much the same manner, too: a single bird at the front, the others trailing neatly behind. No bird ever strays. Periodically, the leader will drop to the back, the next bird momentarily picking up his pace to assume the role of guide as they plough on, the whooshing of their collective wings audible even from inside my *tukul*. A glorious sound to wake up to.

It's late in the second week and I'm up earlier than normal. The rest of the team are still in bed but Paul's already busy, cutting long beams for the new nutrition ward with hand tools before the sun climbs. At our front gate, the best-dressed MSF employee I've ever met—European offices included—has meanwhile arrived for work: our guard, who's this morning back on day shifts, wearing a full black suit with neat business shirt and tie. 'Hi, Dennis,' he smiles, and I smile back: two weeks of cajoling, and we've just moved on from *Shamiane.*

The main hospital yard is still. Nothing like what it'll be in an hour. For now only a few kids play near the fence, and a handful of women are boiling water in the communal fire-pit behind Nutrition, using pots that look like relics from the British colonial era (and that may well be). Beside them, the hospital cook is stirring the patients' breakfasts—mud-brown sorghum, bubbling in a large pot like thick lava—with a length of wood that looks suspiciously like the oar of an old rowboat (and that also may well be). I stop to greet them; then, avoiding the wards entirely, head straight for the main entrance, where David, the watch-tapping health worker from Outpatients, is going to meet me. He's promised to show me his home before rounds.

David and I stroll north, away from the river, and head against Nasir's morning traffic—a single UN LandCruiser, two trucks from the military compound, hundreds of people walking towards the market, and the groups of kids who're hopefully off to one of the schools. A few bicycles are around, too, and even some taxis—also bicycles, these ones adorned with bright plastic flags or boldly painted signs, and whose riders will give you a lift on the back rack for a few Sudanese pounds.

'My house is not a very big house,' David apologises. He shows me into a grass-walled enclosure, one of a small cluster of compounds about five minutes from the hospital. Within it, three *tukuls* and a plastic-roofed shed are arranged around his dry yard, a few goats wandering about. Unusually for an African village, there are no fowl—the Nuer don't eat birds.

David leads me inside the first *tukul* (two single beds, a table and some chairs provide the furnishings), and I'm immediately impressed. They're clearly not easy to build. The wall is circular and mud-covered, but the roof reveals the intricacy of the inner frame—a latticework of thicker sticks bent carefully into shape, dozens of smaller wooden ribs tied across them using natural twine, and thick straw woven over the top of it all. The shape conferred from the outside is that of a giant, grass-coloured Baci chocolate; the larger *tukuls*, used as cattle byres, reach over four metres in height. Seeing hundreds of these near-conical structures on a barren moonscape, all silhouetted against a red sky each evening, is quite other-worldly.

A group of kids jostle in the doorway. 'These all your children?' I ask David, but he laughs. No way, he says. He has only five children to two wives, all of whom live in this compound. He points out his three younger ones and explains that the older one is in Juba, and another son with the herd. 'These other ones, they have come to see you. I think they have never seen a *Khawaja* [white person] so close before.'

I'm inclined to agree. I've become used to the startled reactions of some children to seeing me these past years—the fleeing, the screaming, the transfixed staring or the more adventurous patting and prodding of my skin—but these kids take the prize. Three kneel down and pull gently at my leg hairs. Two of the younger boys have taken instead to rubbing my forearm, and as my arm heats up they rub it more vigorously, faster each moment, and I wonder what on earth they're doing. One of the boys stops to cool his hand with spit but immediately resumes rubbing, even faster this time, and it dawns on me that perhaps they think I'm also black—that beneath a layer of white, firmly adherent dirt, I too have the same wonderfully dark complexion as them.

David shoos the kids away and shows me proudly around the rest of his compound. 'But it is not like your home,' he says. 'I am sure your home in America is big, yes?'

'In Australia,' I reply. 'I'm from Australia. Do you know it?'

He turns. 'Oh—Melbourne, or Sydney?'

This I didn't expect. I tell him Melbourne, and his face lights up.

'Oh! My friend is living in Werringbee.'

I stop dead. *Blown away!*—that this man, who's surely not ever been out of the region, can name a suburb in Melbourne! I ask him if he's been there, and he says no.

'But many Sudan peoples went to Australia,' he says, which is a fact I'd discovered inadvertently while working in a small coastal town a few years ago. Several Dinka families had been resettled there as part of Australia's intake of twenty thousand South Sudanese over recent years, creating a small but highly conspicuous group in an otherwise very white town. What they must have thought when arriving in a rainy, affluent coastal town in the throes of a southern winter, having been recently ushered from a hot, dry, crowded refugee camp, I can't imagine.

Nor can I imagine what the town's people would have thought. Because even having spent time in Africa, I find the Nuer remarkable looking. Take David as an example: six-foot three with long, thin limbs and utterly black skin; a soft, handsome face; and the distinctive dentition of many of the adults here—the absence of his lower front teeth and two upper canines due to ritual extraction during childhood. (These teeth, the Nuer believe, make people look like hyenas.) And then there's the *gaar*—those six prominent scars across the forehead, the incisions having been made so deeply that it's said that marks can be seen on skulls found in the region.

David nods vigorously when I ask if he remembers having it done. He was about fourteen, he says. 'It is when a boy becomes a man, and he must not cry. It is a shame to cry. And he must not move. If he moves, it will not be straight, and everyone will know forever that he was not brave.' He was very much awake at the time, he explains, the procedure having been performed with a sharp knife by the *Gur*, a ceremonial leader, following which—ensuring a truly memorable afternoon—the initiates were circumcised. But it's a proud moment, David tells me, and the point at which a man will be given his first head of cattle.

What I'd really like to ask David though is about the war, and more specifically how he'd survived: Nasir was the scene of some of the worst of it. For decades the northern government armed and encouraged horseback-mounted Arab militias, known as *djellabas* (not unlike Darfur's infamous *janjaweed*), to conduct raids on southern villages. Homes were torched, women raped and children taken into slavery, with many thousands of others killed. As well, the region was bombed extensively by government planes; in Nasir alone, the crowded hospital and UN feeding centres were hit on more than one occasion, a fact to which the twisted beams of metal in the corner of our compound still attest.

Things took an even worse turn here in the early 1990s, when the southern forces—the SPLA, or Sudan People's Liberation Army, a group ostensibly formed to defend the people here—split into two factions: a Nuer faction, and a second, Dinka-based faction. Now, Southerners were pitted against each other along tribal lines, and a war-within-a-war ensued—a conflict every bit as devastating as the north–south war, which meanwhile continued. Both tribes attacked the others' villages. Both were responsible for rapes, kidnappings, and the burning of essential crops. And both continued like this for almost a decade, until an agreement between the respective southern leaders in 2002, just three years before the north–south war ended.

As in all these conflicts, though, it wasn't just violence that caused deaths. Starvation and disease took a greater toll. When MSF first arrived in 1988, a parasitic illness called Kala-azar had killed a hundred thousand people near Nasir—around one-third of that area's population. My briefing documents described volunteers coming across villages that were either deserted or filled with bodies. And then there were the food shortages. In 1988, a quarter of a million South Sudanese starved to death. Barely three years later, another food crisis resulted in thousands dying along this riverbank, with individuals so desperate they were seen to be digging in search of any grain stored in ant nests. In 1998 the region was again on the verge of another catastrophe, and an international aid effort named Operation Lifeline Sudan was set up, carrying out widespread food distributions (mostly by air drops, using Lokichoggio as a base) that at its peak cost donors over a million US dollars a day—the largest effort of its kind since the Berlin airlift.

Perversely, the manipulation of this food aid was a feature of the war, and perpetrated by all sides. The north threatened to shoot any plane it didn't expressly authorise, and southern rebel leaders frequently dictated where and how the aid was to be delivered. In a more extreme example, the leader of the SPLA in Nasir was suspected of deliberately keeping twenty thousand people in a state of perpetual starvation nearby so as to bait further deliveries.

Yet walking around here, as in Mavinga, I find it hard to reconcile such stories with what I see. The kids are still with us (they sneak back within moments of David shooing them away, jostling to hold my hand, one of the smaller ones happy enough with just a thumb), and the oldest would be no more than ten. When I was last in Loki, a colleague had lent me two memoirs, both being the first-hand accounts of young boys who'd fled fighting during the war—boys of about the same age as these kids now with us. These children, having survived the raids on their villages, and being unsure as to whether their families were alive or not, walked for months across Sudan in the late 1980s, arriving in Ethiopia like 'walking skeletons'. Camps were set up to accommodate them, and more generally the growing numbers of Sudanese being displaced from all over the south, but Ethiopia's own security situation deteriorated and they were forced to move again, this time south to Lokichoggio—on foot. Many spent their next decades in the refugee camps nearby.

More than twenty-five thousand children made this journey overall, either alone or in groups, and became known collectively as the 'Lost Boys of Sudan'. Few girls set out. Boys survived the militia raids because they were tending to cattle away from their villages when they occurred, whereas girls were either killed or taken into slavery; and of those boys who did escape, at least one in five died travelling. It goes without saying then that the accounts of their journeys are heartbreaking. Of an aerial bombing raid, for example, one boy wrote that there was a plane standing above the trees, pouring fire on them; another boy noted that during the walk he'd envied those who had a cup of urine to drink, and that the journey had become a game where the object for him was to go as far as he could before dying. I did manage a smile, however: on being given milk and butter as part of his rations in an Ethiopian refugee camp, one boy pondered how the UN could possibly own enough cows to produce such quantities of dairy.

So, could David have been in this group? Very possibly. As too could Joseph, Peter, John, Gatwech, Deng—any of our two dozen health workers. Almost all are men in their thirties and forties, the same demographic as the Lost Boys, and all had to have learned English somewhere. A refugee camp is as likely a place as any. (Birthdays are a giveaway for someone having spent time in them: a significant number of our staff and patients list theirs as being January 1st, a date conferred by unimaginative registrations staff at the camps.)

But I ask David about none of this. I'd hate to upset him. He looks delighted showing me around. And I'd previously tried to ask staff about such experiences, and it hadn't gone well. I'd asked Roberto about the Angolan war, sometime towards the end of my time there when we'd started to banter a little in the afternoons, but he just looked away, said only 'Confusão,' and stayed quiet. It killed the conversation. And I see the consequences of mental stress often enough in this hospital to know that it's an issue here. Since I've arrived, we've admitted a dozen patients, usually women, whose conditions are almost certainly a manifestation of psychological trauma: pseudoseizures—atypical, non-epileptic seizures that tend to respond promptly to a placebo; extreme states of hysteria, including the transient inability to speak, dramatic outbursts followed by a collapse, or other unusual neurological symptoms; or just inconsolable crying. All of which seem to improve with a night on the wards, some reassurance, and the doting of loved ones. (And I wonder as well, with regard to the men, whether these gunfights aren't another expression of trauma—or at the least a result of desensitisation to violence, given a lifetime of exposure to it.)

David looks at his watch. 'Already eights,' he says: time to get to work. I'm not quite ready to head back, though. This is what I didn't get to do enough in Mavinga, just spend time with staff, and I'm quietly intrigued by him, his kids, and really all of these Nuer people. That some of them show symptoms of post-traumatic stress disorder isn't what surprises me—it's that not all of them do. Maurice was right. These people are tough.

David's tapping his watch now. I know, I tell him, but I remind him that he did also promise to show me the fish market.

'Yes, but we will be late,' he says.

I shrug. He laughs; the fish market it is.

• • •

Carol, our midwife, returns the week after walking out. She still doesn't want to talk about it although she at least seems rested, and things have generally settled this week—no more gunfights, fewer deaths, and what I assume is the more normal routine has set in: busy mornings, a long lunch break (staff go home at one and return at four to avoid the hotter hours), and late afternoons spent in the hospital again; and, if we're lucky, pleasant, lazy evenings at the outdoor table, or sitting on the riverbank, or watching DVDs in the room with the bats. Morale seems okay even if people are tired, and there're enough of us here to at least allow for some social variety.

On Saturday afternoon Zoe attends a meeting in town with the UN and local police representatives. She calls the ten of us expats to the outdoor table when she returns, and tells us that they're expecting an escalation of these raids. 'They've seen members of the Lou clan heading this way,' she says, 'so the other groups are moving their herds closer to town for protection.'

There's a collective groan. In a region where banks don't exist, cattle traditionally represent the only significant way for a person to accumulate wealth. Having what's tantamount to gold-bullion-on-legs wandering around us is a sure recipe for trouble—no less given that the two larger clans along the Sobat River here, the Lou and Jikany Nuer, have a long history of animosity toward each other.

'When are they going to get here?' asks Paul, towelling his forehead. 'When can we look forward to this?'

'Two to three days,' says Zoe. 'Maybe longer. They may wait for the next full moon.'

Paul shakes his head. This presumably isn't the first warning he's heard in the eight months he's been here. It's his first stint with an aid organisation, a long-term ambition, he'd told me, and the question that's half-jokingly thrown around among aid workers—'What are *you* running from?'—is, I suspect, largely redundant in his case. He's a successful businessman who turned sixty just last month (no wrinkles yet but his brown beard is starting to grey, although I'm still deeply jealous of it—now a thick, bushy, 'I've been in Africa for months' kind of affair), and he'd left a supportive wife and daughter in New Zealand to do this. And he works *hard*—puts in at least as many hours as any of us who're half his age, but he's clearly anxious to get home in the coming weeks.

'Look,' says Zoe, 'it may all amount to nothing. The police are going to keep a close eye on things, so let's hope. But it's a good time for us to revise our security procedures. So, first thing is the grab-packs. Make sure they're easy to find. Keep them with a small bag of valuables—maybe tie them together, but limit it all to four or five kilos—and place it near your door, somewhere you can find it easily at night. It's a good idea to keep your passports and entry permits with them.'

The grab-packs are something we'd all been issued with in Loki, just after being shown how to assemble a large, rucksack-mounted UHF radio for emergency communications. Each pack is a generic hip bag, filled with survival essentials including a lighter, compass, pocket-knife, thermal blanket, water purification tablets, and, somewhat bizarrely, condoms—not something I can foresee needing while fleeing through a swamp. Even more useless than condoms though is my South Sudan entry permit; despite my having submitted a detailed application form and a dozen colour passport photos in support of it, the official document has me listed as being a seventy-seven centimetres high, black-eyed, brown-haired Australian national—an evil-looking, hirsute, Antipodean dwarf. It'll be interesting to see what a soldier makes of it if I'm pulled aside.

'The safe room is obviously the place to go if you hear gunshots,' continues Zoe. 'If you're on the brick wards or in theatre, stay there, but waiting in the *tukuls* is pointless. Also, I think we should avoid going into town for the next few days. Okay, in terms of evacuation, we'll ideally get flown out, but it takes at least two hours for the plane to get here. And we'll need to be able to get to the airstrip, so it's only possible if things settle. Our second option is the cars. If we need to get out of here immediately, we drive, but there's obviously no way we can get to Kenya. We could drive to the UN compound, but only if we're really desperate.'

As a rule we're to avoid all non-essential contact with the UN. Our security stems from our being perceived as strictly neutral by all groups, rather than from any reliance on armed guards or impenetrable fences. (Somalia is the only context in which MSF routinely operate with that level of precaution.) If people really want to get into our compound here, they will. It's by taking no sides, and by treating everyone—for free, at any time, and regardless of clan affiliations, political allegiances, religion or ethnic group, among other conceivable variables—that we ensure our security. And so far there's been no hostility targeted towards us here. The risk, although small, of being accidentally caught in crossfire during one of these raids is our only major issue—for now.

'Our third option is the boats,' says Zoe. 'Paul and Anwar, you guys please need to make sure that both are ready, and that there's spare fuel. So, nothing we haven't discussed before. Any questions?'

We move on. It's already late afternoon, the sun drawing long shadows across the dry compound. A dozen little birds chirp brightly above us in the branches of the large tree, plopping their contributions onto the table with impressive regularity as Heidi updates us on the Nutrition unit.

'It's always at night,' she says, speaking of the two children who've died in the past week. 'Always.'

'It's classic,' says Zoe. 'Death rates are always higher in these centres overnight. You need to make sure that meals aren't being skipped. Are the mothers waking up to help give them? Is the health worker checking the kids' vital signs regularly? Do they call you or Damien as soon as things deteriorate, rather than waiting until the child's really in trouble?'

'No!' says Heidi, with endearing German feistiness. She reminds me increasingly of Andrea: frustrated by the context, enamoured of the people, desperate to make a difference and at her happiest when working with the kids. (A small posse follow her for much of the day, including a young boy who insists she carry him, and who she's nicknamed 'Breast Man' due to his propensity to grab said object on anyone nearby—men included—presumably for a feed.)

'I am sure the health workers sleep,' says Heidi. 'Last night I got up to check on a young girl, but she hadn't been given milk for hours.

When I asked Gatwech why, he said that the container had run out. So why did he not mix some more? Oh, he said, because it was more difficult to mix at night. He said that there was no rush, that the morning staff could do it! And the mothers? Have you tried to wake them? Some are so difficult! They get funny with me because they want to sleep, and if we push too much they want to leave. One even wanted me to *pay* her to wake up! I really don't get it.'

I agree with her. There are some serious cultural misunderstandings here—from both sides. A few of the parents seem deeply mistrusting of us. We try often to convince mothers not to take their children early, but they're extremely suspicious, almost superstitious. If a child with a nasogastric tube gets worse, mothers will remove tubes from their own kids. If a child dies after drinking ReSoMal, they'll refuse that drink. So we explain the treatment to them. We point to the healthy kids and assure them that they all had the same treatment, then we go in circles, explain it again, then beg, and finally just insist: I tell them that the child will die if they take them home, because any cultural sensitivity on my part is vastly overshadowed by my concern for the kids.

In terms of supervision we float the idea of rostering one of us to stay awake overnight, but it's simply not feasible. We're awake at least every third night anyway. I suggest creating another volunteer position dedicated purely to staff training, but Zoe says it's impossible. Merely keeping these four projects staffed at minimum capacity is challenge enough, and MSF are currently ramping up projects in the Abyei border region, where north–south clashes have increased.

• • •

It's getting late. We wind up the meeting with a quick whip round for any last comments. Anwar, the soft-spoken Indonesian log, is happy, nothing more to add. So too is Maya, the office administrator. Heidi doesn't want to be on call tonight (she was up all of last night), and Marina requests only that she also attend the next meeting with the UN Peacekeeping commander, because he's apparently cute, and she's been stuck in this compound for most of the past months. Carol laughs. Paul meanwhile heads for the latrine, creating an appropriate segue for Amos, our jovial Kenyan water and sanitation engineer, to make his last point.

'I am telling you,' he says, pointing in Paul's direction, 'something is not right. Look at that man. Look! Always, he gets sick. Then it was Damien—who even got a flight!—and now it is me. Something is not right in that kitchen. I am telling you, our cook is doing something strange. I have been coming to Sudan for many years, and I have never been sick so much. Never! Last week, Damien gave me antibiotics, but now, already—already!—I *sheet* all the time.'

The team laugh.

'It is not funny,' says Amos, though he too is laughing. 'I am telling you, if I cannot stop this I will waste away. Paul is already wasting away. And what if I start? I will waste very quickly. Look at me!'

We're in hysterics. Amos is a giant of a Kenyan, tall and thick-limbed, with probably the largest belly in the region.

'It is this food,' he says. 'Something is not right with it. Paul and me checked the water again yesterday, but the chlorine is good. So it is not the water. But it is something. I am telling you. And I cannot go on like this, Zoe. All this *sheeting*—I cannot do it.'

—But still he's laughing.

The generator hums suddenly into life, and a race ensues: if Amos reaches the TV first, it'll be action movies for the night; Heidi, and it'll be chick-flicks or sitcoms. The others fetch beers and stay put, and for the moment it's fractionally cooler outside so I remain here. Not long afterwards the guard calls me through the gate.

'No,' I say. 'It's Damien. D. A. M. I. E. N.'

'*Desmine?*'

I chuckle as he walks me to Inpatients, where Joseph has called for help, while trying to correct his pronunciation once more.

'Okay, yes,' he says. '*Desmien*?'

'No, *Damien*.'

'Demine?'

'Better Dennis,' I say. 'Let's stick with Dennis, okay?'

'Okay,' he grins back, shining his torch ahead, guiding me into the assessment room. I see Joseph here, his shirt still neatly buttoned to the collar even after ten hours in this place. He'd have made a far better doctor than me, I've concluded, if only he'd had the opportunity. As would so many others I've worked with.

'Looks,' he says, unusually seriously. He's standing beside the assessment table, putting an IV cannula into the hand of a young girl. She looks up at us. Her hair's braided with colourful beads, and she's got a simple string ribbon for a necklace. She's naked but for a pair of old white shorts, but we don't cover her up. The Nuer aren't particularly self-conscious about nudity.

'Bad fever,' says Joseph, as I hold her arm steady for him. But the girl pushes us away, rolls feebly onto her side and moans for her mother. We catch her before she falls. The mother takes her for a moment and sits on the floor and cradles her, and the little girl sits in her mother's lap and looks up at her, then blinks, sighs softly, and gently empties her bowels.

Then dies.

Just like that.

Joseph tries gently to pick her from the mother's arms to resuscitate her but the little sister throws herself onto the body; kids bringing up kids, now kids mourning kids; so we leave them. There's no point interfering. I've not ever seen a child resuscitated from this state. Not in these places, not with those sunken eyes and tissue-paper skin.

We give them a blanket. When they leave, Joseph and I start seeing the three other families who've been sitting on the benches against the wall just metres away during all this, waiting to be assessed for their own health problems, and I wonder what they must think. Perhaps that it's just another sad day in South Sudan, because none of them walk away and they're all very grateful to be seen when we finally get to them.

Afterwards, I go back to the compound to join Heidi, who did make it to the TV first, and she asks me what happened. I say only that there were a few admissions, and I instead throw the question at her because she's watching *Friends*, and it's up to the series finale, I think, and Rachel and Ross have got back together and although I never had any interest in the show in Australia I'm taking a keen interest here, suddenly engaged, a lump in my throat and this strange—

Jesus. I'm crying.

While watching Friends?

This is embarrassing.

I never do cry in these projects except for that time we'd operated on Roberto's niece, but I suspect that I should, because something's got to give, or break. Heidi's fortunately too engrossed with Ross, who's now kissing Rachel, to notice at first, but when she does look over she says exactly the right thing—nothing—and just gives me a soft look and asks if I'd like something to eat. I say Yes thanks, and lie back on the mattress, watching as our resident bats fly their sorties down the corridor, past the five bedrooms then back around quickly, bundling over me and into the kitchen like leathery winged golf balls that never so much as glance a wingtip.

But before dinner comes Dennis is yet again summoned. And Dennis cringes even though he quite likes that he's at least being called Dennis these days (and notes too that he's also beginning to refer to himself in the third person—perhaps this is what missions do to you after a while), but when Dennis gets to the gate this time he smiles broadly, in part from relief, in part bemusement, because it turns out this is a good summons. Just some visitors at the gate. The little boy with the beads, and two of his friends.

He came past earlier and stood here quietly, staring, and I never do know what to do with him because he always looks so serious. Trying to make him smile, I picked him up beneath his arms, threw him straight into the air and caught him again, but as soon as his feet touched the ground he ran off—fast—so I assumed I'd upset him.

Apparently I didn't. He's back. And now standing with arms raised (although still looking serious), as are his two recruits. He does a little jump and waves his arms in case I'm not clear about what he wants, but I am. So I do it—I pick them up. I fling them as high as I can, several times each, and the contrast with what just happened on the ward isn't lost on me.

19. AN ANGRY CLAN

It's mid-May when the wet season arrives. Almost on cue to the Sudanese staff's predictions, the first storm blows in at night, a deluge of rain so grand it's as if the gods are trying to make amends for centuries of drought in the next hours—or wash away the huts. I meanwhile lie curled in my own *tukul*, reassuring myself that the sturdily-patted-together walls won't dissolve in the near-horizontal torrents.

And they don't. Surprisingly, none of the huts come apart, and when the storm clears in the morning the air smells clean, washed for the first time of the smoke from those cow-dung fires, although there's now a bigger issue: a sticky, tenacious clay carpets the entire region, and it becomes impossible to walk anywhere without acquiring a few inches in height as wads of thick, brown-black earth cement themselves to your shoes. No ordinary clay, though; get enough of it on you and it exhibits a paradoxical effect, the compound instead becoming a giant Slip-n-Slide.

Mud unfortunately isn't the only thing born of the rains. Within days the insect population explodes in both number and variety. An inquisitive 'Wow, look at that colourful little thing,' is superseded by more desperate exclamations of 'Don't . . . Fucking . . . Move . . .' as winged objects the size of potatoes, that didn't seem to exist last week, torpedo from the darkness. Walking anywhere at night mandates switching off one's headlamp lest it attract them, and if the outside light is left on following any rains, the sound of the constant barrage of insects flinging themselves maniacally towards it sounds like a heavy storm in itself. Indoors, things are little better. A bedside reading lamp quickly becomes wallpapered with bugs, and malaria prevention now seems a minor benefit of my mosquito net—keeping the three or four thousand other creatures in my *tukul* at bay is the bigger. I tuck it in firmly.

The wards too are carpeted in mud. Friday morning of my third week back, and I step over the pile of gumboots near the door (Paul recently gave them to all staff), nudging my way through a crowd to find Joseph. There are twice as many people in here these days, as patients, relatives and passers-by all seek shelter.

Joseph and I begin seeing the newer patients, then the longer term cases. In the far corner we come to Elizabeth, the smile-in-a-red-dress, who's still sharing a bed with her mother. She's now a couple of weeks into her anti-retroviral therapy and gaining a little weight, but says she was up last night with diarrhoea. She looks well on examination, though—no fever and not too dehydrated—so I reassure her that this is just a small setback. But she doesn't seem happy.

'She is very angry with you,' says Joseph.

'Angry?'

'Yes. She is okay with the treatments, but she is saying you are ignorings her. She is saying you have not ever accepted her offerings.'

'What offerings?'

'For marriages,' he says, and the three other health workers laugh heartily. But Joseph persists. 'Really,' he says. 'She is asking what your answers is.'

'Come on, Joseph—as if she wasn't joking!'

Elizabeth fixes me with a look of sincerity as Joseph speaks with her, her bony hands clasped in her lap, no hint of a smile. But the health workers are in stitches.

'She asks why would you think she is jokings?' says Joseph.

'Are you serious?'

'I think you are going to stay in Sudan!' guffaws Mark, who's just back this morning after two days off following a scorpion sting, and who's been affectionately, if somewhat jokingly, nicknamed 'The Professor' by his colleagues—a nod to his propensity to ask unusual questions on rounds. The other health workers start up, too. 'Looks like you will be staying here,' laughs Johnson, the youngest of the team. So I play along and make light-hearted excuses, but Elizabeth just glares. Doesn't see the funny side. She looks away after a moment, then dismisses me with a flick of her hand.

She really was serious?

• • •

My second-ever marriage proposal occurred on this ward as well— just last week, and from an HIV-positive patient, too. Nyawech is the woman. She's the mother of Breast Man and his two older sisters, and for almost six months has been living in a bed in the isolation area, a small, semi-partitioned space at the far end of the medical ward. She's unfortunately not doing well.

As well as late-stage HIV/AIDS, Nyawech is suffering from Kala-azar, the illness caused by the *Leishmania* parasite that's transmitted by the bite of infected sandflies. It's almost always fatal without treatment. Twenty-eight days of injections with an old, side effect laden drug will usually cure it (the two tents behind the surgical ward currently house eight patients receiving it) but Nyawech has relapsed twice. The HIV makes it difficult. An expert in Amsterdam is advising us and we've now got her on a combination of expensive second-line drugs, but she's still not improving, battling with high fevers, severe anaemia, marked weight loss and worsening diarrhoea.

This morning there's no more talk of marriage. Only a forced, crack-lipped smile from her, and an apology that she's not good. Just weak and achy, she says, and asks if she can have some Plumpy'nut, the oily, peanut-based high energy supplement we give the kids in Nutrition, because she loves the taste and can't eat anything else. We really shouldn't give it—if the rest of those on the ward see us we're going to be stuck handing out Plumpy'nut until next Wednesday—but we do. We sneak a box from Nutrition and slide it under her blanket, only the younger paraplegic woman crumpled in the opposite corner sees us and she'd also please like some. So we fetch a few more sachets and give them to her, discreetly, as if it were an illicit substance we were trying to sneak past Customs, only now the old lady with the swollen belly beside her sees it and wants some, and the man in the first bed of the main ward pokes his head around—

'Jesus, Mark! Hide it!'

—and he *does* see it, and now we're in serious trouble because he makes it known to everyone else . . .

• • •

This third week has been mercifully easier. Not without problems, though. We've had a few deaths, and the medical ward remains full—partly because I still struggle to send home patients who're desperate to stay for the food, the attention, and the respite—but it's been a better week nonetheless.

The workload remains heavy, but from an academic point of view this place is unparalleled, these wards a master class in tropical diseases. Cases seen just this morning, on the left side of our unit: brucellosis—a disease contracted from the consumption of unpasteurised milk (or from blowing into a cow's vagina, according to my reference book, as a practice that alters their fertility); HIV/AIDS, with extensive skin lesions; Kala-azar, requiring blood transfusions; leprosy, with severe nerve complications; pneumonia, with the affected child receiving oxygen via our small oxygen concentrator (a noisy, compressor-like device); typhoid fever, the patient recovering well; acute paralysis of the legs, highly suspicious for polio (the boy is being moved to a tent); a snakebite to the ankle, with marked swelling; probable exposure to rabies, the third such patient this week following a spate of dog attacks; and two older women, each with a litany of non-specific symptoms and a hankering for Plumpy'nut, and who've been diagnosed with, according to Joseph's notes, Generalised Achings. Notable is the absence of any malaria, although the rains will likely change that.

Contrary to what I'd expected, staff here have proven relatively easy to work with. Their medical knowledge is poor but they're aware of this, and for the most part are keen to learn. Teaching sessions are a delight; attendance is good, questions asked, notes taken and future sessions planned; but the issues in Nutrition, and of the frequent night calls, continue to be significantly troublesome.

Language is another major challenge. Less so for me because I get to speak English all day, but the health workers need to make themselves understood, often regarding complex presentations, in a tongue they hear only at work. I empathise wholeheartedly with them; I know well the frustrations of trying to make yourself understood to a bewildered audience, and they handle the difficulties with patience. That said, the confusion does lead to amusing exchanges.

'Chest pains,' says The Professor, presenting a patient a few beds down.

'The baby?'

'Yes.'

'But she's four months old. How can she have chest pain?'

'She told me.'

'Oh?'

'Yes.'

'This four-month-old girl *told* you she had chest pain?'

'Yes. Before.'

'The thing about chest pain, Mark, is that—'

(The baby coughs.)—'There!' he says. 'She did it again!'

So I learn this morning that chest pain, at least in our little hospital, means 'to cough'.

Later in the afternoon, Peter and I meet to do a round of the TB village. Within minutes we're mired in a fine example of the difficulties of translation, this time involving three of us.

'How's her pain?' I ask Peter, as we review an elderly woman in one of the huts. She's now in her fifth month of treatment for pulmonary TB and looking well, but every time I visit her she complains of an ache. And every time I ask, the ache is somewhere different.

'Yes?' asks Peter.

'The pain. How is it?'

He speaks with her in Nuer. She gestures with her hands as she replies, and Peter asks another question. She then embarks on an animated monologue for several minutes; after a while I ask what she's saying. 'Not much,' replies Peter, and they continue. More questions and lengthy explanations follow, all in Nuer, and if the woman's facial expressions are anything to go by she's recounting something truly remarkable—what seems to be a journey of sorts, certainly something evoking a range of emotions. It's fascinating to watch, the people so delightfully expressive when they talk.

Peter turns to me when she's done. 'Yes,' he says. 'She does have aches.'

'What else did she say?'

'Not very much.'

'Anything?'

'No.'

'Hang on—you spoke for five minutes! She looked like she was giving you her life's story, Peter. She must have said something else important.'

'Not really,' he laughs. 'Because, she is just talking about things.'

'About the pain?'

'No. Not very much.'

This happens frequently. Particularly in Outpatients, health workers will have lengthy discussions with patients and summarise it all back to me in a sentence or two. Not that they're being lazy—I'm sure the patients digress, or explain concepts for which there is no direct translation, or perhaps the health workers don't know the right English word—but there's little doubt it leads to errors.

I look back at the woman. The confusion now ramps up a level. I ask Peter where the ache is. He asks her, and she points everywhere. He asks her something else, but she again points everywhere. He questions her gently and she raises her voice, and when he tries politely to interject she shouts at him.

'Because, this is the problem!' he laughs, rolling his eyes. 'She is never making sense. So many of these peoples, always, they point everywhere!'

She does seem to be favouring her left knee as she waves around, though, so I examine this. It seems normal. I examine her more generally but find nothing of note. I explain to her that nothing serious looks to be going on, and that we'll keep a close eye on her and in the meantime prescribe gentle painkillers. Peter relays this, and an argument ensues. The woman's unhappy. She shouts at Peter, but he just looks over at me and throws his hands in the air, and I can't help but laugh. The guy's over two metres tall—the hems of his surgical scrubs would dangle well over my feet, yet they hover well above his ankles—and of the most jovial, soft-natured disposition. To see someone scold him is quite unexpected.

'She giving you a hard time, Peter?' I ask.

'Because, she says we are not finished examining her yet,' he says. 'She is crazy. She says you have not listened to the knee.'

'*Listened* to it?'

He points to my stethoscope, dissolving into hysterics. 'Listened,' he hoots. 'She wants you to listen to the knee!' Between fits of laughter he explains that the previous doctor used to do this (I can only hope it was to appease the patient, rather than for any perceived medical reason), and Peter says that he's now been trying to tell the woman that it's pointless. We're clearly not getting anywhere, though, so I do it: I crouch down, place my stethoscope on her knee, and pray that no one walks in. And after a long moment I smile and give her the thumbs up, which pleases her no end.

Not all is as light-hearted in this little village. Peter and I continue through the huts—tin-roofed, poorly illuminated, wet-hot spaces— and by the end of the afternoon we've seen only half the patients. Most of them are recovering well from pulmonary TB and will go home cured, but many others won't. Like the paraplegic man with a twisted spine, for whom we can kill the TB bacilli in the bone but do nothing for the nerve damage—*if* it's TB that he's suffering from; or the elderly woman with the swollen belly, who may actually have cancer instead; or the handful of others in here with unclear diagnoses. So why then admit them? It's a difficult decision. Like many diseases here, TB can present in unusual ways, so treatment becomes a balance between committing someone to six months of potentially unnecessary therapy with powerful, side effect causing drugs, versus missing the only opportunity they may ever have for a cure—even if that possibility is small. And the patients are almost always desperate to try anything. It never ceases to amaze me when we tell someone about the therapy. 'You will need to live here,' we say. 'You will get free meals, free blankets and free tablets, but you must stay for the whole period.'

'But I have children.'

'They can stay as well.'

'And my wife?'

'She's welcome too.'

'Okay.'

No arguments. No debates. (Ignoring the young man who'd walked out for a night.)

It's a fascinating place, this little village, as if all the challenges of practising medicine in the developing world had been compressed into these dozen huts. For the kids, it's a thrilling rabbit warren of a playground; for the patients, their last ever hope. Many are touchingly grateful even though we do little more than give them medications and see them weekly; others complain about their persisting symptoms, or the heat, or the lack of space. In the corner of a hut, an eight-year-old girl has done up her family's dank little patch, placing a little throw rug—a piece of white plastic—on the dirt, sweeping it neatly with a bundle of sticks as we come past; in the opposite bed, an old man clambers up and spits lightly on my head, in what Peter assures me is a sign of respect. You can't possibly come through here and not be moved. And you can't come through here and not be humbled, having to tell people sorry, that the tablets should hopefully work, but if not there's little more we can do.

Sometime after I'd got home from Mavinga, a friend had asked me if aid workers had a 'God Complex'. If we thrived on the responsibility of life-and-death decisions, of being in control of such large numbers of patients and staff in difficult situations—a degree of responsibility we'd never have at home. If we delighted in being flown to places where we're ostensibly important, highly regarded and very much *needed*. Narcissists, even. To which, I'd said that some may. I can't speak for them. But if they do, then what I'd suggest they have, above and beyond a God Complex, is a complete lack of insight. Because walking around this village, as with everywhere I've worked,

I'm conversely overwhelmed by the scale of needs. And by my inability to do anything much lasting about it.

· · ·

Marina leaves in the fourth week, still no replacement surgeon found. Most of her patients are fortunately stable, and Thomas, the head surgical health worker, knows them well, as does Heidi, so managing the ward is relatively straightforward.

Then the acute cases begin arriving. No Roberto-like *clinicos* here, so Heidi and I take the smaller things to surgery—a few large abscesses, a badly broken arm (from an alleged police beating), and a partially amputated finger (from an accidental gun discharge)—and when a man arrives with appendicitis, we arrange a plane to fly him to the other MSF hospital with a surgeon. So far, so good. The lack of a surgeon here adds significantly to the workload, but I'd be lying if I said I didn't like the variety. Until a week later.

On a Sunday morning in late May, the victims of a gunfight are bundled in. Two of them this time. Both men, and both with significant limb injuries. Others were also injured at the scene, but they've since died. (My fears about having to deal with severe abdominal and chest injuries were partly allayed by Marina, who'd explained that nature does the triaging here; critical cases generally die en route, so if someone makes it to the hospital they're likely to be relatively stable. The mainstay of our treatment is the debriding, cleaning and dressing of wounds, rather than any complex surgery.)

The morning the two men arrive, I take them to theatre to clean up the wounds, then admit them for antibiotics and dressings. Again, so far so good, but things get suddenly more complicated when a third man is carried in—this time by the opposing clan. Word spreads quickly. Much commotion ensues as men from both clans gather outside our gates. Police arrive and our guards watch the wards, and

Thomas says there's no way this third patient can stay here. He's a security risk to everyone. Whatever his injuries, he needs to go. Zoe makes phone calls, and within hours a plane arrives to transfer him.

Three days later, a fourth man is carried in, a victim of the same fight. For reasons unknown he'd chosen to treat his wound at home, but the delay may cost him his life. His lower right leg has an extensive, gaping wound that's about fifteen centimetres long at the front, and that involves bone; shards of his tibia adhere to the dressings as I pull them off. The surrounding tissue has already become grey-green with gangrene, and he's showing signs of sepsis, or 'blood poisoning'. He urgently needs an amputation.

I call for a plane, but our airstrip is currently a kilometre-long puddle. There's no chance of a landing in this rain, no other transport options, so I pull out the surgical books and brush up on my anatomy, then take the patient to theatre with Heidi and one of the Sudanese assistants. There, I cut away large sections of green, putrid flesh, working around the shattered ends of his tibia and going as close to arteries as I can safely go. None of it will save his limb or cure his sepsis, though. By debriding this and giving fluids and antibiotics, I'm merely trying to buy time until the plane can land.

On day two he's worse. The plane still can't land, so we repeat the process—and hope desperately for a change in the weather.

On day three he goes into shock. The airstrip's fractionally drier but still not safe, so there's simply no choice: if we don't amputate, he'll die. His dozen companions on the ward don't see it that way, though.

'Three days,' says one of the men, standing a foot from me, a pair of sunglasses hiding his eyes. The smell of millet beer is strong on his breath and he's becoming agitated. 'Three days, and *still* this is not fixed!'

We're going in circles. Thomas has been speaking with them for half an hour, but the man, who's the patient's older brother, refuses permission for the amputation. The others crowd behind him and agree. I explain the options once more and Thomas translates, but voices are raised. Their decision remains. No amputation. 'He is a herder,' says Thomas, who's himself a tall, well-respected Nuer man. 'They say he cannot lose his leg. They say this is a hospital, and they want it fixed. I have explained this is not possible, but they do not believe it.'

I fetch gloves and take down the dressings, hoping the sight of the leg will convince them otherwise. The smell fills the room. A woman cries out, but the men are unswayed. 'Not acceptable,' says the brother. 'Look at all this! All this mess! We want it fixed. *Now.*'

Thomas speaks with him at length but the shouting starts up again. 'No way for an amputation, Doctor,' he says, looking flustered. 'No way. They will not allow it.'

It's an aspect of this place I'm growing to seriously dislike, this machismo, or bravado, or plain aggressiveness, or whatever it is. In as much as the people here are open and expressive in their warmth, it holds true for the opposite: if they're unhappy, they'll be sure to let you know. There's no holding back. Last week I was severely repri-manded by a man for draining his daughter's neck abscess, a quick, easy procedure, because I did it with only his wife's permission: I'd undermined his authority. And twice now I've been threatened; once by Gatwech, one of our Nutrition health workers, when I pulled him up for not attending teaching ('You ever tell me what to do again,' he'd stammered in a rage, 'and I will kill you!'); and on another occasion by the parents of a child who'd died on our ward, accusing me of giving the wrong medicines. Both were obviously empty threats— Joseph had reassured me as much at the time, and I'm still here—but I found them deeply unnerving. Expats have been evacuated follow-ing such incidents in the past. In the Somalia briefing, I was told that a threat means the end of your placement—or worse. So how then does one know which to take seriously, which to laugh off? Seems to me that it's a retrospective assessment: if you don't get hurt, they probably weren't serious.

What I'm struggling even more with, though, is this culture of gunfighting. I've tried my best to understand it. I finished that book about the Nuer and I appreciate the significance of cattle and the cultural factors behind these raids. But what I read, and what I see, are two different things.

What I read is that cattle are not merely a source of wealth. Rather, the Nuer's daily routines and seasonal migrations revolve entirely around the herd's needs, with the animals said to be utterly doted upon. Only rarely are they eaten, and almost every part or product derived from them is traditionally put to use—even urine for hair washing, and the ash of dung for teeth brushing. Men compose songs about their favourite beasts and are said to be able to recite the ancestry as if they were relatives, and there's a significant spiritual component to the animals, too, with beasts being dedicated to the ghosts and spirits of ancestors—becoming wandering shrines, in essence. It's an entirely cattle-centric view of the world, perhaps best summed up by the Nuer word for foreigners, *Jur*, which means 'entirely cattle-less'. Easy then to see why they'd risk death defending their herds.

What I see, though, when standing at the end of the victims' beds each morning, is petty squabbling among armed men, who're willing, despite decades of hardship, to risk not only their lives but also those of innocent bystanders—for animals. It's not my role as a foreigner, and particularly not as a health worker, to question such things. I know this; the practice has been going on for thousands of years, albeit without guns, and is part of the culture. Yet I do question it. More each day, as I review the consequences of it all on the ward.

Thomas turns back to me. The brother's adamant, he says. There can be no amputation.

I go to the office and try again for a plane, but they can't send it.

I talk to the surgeon in the other project, but all he can suggest is to get the patient out.

I feel ill.

We set up theatre, then carry him over. The clan follow and wait outside. I'm still not sure what I'm going to do. If we leave him, he'll die. If we amputate, there'll be consequences. I'll just have to try to trim away the spreading infection again.

We lie him on the table. Paul runs the generator. Gatluak, the surgical assistant, prepares the instruments, and Heidi draws up the anaesthetic. I scrub and don gloves and gown, and while I'm prepping his leg with iodine and musing aloud as to whether things could possibly get any worse, the question is answered with a resounding 'YES!' when Heidi gives the first dose of ketamine and his throat clamps and he stops breathing.

I drop the iodine and run to beside his head where Heidi's apologising furiously. She gave the right amount; this is a rare but known side effect. She hands me the laryngoscope to look down his airway and to try to secure it with a tube but a herd of wild horses couldn't pry open his mouth right now, it's clamped so tight and the oximeter beeps faster as his blood oxygen concentration drops and it's already below ninety per cent *Jesus* in a couple of minutes it'll be in his boots and he'll arrest and we'll have no chance of getting him back.

I can't ventilate him. I discard the laryngoscope *fuuuck there's no one to call for—*

Back to basics.

First principles.

A rubber bag and mask.

It's all we need to move air.

Nothing.

Like trying to blow hard through a blocked straw.

'Seventy per cent,' says Heidi. 'Oxygen is seventy.'

Christ.

Everything so slow.

Diazepam . . .

Diazepam has muscle-relaxing effects and we don't have any other drugs that could be of use right now so I ask Heidi to inject a couple of vials into him to relax the spasm in his throat and jaw, but I can still barely move air through his lungs—

'Oxygen's sixty per cent.'

—so we just empty more vials into him because the side effect of too much diazepam, to stop breathing, seems an ironic and irrelevant one at the moment, *Jesus what am I doing in this place,* this man's family are outside the theatre waiting for him to come out and I have no doubt in my mind that they'll lose *their* minds if I walk out and say that he just died but the good news is that the leg's still on, we didn't perform an amputation, and I inflate-deflate the rubber bag as hard as I can while the diazepam runs into his veins. His oxygen level is now so low that the machine's stopped trying to calculate it and I'll be honest that a part of my mind is trying to work out how we'll get to the boat from the operating theatre and downriver without going past the clan if we screw this up because I can't comprehend what those younger guys will do, because if Gatwech threatened me for merely pulling him up over a missed teaching session, then imagine what'll happen if this guy doesn't—

Air starts to move fractionally more easily.

'Sixty-five!' says Heidi.

I can feel the spasm in his throat relaxing.

'Seventy!'

His oxygen levels slowly come up . . . 'seventy-five' . . . and maybe we won't have to leg it for the boat after all . . . 'seventy-nine per cent . . . no, it's eighty-two per cent!' . . . I suspect that now we're out of the woods, and it's probably been only five minutes, this whole ordeal, but my scrubs are soaked with perspiration.

It becomes gradually easier to ventilate him. His levels climb to the nineties, which is where they stay. For the next hour Heidi and I stand with the rubber bag to assist his breathing as the drugs wear off, and we call Paul to set up the oxygen concentrator to help his breathing. There's clearly no way I'm going to be able to do anything about this leg now. We just re-dress the wound and fashion a new cast.

As the patient wakes up we move him back to the surgical ward. He seems to be okay. The family are oblivious to the near-disaster and actually quite happy with the look of his new cast, so I head to the office to call Loki again and upgrade the flight request from *Urgent* to *Get The Fucking Plane Here Yesterday* status because this has now become a security situation as much as anything else. And when I finally go to bed, I become transiently but deeply religious, more even than when I board these small planes out here, and pray that the airstrip isn't too muddy in the morning.

And, for reasons more selfish than I should admit, that he actually survives the night.

20. THE ASSASSIN

The rain holds off the next morning. It's still cloudy, but Paul checks the airstrip at dawn and thinks it'll be fine. We radio Loki. They send the plane, and I stare anxiously at the dark clouds brooding to the north, would blow them away if I could because the plane can still turn back, but they stay put and the flight lands safely. The patient and one relative are evacuated. A couple of hours later I phone the surgeon receiving him, and he agrees that the leg is beyond salvage. He's a Congolese man, though, so I can only hope that the family will respect a fellow African's opinion more. He'll let me know.

And we were lucky, it seems. In coming weeks rains of almost biblical proportions regularly batter the town, causing frequent flight cancellations (more cases need transfer but none are as urgent), although I do enjoy listening to the storms. Especially since moving into a bedroom in the old missionary house. I sleep better knowing the walls aren't water-soluble.

By mid-June the river's visible from our kitchen window, lapping not far from the top of the banks—the same banks on which our compound is built. The current is swift, sweeping clumps of water weeds silently west along the muddy surface, and the dugout canoes that ferry people and goods across it are now carried hundreds of metres downstream during just the short crossing. Beyond the far bank, what was until recently an endless expanse of dry land is now a large, shallow lagoon pooling alongside the river, its surface broken by a series of low islands and peninsulas on which lush grasses are already thriving. And all this is within just a month of the first rains. It's testimony to how completely flat this region is; although water levels in the Sudd's channels rise by only a metre and a half in the wet, even this small change will lead to a quadrupling in the size of swampland. Many Nuer will now move from the lowland cattle camps of the dry season to their higher, wet season villages, planting sorghum and maize in anticipation of an October harvest.

'Does it ever flood in here?' I ask Amos. It's the Tuesday of my ninth week. He's heaping plastic spoons of instant coffee into a mug, just beside me in the kitchen.

'It does,' he laughs, and he'd know. He's worked in these South Sudan projects for much of the last five years, returning home every few months to spend time with his family in Kenya. 'Sometimes, the water will come right in here. Right into the compound.'

'Seriously?'

'Oh yes! You will be living in those boots, my friend. Get used to them!'

I grab a biscuit and jump the low windowsill into the bats' room—one of two entrances to our main corridor—then head through and wait outside the shower for my turn, sitting on one of the large food storage containers. Paul soon comes around the corner, his pants muddied and face a little off-colour.

'Sick again, mate?'

He nods.

'Squirts?'

'Yeah.'

'Badly?'

He shrugs. 'Same as two weeks ago.'

'I hope that's mud on your pants, Paul.'

'Not that bad,' he smiles.

Either way, it seems that Nasir's Frequent Traveller Club is well and truly open for business this month, the *isle if la'trine* its exotic and only destination. Paul's looking gaunt, having lost a noticeable amount of weight since I arrived. Amos is sick again, too, and I've now shed a handful of kilograms since Mozambique. We still can't work out the source of all this. Amos is confident the water's good, and I doubt that the problem's coming from the hospital—Heidi's in there all the time and never gets sick, and neither does Carol. It must be the kitchen. Washing dishes outside is going to have to stop. Paul and I agree that one of us should spend an afternoon with the cook to see if she's washing her hands and where she's getting water from.

'I'll get that proper sink installed by the end of the week,' he says. 'I've been meaning to do it. Hey, you ever noticed that none of the women ever get sick? Zoe, Carol, Heidi, Maya—they always seem fine. You ever seen any of them ill?'

'Never, actually.'

'Seems a little weird, huh? I mean, we're all eating the same food, and—'

'She's trying to pick us off.'

'Huh?'

'The cook. She's trying to get rid of us, Paul. You, me and Amos. Anwar's gonna be next. Then Ben. You watch. She's trying to take us out, all the men.'

'Seems that way,' he smiles. 'Like an assassin, you reckon?'

Exactly. Not that she's necessarily causing the gastro—the multitude of flies and proximity of our dish rack to the latrine may have more to do with that, in fairness—but at the very least she's ensuring that we don't regain any weight. It's an objective that's accomplished using a series of unusual though apparently well-honed cooking techniques. Like the boiling of spaghetti, for example, to a paste that, when left to cool, moulds itself to a glutinous mass replicating the inner shape of the pot in its entirety, and that can only be pried from its crucible with a manoeuvre involving the sequential levering of a series of well-positioned spoons—not unlike removing a bike tyre from its rim. Or the frying of fresh meat into dark, mahogany-like pebbles, the ingestion of which harks back to a distressing childhood incident involving the accidental swallowing of a Lego block; or the transformation of freshly purchased Nile perch and its less palatable flatmate, the catfish, from appetising foodstuff into golden, oily goop. And then there's the accompaniments. Just last night: canned chick-peas, boiled eggs and a jar of curry sauce, all served cold.

Paul stares flatly out the nearby doorway, looking drawn. I ask him why all the mud on his pants; it's now just before seven, even by his standards a little early to have been working for long.

'Had to do some digging,' he says.

'For that new ward?'

'For a grave.'

I'd not expected that. 'For the young boy?' I ask.

'Yeah. Father's not around, so the mother asked us to help with the body. Said she couldn't carry it.'

'Sorry, mate.'

'Yeah.'

'The local guys couldn't do it?'

'I didn't want to put it off any longer,' he says. 'Not in this heat. He'd been lying in that back room all night, you know? I though it'd be better to just get it done.'

'I'm really sorry.'

'Yeah, well.'

The boy had been another far-too-late presentation to Nutrition, dying within minutes of arrival. His was our first death here for days. We're still seeing plenty of sick patients, but nothing compared with the sustained tragedy of those first weeks. Nineteen deaths had occurred in total that first month, but we'd found no obvious pattern, no consistent underlying cause. Nevertheless, MSF's regional medical coordinator is coming out from Loki in a couple of weeks anyway, to have a look at things.

Paul's still staring out the doorway. We stay quiet for a while, bathed in the grey light of an overcast morning. Some kids laugh beyond our fence. A bull bellows across the far bank, and in the background there's the gentle lapping of the river; a soft, ceaseless gurgling.

'The mother wouldn't let go of him,' he says, after a while. 'I dug the hole and stood there, just waiting. She couldn't let him go.'

'Jesus, mate. I'm sorry.'

'Yeah.'

'You okay?'

He says nothing. We sit quietly.

'They really don't know what to do, Paul. These mothers—it's really sad. They stay at home too long, inadvertently feeding the wrong things, giving bad water, then they see those quacks at the market that sell them aspirin or any old rubbish and they buy it because they think if they're paying it must be good. Then the traditional healer charges them a cow to make incisions or give herbs or remove a spell, and they pay it, and when it doesn't work they bundle them in here, three in the morning, on the verge of death when it's all too late.'

Paul says nothing.

'Mate, you okay?

A long silence.

'The sister,' he says, after a while. 'His little sister . . . she really clung on, too.'

He removes his hat and walks off to his bedroom, and I think: Nine months ago he was a successful businessman living with his wife; today, he buried a child. I wonder how he'll fare when he gets back. I wonder what he'll say at the office when people ask. And I wonder too what happens if you do this often enough, if you spend year after year in the field, repeatedly living its unbeatable highs and unrivalled lows. Does your emotional barometer simply reset itself? Is it irreversible? Is there a line you cross, beyond which a 'normal' life at home becomes impossible? When you *have* to return to the field, simply because you don't experience things to the same degree, for better or worse, back home? Like a Disaster Gypsy, maybe, just floating from one international crisis to the next . . .

I worry that that's where I'm headed.

. . .

More rain during the week, but not everyone is lamenting the mud. On the contrary. While adults grumble as they *schlurp*, skid and clog their way around town, kids are having a blast—and understandably so: several thousand tons of high quality, ultra-gooey, extremely mould-able play-dough has just presented itself for their unlimited use, and young imaginations aren't short of ideas. I discover this while heading past the TB village on Saturday morning, frantically called over by the kids.

'*Khawaja!*' a young girl shouts, and I wave back, heading past her to the ward.

'OI!' she yells, stomping her right foot—what appears to be a rebuke aimed my way. '*KHA! WA! JA!*' she calls again.

I've been told. I change course and veer towards them, a trip very much worth it. 'You built all this?' I ask, in reply to which muddy little hands clasp big white ones, and excitedly, breathlessly, give the *khawaja* a tour of their play area: the construction site of a replica Nuer village.

Football-sized *tukuls* have been styled from mud and clay—some remarkably detailed, others a little less convincing—and a group of boys are currently working on a thatched roof for one, trimming straw to length. And what good is any home, replica or otherwise, without a befitting entrance? None, of course—every six-year-old knows that!—so the larger *tukuls* have accordingly been given little stick doors, their twig 'beams' hitched side by side like the poles of a raft and bound together tightly with thread. Nearby, little mud people tend to their little mud animals, and transport options have even been provided by little cars with little straw axles and clay wheels that actually roll when pushed! The site is still very much a work in progress, though; lumpy foundations allude to forthcoming develop-ments, and the dozen-strong work crew are still in a flurry of activity. And *what* a work crew: ignoring that a few of the younger plaster-ers have arrived without uniforms (completely naked, in fact) and that madam foreperson is directing it all without shoes (but wearing a bright orange dress, although her young sister has sourced shoes—a pair of adult-sized gumboots that I suspect have been borrowed from the medical ward) they're as coordinated and efficient as any I've seen. It's just delightful. I consider taking the day off to join them. Many of these kids are the children of TB patients, although a couple are unwell themselves. Either way, they've all been in this hospital longer than me, and as far as they're concerned *they* own this place. I've come to know them all by greeting now (some prefer a high five, others a lift and a few just a hug, although a couple would please like to hold my hand), and today I'm expressly forbidden from heading to the wards until I've opened each of the doors, looked in every *tukul*, then tried all the cars.

· · ·

Outpatients closes at lunch. By now all the inpatients have been reviewed, and Thomas, Joseph and I have attended to a dislocated shoulder—a satisfying and easy fix. This may be as quiet as things get for a while.

'Market?' I ask Heidi, who's busy in Nutrition, but she needs no convincing. She pries Breast Man from her hip and grabs a radio, and like a comet we're out the front gate, stopping for no man, our tail a dozen kids trailing us from the unit. They follow us out the gate but we redirect them to their mothers, then squelch our way east along the riverbank for this, our twice-weekly exercise session and part cultural tour of Nasir . . .

First point of interest is the small brick church to our left, where the missionaries who'd arrived a century ago gave their sermons, inadvertently becoming advanced students of linguistics as they struggled to get a handle on this previously unwritten language—a language in which gender-specific pronouns such as *he, she,* and *it* are represented by a single form (accounting for such honest mistakes by our staff as, 'Him, with the pregnancy pains'), and in which the same word can have completely opposite meanings depending only on the tone used. There's an interesting aside to the church, too; in a smaller mud chapel not far from here, a British aid worker controversially married the leader of the rebel Nasir SPLA group in 1991 ('The Warlord's Wife', the media called her), subsequently staying on to live in his *tukul* until she was killed in a car accident.

We continue up the bank. Thick clouds, heavy humidity—there'll surely be another storm tonight—and Heidi averts her eyes from the group of young men washing on the edges. A minute later I avert mine as we pass the women's bathing section, then we both avert everything as three men in baggy fatigues pass us with AK47s slung over their shoulders. Better not to make any eye contact, I'd think.

Ahead of us is the crashed plane, bold tufts of grass bursting from its broken cockpit windows, its right wing being bounced by children. Not far from it, a fishing crew are at work: two men in underwear, casting small throw nets from the shallows; beside them, a handful of empty dugouts are tethered to a tree. We pass them and head further along, towards the fish market, but before reaching it we cut across a large muddy clearing to the main market. And here, I'm again distracted by a group of men brushing past wearing their open shirts and dark glasses, all with rifles over their shoulders. One of them points to the camera slung over my shoulder and makes a menacing gesture even though I'm clearly not photographing anything; I don't argue the point, just take it off and place it into Heidi's hip bag.

'Coke?' we ask an elderly shopkeeper. He's one of the few lighter-skinned Arabs in town and dressed in a long white *jallabiya*, and he runs one of the handful of little tea shops clustered at the market's periphery. He nods and puts out two plastic chairs beside a small table for us, then pulls two bottles from the rusty chest freezer inside. A small generator sputters nearby, powering his and other stalls, and as I put my feet on the corner of Heidi's chair and look around, I think: this could almost be a normal town. Teapots whistle on top of coals, just across the track. People stream through the dirt laneways, browsing the same variations of goods seen laid out in wooden stalls all over this continent—batteries, radios, donated clothes and newer knock-offs; foodstuffs in sacks, bags or cans; combs, mirrors and unstrung beads in every conceivable colour, and dozens of other items. Ahead of us, a few of those bike-taxis sledge their way unsteadily through the mud, and to our left the driver's seat of an old truck has been fixed to a wood pallet, placed before a lopsided counter that's bearing a straight-blade razor, scissors and small mirror—the barber's shop. And beneath a large tree to our right, a game of dominoes is attract-ing a small crowd of men around a table. Breaking any illusions of normality, though, rifles rest casually beside them.

'You hear the carrying-on in that *tukul* last night?' I ask Heidi, and she laughs. She says she didn't, but that she suspects she knows who it was. I'm still discovering all of this, because never mind love triangles—what's going on here resembles more of a large, misshapen polyhedron. Unlike in Mavinga, volunteers from the South Sudan projects tend to meet often enough during briefings, evacuations or holidays, passing each time through Loki and often being delayed, to create a bit of a dating scene. As weeks go on, details of any relationships at home become hazier, and a What Happens On Mission Stays On Mission attitude seems the rule.

Heidi looks up suddenly. 'Shit—do you think we're both going to end up with MSF'ers? Or *marrying* MSF'ers?'

I laugh. It's not unlikely. That, or another field worker, or a national staff member. We ponder this as we hand the shopkeeper a few Sudanese pounds, and I think of that recent night when the girl died, how Heidi had known exactly what the trouble was. It'd be far easier to be with someone who's worked in these places before. 'But that means *twice* the baggage in one relationship, Heidi!' I laugh. 'Can you imagine? Twice the maladjustment, twice the strong personality type, and twice the eccentricities from being isolated in these places for too long'—and I tell her about Maurice.

The mother of a former patient recognises us as we pass down a side track, calling for us to join her where she's making *injera* flatbread on a small cooker on the ground. There are no chairs, so she puts out cardboard for us to sit on, then shouts for others to join us and directs the older daughter to prepare the *injera*. A few of the younger kids climb onto Heidi's lap and a small crowd gathers, and as I watch the cook I sense another bout of gastro looming. Her muddy little hands marry grey-brown sorghum with turbid water in a metal bowl. Next, a stick frenziedly whisks the mixture as her bright eyes dart proudly between it and the unusual customers. The batter is then poured into an oiled pan and the pancake-like bread smokes; and, not long after, we *khawajas* smile warmly but apprehensively as the chef's assistants—the kids on Heidi's lap—break up the bread and hand it to us, watching as we chew the first pieces.

'Lovely!' we say, 'Very nice!' which only leads to a repeat of the whole process. This time though the batch is wrapped up for us as takeaway, but we're not yet done—the teapot is on, and it too is filled with turbid water. More kids come, more of the woman's friends gather, and people chat in a language of which I know less than a dozen words so we all mime and laugh, and it's moments like this when I'm utterly at peace, thrilled to have had these opportunities. Two cultures that in many ways couldn't be less alike, yet here we are . . .

After tea we thank our hosts and pack the takeaway, and as we stand up to go I realise I may have thought all this too soon. Another group of armed men passes. Three this time, scowling, no uniforms but with AK47s strapped across a shoulder, and as they look over I both cringe with unease and seethe with anger. They're like belligerent teenagers with something to prove, these guys, answering to no one and acting up—albeit with guns. *And right beside the kids!* Have they not had enough? After thirty-nine years of war, wouldn't they just have flung their guns into the river at the first opportunity? Yelled, '*Ha! We're done! We survived! Take these shitty things back!*'

This moment sums the place up for me. Gorgeous kids, capable of anything given a chance; armed men, threatening again to ruin it all. After two months here, all I can conclude is that this place is a sad contradiction. Either bone dry, or flooded; at war with its neighbours, or more so with itself; filled with happy kids, but so often they die; and watched over by the international might of the UN, yet they can do nothing to intervene in the clan violence. The town was even born of paradox, founded when an Arab slave trader was commissioned by the British to lead their *anti-slaving* efforts here; an inauspicious beginning if ever there was one, and it still bears his name.

But what I struggle to understand most is this: that life is so precious here; that these people battle to coax an existence from this severe land, to raise their kids, to carry a sick relative for days to a hospital and then sit by their side for weeks; yet life is equally so cheap. Disregarded during a cattle raid, valued secondary to a clan's honour, and constantly threatened by these armed men—even if the majority of people would rather get on with things.

The drain on our project's resources due to violence is dispropor-tionately large. Flights are frequently chartered, or diverted, to transfer the wounded at a cost of thousands of dollars each time (normally only two of the four projects have a surgeon). Worse, transfers are sometimes made for security reasons rather than medical, purely to keep rival clan members separate.

And what we could otherwise do with this money: educate women about nutrition and hygiene, so that the kids we discharge from Nutrition don't bounce back in an even worse state because of poor feeding practices, as a percentage invariably do. We could run an HIV education program, because preventing the infection of someone like Elizabeth is surely more efficient than providing anti-retrovirals for two, three or five years, or however long until we hand this project over. We could teach women about family planning and provide the services, because preventing unwanted births makes more sense than re-feeding a child who's malnourished only because he's the eighth son, born unplanned to parents who struggle to feed their seven other kids anyway. We could train health workers like Joseph, put them through a full-time course so the hospital doesn't rely so heavily, and so unsustainably, on expat staff, because there's no doubt that if we left tomorrow the project would quickly fall in a heap.

These aren't original thoughts I'm having here. Not by any means. I've heard them before, thrown around dinner tables in Mozam-bique, Angola, or in European offices, and I wonder now how many thousands of other volunteers and professionals have stood in these same places, pondering exactly the same things, in decades gone by. Or how many more will do so in the years to come. I wonder as well what impetus there is for any of these governments to step up and treat their own cholera patients, or to respond to their own floods, or staff their own hospitals properly, or to do much of anything, when

they know well that we'll simply rush back at the drop of a hat, with
no strings att—

Heidi's giggling. I'm ranting, she says. 'So cynical, Dennis! My
God! How on earth did you come to be so full of shit?'

I laugh. She's right; I am ranting. And largely pointlessly. Whether
we should be here is something I don't question. This place is not just
rebuilding itself, in many ways it's starting from scratch. And while
infrastructure and services are being put into place, and an entire
generation of people are educated, we *should* be providing a safety net
of health care. This I don't question. So I'm clearly going to have to
get over my frustrations if I'm to keep working with this organisation,
because this is exactly what they do, and what emergency intervention
is. They bite off only what they can chew—which here means running
four major hospitals and a dozen outreach sites, keeping an emergency team on stand-by, employing forty expats and four hundred
and fifty locals, and allocating six million euros to cover it each year.
By any standards it's impressive—and ambitious. No less given the
logistic and security constraints.

Heidi and I head back across the mud. The sky's darkening. Over
my shoulder I can see the black rotors of the UN helicopter through
their fence; ahead, a young boy leads an elderly blind man across the
field, each of them clutching opposite ends of a stick—the sum total
of sight aids in such places. And cutting across our path, another man
with a gun. Everywhere, these fucking guns.

• • •

Joseph's on the ward when we return. 'One very big problems and
four admissions,' he says.

We get straight into it.

First, two kids with a cough. We'll see them last.

Next, a young boy bitten by a snake two weeks ago, and whose hand is black and already dead. We'll fly him out for an amputation.

Next, a teenage boy, screaming in the yard. 'Crazy,' says Joseph, who knows him well. 'Always, he is shouting.' The boy's hands are tethered together with a coarse rope, the father holding one end. He's normally tied to a long lead at home, explains Joseph, but last year he'd freed himself and wandered into a neighbouring village and was stabbed (out of malice or mistaken identity, who could know). I'd object that this is inhumane, that the calluses and cuts from the binds are unacceptable, but what'd be the point? I've seen this before. I saw it in Mozambique, in a village we'd visited. What else can the families do? What mental health teams can they access?

The father looks worn. He says the boy's been distressed for days. Neither of them have slept. We sedate the boy with an intramuscular antipsychotic and take him to the side room near theatre; I'll reassess him when he wakes.

Next: the one very big problems.

Joseph leads me to the little isolation room where Nyawech, the HIV-positive woman with Kala-azar, is sleeping. He crouches down and retrieves an old Plumpy'nut carton from beneath her bed, opens the lid to show me the contents. Inside is a sizeable collection of pills— all of her medications for the last two weeks, at least.

We wake Nyawech. She rolls over, weak and red-eyed, and shoos us away with a flick of her wrist. Joseph speaks with her but she doesn't reply, just rolls further away. Joseph taps her shoulder but she ignores him. Nyawech's mother is sitting on the end of her bed, cross-legged on a corner of their blanket, and she now leans forward and slaps Nyawech.

Nyawech cries. She turns back towards us, mewling unsettlingly. We ask her what she's doing, why she's stopped the tablets.

Go away, she says.

Joseph explains to her that she'll die without treatment.

Go away, she yells.

'But Nyawech, what about your children?'

She sobs.

'Nyawech, why are you doing this? Are the tablets making you worse?'

No answer.

Nyawech has had enough, I suspect. Two relapses and a dead husband. She doesn't want this anymore.

Joseph speaks with her for a while and Nyawech glowers, her face a sad picture of rage although her body is feeble and wasted. The mother becomes furious. She gets up and slaps Nyawech around the torso and head, slaps her hard, and she shouts at Joseph. Joseph then steps out and calls a handful of the other health workers to the bedside, and under the mother's direction they grab Nyawech's bony limbs and restrain her. The mother pries Nyawech's mouth open and these two women yell at each other with eyes wide, shrieking with all the anger and bitterness of this shared tragedy, and Joseph selects an evening's dosage from the box and places them into her mouth. Nyawech spits and chokes as the mother holds her mouth closed, it's an unsettling sight, this woman who two months ago was tall and graceful as she strolled the compound with Breast Man, now a gagging skeleton with no shred of dignity because look at what we're doing. So I turn my back and leave. This isn't my culture. It's not my place to interfere, and the longer I stay here the more confused I become.

Later I return to check on the crazy boy with the rope handcuffs, but he's gone. His father already carried him home. Presumably he'd got the brief respite he sought.

21. CATFISH AND COW DUNG

I'm a shoo-in for June's 'Slimmer of the Month' award in the Assassin's weight-loss classes. Despite strong competition from others in the team, I've maintained my months-old head start. Paul is out (he left a few days ago and is currently heading back to New Zealand), although Heidi's made a late bid, and Amos remains a solid favourite with the bookies. I'm meanwhile sneaking the odd sachet of Plumpy'nut to boost my weight, and my breath-holding capacity rivals that of a world-champion free diver: the little latrine doesn't bother me much anymore. That said, this constant gastro is wearing me out.

Now midway through my eleventh week back, and another swollen sky greys the town. Heavy rains this morning have so far kept patients away but it's no reprieve for the Outpatients health workers. It just means that this afternoon will be twice as busy. The five of them are on the outside benches when I pass, listening to a radio—a blue, dynamo-powered plastic handset with a crank handle, the type given out in camps—and they call me over to talk, but we're promptly distracted by the sight of a young boy who's squealing loudly as he sprints past. His arms and legs pump frantically as his little body hurtles across the soggy compound; 'KHAWAJAAAAA!' he yells as he whips past—plea for assistance or merely an observation, I can't tell—and squeal becomes shriek as he turns to look back over his shoulder. There's trouble: not far behind him, a posse of a half-dozen other children are in hot pursuit, and the gap is closing fast.

The little boy tears past the nutrition centre. He weaves between bystanders and hurdles a low lump of mud that's maybe a half-foot high, just clearing it (he'd be about three years old), then makes a risky move: he disappears into the crowd of people collecting water from the taps outside the surgical ward. It works. The posse are thrown. They disband as they momentarily lose sight of him. Kids fan out around the crowd—a classic pincer movement, two at the front, a couple on either flank and one penetrating the fray—but not long afterwards the boy reappears on the far side. He doubles back in a broad loop around the surgical ward, having regained his lead, and still holding in his right hand the cause of all this and what must by now be the last of such items remaining in Nasir: a half-inflated rubber balloon. It's the remnant of a fascinating recent incident here in the hospital, and one which confirmed to Heidi and me the importance of that old adage, *You don't give one and not the other.*

These South-East Sudan Balloon Wars began late last week, following the unexpected death of a child in the feeding centre. Heidi, distressed by the loss of another patient she'd spent so much time with, tried to lift the mood by arranging activities for the kids in the centre and distributing the small stash of balloons she'd brought from home. The intention was good, the time spent inflating balloons nothing short of noble, but the gesture quickly backfired: within hours, every other kid in the hospital, outside the hospital, and throughout what seemed to be the entire region who didn't get one wanted one. What followed was unexpected.

In scenes reminiscent of the upheaval caused by that single glass bottle in *The Gods Must Be Crazy*, kids quickly turned against one another. Compound yard squabbles took place, interspersed with high speed chases or extended periods of hiding by some in an attempt to hang on to the precious bounty. During ward rounds, children could be seen peering under beds, opening doors and combing every corner for a balloon, and the behaviour continued like this for several days until all balloons had seemingly been accounted for: either burst, lost or stolen, at which time calm once again descended—on the paediatric population of this town, anyway. So, run hard, little man! God knows how you hid that balloon for an entire week, but hang on to it! *Run like the wind!*

• • •

Joseph's examining a patient when I enter the ward.

'Any news about the new woman?' I ask.

He finishes what he's doing and looks up. 'Not yet. The families is still making problems.'

We walk to the far corner, where Carol's crouched beside a new patient, a pale, quiet twenty-something woman. The patient's brother is standing on the opposite side of her bed with a handful of other men. I ask how she's doing.

'Weak,' Carol says. 'Very weak.'

'Has the brother decided?' I ask.

She shakes her head, looking flat. 'He's still refusing.'

'He won't even let us screen for a transfusion?'

Carol shrugs. 'What can I do? I have told them everything. They know how serious this is.'

The woman was carried in just hours ago, having gone into premature labour during the night. But rather than delivering a foetus, she's been passing numerous small cysts, the consequence of a molar pregnancy—a rare, unviable type of pregnancy where clumps of poorly formed embryonic tissues develop instead of a baby. She bled heavily at the time and her haemoglobin has fallen to forty—three times the lower limit of normal, a life-threateningly low value—and she's still bleeding. She urgently needs a blood transfusion and the removal of the remaining tissue in theatre, both being straightforward procedures that would fix the problem. But the brother is refusing both. Why? He won't say. As for what she wants? She can't say. The men have forbidden her from speaking.

In anticipation of a transfusion, we've screened a few staff members for compatibility (as usual we have no spare stocks in the fridge—people generally won't donate unless it's for a close family member) but haven't yet found a match. The brother has refused to give blood or allow his companions to do so, but the situation's becoming critical. We ask again.

'No,' they say.

'What if we just try among the staff once more?' I ask. 'Would you be happy for one of us to give a unit?'

Joseph translates, but the brother looks uneasy. No one is to do anything until the husband arrives, he says.

'But where is he?'

They're not sure. But someone is out looking for him, he says, so not to worry.

The morning wears on and I become more impatient. She's bleeding to death. Theatre is set up and ready to go and I could have performed the procedure a dozen times by lunch, but the men continue to forbid us from doing anything.

I try to explain the situation again. I explain it patiently, and simply, but they say no. I explain it with a little more urgency, and they say no. I ask them to step outside, and I tell them bluntly that they're going to be responsible for her death. 'Do you understand that?' I ask. 'She will die while you just stand here wasting her time. It's that simple.'

The brother remains adamant, if nervous. Not until the husband is here, he says. Only he can decide.

'And the woman? What if we get her consent?'

'No,' he says. 'It is for the husband. Only he will decide.'

Meanwhile, here she lies, seeping away into a sheet.

I try to get on with the day. I take a few minor cases to theatre—abscesses, wounds, all small things—and make my way through the rest of the ward, then the Kala-azar tents. Sometime mid-afternoon I get called back to the medical ward: the husband is here. I run over. The man's tall, six-foot five at least, wearing dark glasses, nice business shoes and a pair of silk pyjamas, top and bottoms, and his expression suggests he's very serious.

Joseph, Carol and I go through the situation with him. We explain what we need to do and how simple it will be, and what will happen if we do nothing.

'No,' he says.

I couldn't possibly have heard right. Joseph speaks with him again at length.

'No.'

'But do you understand that if we don't do this, she is going to *die*?'

He again refuses.

My heart thumps. Maybe they're misunderstanding me. I talk with Joseph and he again translates, but the husband reiterates his answer. The brother and four other men stand behind him.

Fuck them, I think, and ask the woman what she wants. Why should the men have a say in this at all? I crouch beside her where she's lying on her back in a long green dress, covered by a sheet that Carol changed not long ago because the previous one was bloodstained. Her eyes are too white—dangerously anaemic—and she's too weak to reposition herself. She looks away from me and up at her husband as I speak, abdicating all decision-making as she puts her life in the hands of this man, and I wonder if she's more scared of speaking against him than of just bleeding to death on this mattress. I watch them both. He regards her for a moment. They don't touch, and he doesn't speak with her. He looks irritatedly back at me.

'I've said *no*.'

Jesus, maybe it's me? Maybe I'm explaining it all very badly. Maybe it's my manner; I'm being too forceful, I look too young. I leave Carol to speak with him in private for a few minutes, hoping he'll be more persuaded by an older person's take on this. But she walks out a few minutes later and tells me again, No.

I call Thomas from the other ward to try. Thomas is used to consenting patients for surgery. He knows the ins and outs of theatre far better than Joseph so maybe he can explain it better, spin it and deal with whatever misconceptions the rest of us may be oblivious to. But the husband again says no.

Why?

'He is giving no reason,' says Thomas. 'Just, "No".'

I try bargaining with him. I ask him if he'll allow only the transfusion for now; he can decide later about whether to allow me to do the curettage. I offer to show him the theatre and the instruments we'll use, but as calmly as if declining an offer for coffee, he again says no.

Christ! This makes no sense! My hands begin shaking and I lose any self-restraint and step closer, and I find myself shouting with pointed finger that he's about to murder his own wife, and I wonder if maybe she's brought shame on him or frightened him for having borne this unsightly complication instead of a healthy child, because bearing children is a woman's most important role out here—no marriage is complete until the woman has had at least two children for her husband—but I couldn't give a damn about cultural considerations at this moment because hers is one life we can actually *save*.

I ask Joseph to tell him that she's going to die soon because of his decision and that we can't just stand here and watch it happen, so the husband has three options. One, we take her to theatre and fix this; two, we just give her the blood, *Christ*—our blood if he wants; or three, we do as he says and don't treat her, but in that case he's to stay beside her all day on this ward. He's to sit here and attend to her, and he must watch the consequences of his decision play out. He doesn't get to walk away. Not from this. Not from his wife.

The ward is silent. I'm trembling. The man glares and I'm hot-wet with nerves. Joseph's unsure of what he should translate but I tell him all of it, every word, this man is to understand the gravity of his decision, and in this moment I feel more anger towards a person than I've known before. I hate this man and what he represents; what these women, these children and so many other men have to put up with because of people like him, the *strongman*, the self-righteous minority of men who impose their wills on the rest. The Administrator in Mavinga, the gunslingers in our market, the bombers in Somalia, the post-election gangs in Kenya—the mentality is just the same.

The woman lies quietly. My eyes meet hers and I don't know if I'm more heartbroken for her or outraged with him.

'He will takes her home,' says Joseph. 'He says if she dies, that is God choosing. Not him.'

A wave of heat runs through me. *Jesus Christ*, I want to grab the man, I've not ever lost it like this before and I step closer and point angrily at him and raise my voice and I couldn't give a fuck right now if he or his posse threaten me. 'Make it *very* clear to him that God's got nothing to do with this, Joseph. If she dies at home, it's the husband's doing—*he's* doing this. He's responsible.'

The men talk for a moment. The husband pauses. He puts on his sunglasses, and his shoulders relax. He talks with Joseph more softly now, and I ask him what they're saying.

Joseph shakes his head and speaks quietly. 'He is wanting to borrowing something,' he says. 'Something to carry her in. He wants us to gives him a sheet, so he can carry her home.'

I'm speechless.

Carol walks out.

Joseph gets a sheet.

And the husband just waits, looking as unfazed as when he'd first walked in, still in his business shoes and patterned silk pyjamas.

A ridiculous-looking prick.

• • •

The sky's unchanged when I step outside—heavy, gloomy—but my watch tells me it's evening. I'd like to keep walking; past the compound, the fuck out of town and away from this entire volunteering thing, try to remember why I wanted so much to do this work in the first place.

Amos is at the outside table when I return to the compound. Today's the birthday of Maya, the office assistant, and Amos is opening a box of cask wine, wrestling the plastic tap through the little cardboard door. A moment later he fills an old coffee mug and swirls it under his nose, inhaling deeply like a sommelier. '*Yessss!*' he laughs. 'Very nice!'

'That good boxed wine, Amos?' I ask. 'You look very impressed.'

'My friend,' he says, a smile igniting his face, 'in Africa we say that a lion that cannot find meat, he must sometimes eat grass to survive!' He throws his head back and laughs—that big, deep, African belly-laugh the way that only they can do—then offers me a glass.

The rest of the team gather around the table, about a quarter of our stock of candles providing mood lighting. The bugs fling themselves at us and the cask wine flows, and the Ethiopian beers are chilled; not a bad evening. On top of it all, I'll be out of here in thirty-six hours, off for my scheduled break.

I go to bed early. Just before dawn I'm called to attend a breech delivery with Carol, seeing in the new day by repairing an episiotomy by the light of my headlamp. Afterwards, I steal another hour of rest—a fitful, sweaty, uneasy sleep—and when I get up the clouds have broken for the first time in days, and two new patients have arrived: a gasping infant and a comatose young girl. We do what we can. The infant hangs in there, but the girl's serious.

'Meningitis,' I tell the worried-looking parents. Her neck is arched, her back as stiff as concrete.

'Is it serious?' they ask.

'Very. I'm sorry.'

We start treatment for the girl just as Mark, The Professor, walks in. He's usually quite the clown on the wards but today looks solemn, and he says I must come to isolation. I follow him to the little room, to the corner where Nyawech lies.

She's dead.

I go over to the bed. Breast Man is next to me. The child clearly doesn't know, or doesn't understand; he wants me to pick him up and throw him, and while I listen in vain for his mother's heartbeat, he sits on my hip, clinging to my T-shirt with all the dexterity of a little monkey. I wonder where his sisters are. 'There's not a father, is there?' I ask Mark.

'No,' says Mark. 'He is dead. But the grandmother is coming back soon. She can maybe look after them, Doctor.'

Three more kids orphaned by HIV/AIDS. Three more to add to Africa's growing generation of them.

We pull Nyawech's blanket up, over her face, but she's too tall. Her feet peer out. I cover them with a separate piece of clothing. The paraplegic woman in the corner drags herself over to see, and she shakes her head, and Elizabeth looks from around the corner, and she begins to cry. The two had become friends. They've lived together in here for months.

But Breast Man's still oblivious.

I tell Mark that I'll be back soon. I'm just going to have a quick drink, I say, because I need to get some air, wash my face, fucking *breathe* a little, but an irritated young man yells to me as I step past.

'Hey!' he says, lying bare-chested on his bed. 'I'm not any better!' He points to his IV. 'This thing does nothing. I want to go home.'

He arrived yesterday, and he already seems a lot better to me. I pick up his notes and show him that his fever's down. Mark explains this to him.

'I get no attention here!' he says. 'I want to go home!'

We explain that fluids and antibiotics are running constantly via the IV, but he becomes more agitated. 'Take this out,' he says, gesturing at his IV. 'I've had enough. You are doing nothing for me.'

Mark talks with him, but the man still wants to go. 'Take it! I've had enough!'

So I pull his IV out. Right here. I slap a piece of gauze on it, don't even bother with the tape. 'Go home then.'

Fuck off. I've also had enough.

I storm across the yard and into the living compound but I can't find Heidi. Zoe's going through paperwork on the outside table. I tell her I need to talk as I take a cigarette from the box in front of her and pull up a seat.

'I'm losing it,' I say to her.

'Huh?'

I tell her about Nyawech's death and having just kicked that guy out, and that I'm not dealing with this stuff like I should.

She shakes her head. 'Are you serious, Damien? Jesus, how do you think you should be dealing with all this? It looks to me like you're doing well under the circumstances. Don't you start beating yourself up, too. This is a tough place, and you've had a bad run—*and* we're down a surgeon. MSF don't give us more holidays here than most other missions for no reason, you know. And you're off when—tomorrow? Honestly, I was the same as you before my last holidays.'

It's not just fatigue, I tell her. I fill her in on my conversation with that woman's husband yesterday, the one who'd refused treatment, and explain that I'm losing my patience with people. I can't help but wonder if the outcomes would've been different if I'd handled these cases better. 'It's hardly the ideal work manner for a doctor, Zoe. I know I should be the last person to judge these people. We're guests here, I get that, and I know I shouldn't take this stuff to heart all the time and expect that they ought to act like I would. I mean, aren't we *humanitarians* supposed to be these unconditionally compassionate, caring people?'

She smiles slightly. 'Ideally.'

We talk for another hour. Daytime confessionals, beneath the berry-eating birds that shit constantly from the big tree above. I hunch in my chair and admit to her that I'm scared, that these guns and increasing clan movements frankly worry me; two of the other projects have been partially evacuated this week. I tell her that I'm tired from all the on-call, from the bouts of diarrhoea and the constantly broken sleep, and that I suspect I'm going to make a major mistake—security-wise, or with the management of a patient: either would be disastrous. And on top of it all, I confess that I'm losing my desire to be here, to do this work, or to even care about anyone else anymore. Compassion Fatigue, indeed. What a pathetic term.

Zoe listens quietly.

I ask her what the end-point of all this is. Do we all spend the rest of our lives flying around, trying to visit these thousands of impoverished towns, spreading ourselves so thin as to be almost useless at times? And at what personal cost? And why should this be my battle, anyway? Wouldn't the more sensible thing be to get on with life at home, to at least take full advantage of the opportunities that *I've* been given? Why then this burden of white middle-class guilt we all seem to have?

Zoe's silent. I look up, watch the birds quietly.

'I'm not sure I'm the right person for this anymore, Zoe,' I tell her.

'I disagree. But what are you saying?'

'I've been away for six months already, and I've got six more in Sudan. I can't do it. Two to three months is all I've got left. I'm really sorry. Please ask them to start finding a replacement.'

· · ·

My last day before holidays passes quickly. A fill-in doctor will fly in tomorrow to cover for me, but there's a ton of loose ends to tie up.

Joseph and I review all the medical patients once more; the new infant who'd arrived gasping this morning is looking much better, managing to breastfeed a little, but the girl with meningitis is as rigid as a pole, still unconscious.

I visit the TB village with Peter, who, incidentally, is getting an office renovation, and by a work crew unlike any I've seen. Four Nuer women are delicately patting handfuls of mud and chopped straw onto the wall frame—two mud-patters and two mud-mixers, all in dresses—and they're only too delighted to pose for a photo. After-wards, Peter and I pass through all the TB *tukuls*, following which he lodges a request for annual leave.

'What? *Tomorrow*?'

'Yes!' he says.

'Really, Peter? *Tomorrow*?'

'Yes. Because, after from today.'

'But why are you only asking me now?'

'Because my brother, he is only telling me the other day he is getting married again, next weekend.'

'He only told you the other *day*?'

'Yes!' he laughs.

'So can't you hold off until that weekend then? It's going to be impossible to get one of the other health workers to replace you by tomorrow, no?'

'Maybe,' he chuckles.

'And you're a hard man to replace, Peter. No one knows what's going on in this place more than you.'

'This is true!'

'I know it is. You've got a monopoly on it.'

He laughs as I explain the term, clasping my hand in his. 'But, I do needs tomorrow for holidays, Doctor. Really.'

'Why?'

'Because, we needs to get the cattle.'

'Cattle?'

'Yes.'

'Why *cattle*?'

'For the bride,' he states matter-of-factly. 'We needs to give cattle for the bride,' he says, as if it were the most normal reason in the world for a day off.

(And I suppose it may well be out here.)

After the TB village I head through the surgical wards with Thomas, where I find myself reprimanding two young men, each fixed to traction devices, for smoking in bed. In fairness they can't get up and go outside—not for the next few weeks, in fact—but come on: this is a hospital! 'For every other cigarette you light in here,' I stir the pair, 'we'll add another brick to that rope. Deal? And if you start drinking, the traction goes on the other leg as well. Then the arms. *Both* arms. And then you'll be really stuck. Okay?' I mime what they'd look like with all four limbs weighed down and they laugh, their young faces lighting up and those gaps between their teeth smiling through. They're lean, good-looking guys—just a pair of cheeky teenagers, it strikes me. Teenagers that were recently out shooting, and being shot at, on the weekend.

Evening falls and the sky remains clear. I head to our compound and throw the Frisbee with Heidi, then take a last walk around the hospital before dark. It's now a different beast. Kids run around in the cooler air, while adults lean against the outside walls or squat in the yard, chatting, smoking, laughing and spitting as they habitually do here. Two of the night workers are also sitting outside—*reclining in chairs!*—but hey: it *is* a killer sunset. And mothers are now gathered around fires behind the feeding centre, boiling pots of water and stirring meals as their kids smear the evening packets of Plumpy'nut over T-shirts and cheeks.

And then, once more before my holidays, I stick my head over our grass fence. The river's lapping only metres away; behind it, a full moon's rising into an orange-pink horizon, reflecting off the water that's on its way to join the Nile somewhere, and clouds of smoke drift from the cattle herders' fires on the far bank. It's stupendously beautiful. I stand and soak it all in, but there's a tap on my leg.

'*Malé, khawaja,*' says a voice. Hello, White Man.

I look down. It's the little boy from our TB treatment village, still naked but for his strings of red and white beads. He'd be only three but he still always greets me like a gentleman, oh-so formally, talking softly in Nuer as he extends his hand to shake mine. I wish I could speak his language. He looks like he'd discuss something very adult with me; the weather, perhaps, or maybe the cattle he'll inherit one day.

He raises his hands.

'Throw?' I ask.

He nods enthusiastically.

'Just one, okay?' I lift a single finger to clarify.

He shakes his head, puts up three fingers.

I put up two.

He ponders this for a moment, a businessman considering a counter-offer. He tilts his head, and I notice that his haircut is the same as when I'd first met him months before—shaved, with just a square tuft of hair left at the front. It's a popular style for the young boys here, and I remember reading in one of the Lost Boys' memoirs that this tuft had been likened to a handle: a handle with which God could pull the children up to heaven, the writer had said, because God was taking so many of them in those days.

The little boy taps my leg again. He nods, raising two fingers. We shake on it, so I do—I throw him twice; and when we're done, I hold him up to see over the fence, where a group of children are yelling excitedly on the riverbank. They've just caught a large catfish in a nylon throw-net and they're slipping breathlessly on the mud as it flaps and squirms, grasping at it as they try to drag it up, clearly determined to take this one home for dinner. Meanwhile, not far behind them, a scene of rare tranquillity: a man paddles upstream silently in his wooden dugout, the moon shimmering in its wake. I dare say it's a perfect moment.

Except that it's soon shattered by gunshots.

• • •

The first victim of the fighting arrives in the early morning. He's the only one to be brought in—the others are dead.

His leg is badly wounded so we set up theatre, but we're going to have to rush—my flight out will be landing soon. We give him an anaesthetic and clean the debris from the wound, and as I drill a steel pin through his tibia so we can set up traction, something happens. The pin slips. It breaks, and a sharp pain shoots up my arm.

Damn it. I wasn't concentrating.

I look down, hoping desperately that the pin hasn't pierced my glove.

It has.

It's lodged in my palm. And it's covered in blood from the man's leg wound. Heidi comes over and walks me to the basin to pull it out and scrub my hand, and as she does I look back at the patient: a young male, in sub-Saharan Africa, who may well have been a soldier. What's the likelihood of HIV?

I scrub my hand again. Nothing else I can do right now. I re-glove and finish setting up the traction, and the plane lands as we get him back to the ward. I need the man's permission to run an HIV test on him, but he's still unconscious; Heidi will chase it up for me, she promises. She'll call the result through. We hug warmly and she asks if I'm okay, and I lie. Of course I am. In ten days we'll get to do this together again.

I board the little Cessna, landing in Loki a few hours later. For the moment, though, I'm less worried about HIV than about making the trip back to Nasir in ten days. The door came open during that flight. *Wide* open. A hurricane of wind, papers and shouting in the cabin, with nowhere to land nearby. Could we even land like that? No matter; the pilot dropped his speed and climbed back over his seat, helped wrestle the door shut with a nearby passenger and then continued steering us between thunderheads.

I step out, onto the tarmac at Loki. The MSF driver meets me and takes me back to the compound, where the evacuated team members from two of the other projects are still killing time. They're unsure when they'll be returning to the field. Security there remains problematic, but if nothing else there's at least plenty of company.

By the time I manage to contact the team in Nasir, it's late afternoon. Zoe picks up the phone. The good news is that the HIV test was negative, she tells me, but I'm to bear in mind he could still be in the window period. The bad news, she says, is that just after I'd left, clan members came into the surgical ward and stabbed that same man I'd taken to theatre this morning. He's alive, but severely injured. The hospital has meanwhile shut down; the gates are locked and police are around, and Outpatients is closed. All staff are okay, but no one's sure what will happen next. Evacuation may be a possibility.

A night of catch-ups ensues in Loki, but I can't relax. Nor sleep. I get up to phone an infectious diseases colleague in Australia for advice about my needle injury, and he tells me to start anti-viral prophylaxis immediately. I check our inventory, but we don't have the drug he suggests. So I wake the other doctor out here in Loki for an opinion, and she says I'm being paranoid. She wouldn't take anything, she says. Either way, I find a prophylaxis kit from the warehouse. But do I start it? Committing to the month-long course of these old medications will mean blood tests, probably in Nairobi, and some potential side effects. *But not taking it—?*

I'm not thinking clearly. I don't trust myself anymore. And yet I'm the one who's supposed to be making medical decisions for others.

The next afternoon, I'm preparing to head to the coast when we get the news that there's been an aviation incident in South Sudan. A Canadian pilot, a guy I know well from my previous times in Loki, has made a difficult landing and suffered a broken arm, among other injuries. The plane's too damaged to fly, so he's walking to an airstrip some hours away so that a rescue flight can fetch him. He's apparently got a GPS handset to guide him.

All I can think is that we use that aviation company.

Boarding my own flight out, I'm worried. None of this is right. Is this the tail end of a bad run, or just the start? I'm not sure. It's been an unnerving, frustrating six months, and I think I'm pushing it. I'm ignoring signs, and I don't think I should be here. Or I'm just being paranoid. I can't tell which—but I never felt this in Mavinga.

Later that afternoon, I arrive in Nairobi and check into a motel room, but again I can't sleep. I don't know what scares me more: the needle injury, the recent flights, or my growing lack of desire to go on with the aid work right now, or to have to actually care about anyone else. I've not thought like this before.

I call Zoe the next morning. She tells me that the team are okay and that their evacuation has been postponed, and she says also that a permanent surgeon is confirmed to be arriving within days.

'Definitely?' I ask.

'For sure. He's already in Kenya. You'll probably cross paths in Nairobi.'

I ask her if the doctor covering me can stay on for extra weeks, and she asks why. I ask her to please just check, and when she comes back and says that she probably can, I say that I'm really sorry.

'Then please ask her to do so, Zoe. I'm really sorry. I'm out. I can't do this anymore.'

22. HOW YOU GETTIN' HOME?

My belongings will be flown out on the next charter. While waiting for them I take a few days' break on the east African coast, relieved by my resignation, embarrassed for having done it.

I speak to my parents, but the mention of gunfights and aviation incidents predictably garners frantic support for my decision. Mum's beside herself. I shouldn't have mentioned the guns.

I recount some of the more benign recent incidents to a group of travellers I meet in a Kenyan bar—South Africans at that, and well travelled in Africa—and they're wide-eyed.

And I'm bored by everyone else's stories. Disaster Gypsy, here I come . . .

Maurice is in Loki when I arrive to fetch my bags. Maurice isn't impressed. Maurice, he says that South Sudan is one of the last truly remote, truly tribal regions on earth, and that surely one doesn't come here as a volunteer and not expect difficulties. One can't sign up for this and just walk out when it gets difficult, and particularly not when it'll affect the team and cost the organisation money to find a replacement. If every volunteer just walked out when things got difficult, asks Maurice, what mission would be left running?

He's right.

I brace myself for more of the same when I pass through the head offices for my debriefings, but it doesn't come. A manager in Amsterdam listens quietly as I recount the past months' events and make my excuses; afterwards, she concedes that my departure is a significant inconvenience, but adds that this is preferable to dealing with a meltdown in the field. Her only criticism: that I'd put my hand up for Sudan rather than going home after Mozambique. That was short-sighted. I'd pushed them too hard for another placement.

In the Sydney office the reaction is much the same. They insist only that I meet with an experienced psychologist—at their expense, and confidentially—and tell me they'd be happy to have me back, but only after a good few months' break.

So that's it. I take another flight home, then slide back into that other universe. To dine, to date, to decompress, and to spend time with friends and family. And, after a month or so, to head off to work . . .

. . .

. . . Which, in short, is how I come to be standing in this outpatients department almost a year later. This is the hospital I've been working in for much of the previous twelve months. And, somewhat predictably, it's in the one environment I've come to know well these past years—an isolated, dusty, troubled outpost, somewhere back in the centre of this vast continent.

'Betty?' I call into the room.

A half-dozen black faces look over, but no one says anything.

I try again. 'Betty?'

There's a cough and a shuffle of bums, but still no answer. The old man sitting on a plastic chair nearest the door looks up at me, swats a fly buzzing around him and squints from beneath his hat. 'Nuh,' he says, and looks back down. The handful of kids playing on the floor continue their games. No one else answers.

'*Namatjira*,' I try. 'Betty *Namatjira*?'

Still nothing.

I walk towards the main door to see if she's sitting outside. People often wait there after registering with the triage clerk—on the grass, the steps or beneath one of the tall coconut palms lining the road—because this hospital, being better equipped than those in Nasir and Mavinga, possesses luxuries like air-conditioning. Ironically, though, many of the locals dislike it: it's far too cold, they complain. Which is quite a call, because this little town is located dead in the middle of one of the hottest, most arid parts of this continent. Cold is not an adjective one often hears.

A group of locals is sitting near the entrance, chatting quietly.

'Betty with you?' I ask.

No, they say. They've just been visiting a relative on the ward.

'You seen her anywhere?'

'Nuh.'

'You seen any of her family?'

They shake their heads.

I'd normally stop now; I'd not look much further for a waiting patient—they frequently head off after a short time and return later, when the department's emptied a little—but the triage clerk said that Betty had some young kids with her. So I keep looking some more, walk a few metres towards the street, but I see no sign of them. It's already late evening and the last of the day's light is draining into the western horizon; only a faint purplish glow lingers. A block to my east, the metal security grates by now will have been pulled over store windows and business fronts along the main road, and the town's population of white people will have settled into their houses, or behind a table at one of the two social clubs here.

'Betty?' I call.

I hear shouting further down the road. There's movement near an open clearing, about fifty metres away. I step closer and can make out the silhouette of a small crowd of black people weaving their way towards town. Dogs bark. Someone in the crowd yells at a passer-by noisily, aggressively—Betty and the kids are hopefully nowhere near the group—and it dawns on me that today is Thursday. Payday. A great day to be a pub owner, but a bugger of a day to have to do the night shift. The main street will be buzzing with people, and there'll undoubtedly be fighting. Of some consolation, there aren't many guns in town, but the sticks, boots and fists that will be used will cause more than enough injury, anyway.

I head back in.

'Oi, fella,' calls the old man with the hat, nearest the entrance. 'She 'roun there,' he says. 'I jus' saw 'em. She there, with 'em kids.' He nods towards the far corner, where a passageway leads to the wards. I walk over and find a round-shouldered, squat old woman hunched on a plastic chair, a shock of grey hair bursting from beneath her yellow beanie.

'Betty?' I ask.

'Yeh.'

'Great. Come through.'

She straightens her dress and reaches for the two plastic shopping bags on the chair next to her, knots the tops carefully and calls to the three kids playing nearby. Patients generally arrive with much of the family in tow—the 'mob' as they call them up here—even for small presentations, and there's no sitting quietly like on the benches in Mavinga. The adults will, yes, but kids generally lay siege to the waiting room, whirling through like little cyclones of inquisitive destruction. In the wake of just these three: food packets, paper towel, two soft drink cans and a trail of unused medical gloves. The older of the trio is still occupying himself with the latter, a fistful in his right hand and a semi-inflated one in his left (they make great balloons), while his younger brother has his hands under the nearby washbasin, splashing away with the taps turned on full. What I presume is the sister—each of the children has the same charcoal complexion, skinny limbs, big eyes, and dark, tightly curled hair, the tips of which are sun-bleached a golden yellow—is flicking through an old magazine.

'You got enough gloves there?' I ask the older brother.

He stops and looks at his right hand. The gloves jiggle; he looks back up at me uncertainly.

'You leave any for us?' I smile.

'Yeh,' he says, and promptly marches over to the cardboard dispenser on the wall. He stands on tiptoe and tries to jam the handful back in, but they fall straight back out and flop to the floor. He quickly bends down to retrieve them, then hands them gently to me. 'Here!' he says brightly. Betty meanwhile lumbers toward the assessment cubicles. The rest of us follow. I direct her to the only room that's free, where she settles into a chair, and I grab her medical notes from the bench. The kids immediately make their respective beelines for the nearby glove dispenser, otoscope, and sink.

'I've met you before, Betty,' I say. 'About a month ago.'

'Yeh.'

'Diabetes, I think it was.'

She nods.

'What can I do for you today?'

She adjusts her beanie and pauses for a moment. 'Not jus' me,' she says. 'All 'a this mob, too. All 'a them crook.'

'The kids?'

'Yeh. They crook.'

'All of them?'

'Yeh.'

'And they're your grandkids, yeah?'

'Yeh.'

'You look after them normally?'

'Yeh.'

Many of the grandmothers look after the children around here. For various reasons, some of the mothers aren't up to the task.

'And what's been the trouble with the kids, Betty?'

'They got 'em bug, y' know?'

'What, like the 'flu bug?'

'Yeh.'

'And you?'

'Yeh.'

'Flu?'

'Yeh.'

English is clearly Betty's second language, as for many of the locals. Most speak it well, if heavily accented, but some from the smaller and more remote communities don't speak it at all. And cultural factors mean that Betty's unlikely to look me in the eye and speak to me as openly as she would to one of her own people, so I pause frequently, ask closed questions and wait for her to elaborate, although I know from my months up here that she seldom will. There's a translator in the hospital during the day, but to be honest I rarely use her other than for complicated presentations. And for now we should be fine. Betty understands me well enough. We'll get there.

'How long you been crook, Betty?'

'Long time.'

'When did it start?'

'Long time,' she repeats.

'A few days ago? Or a few weeks?'

'Yeh.'

'Which one—days?'

'Yeh. Five, six days.'

'With what symptoms? What sort of problems?'

She looks down, adjusts her beanie again and gazes across the room. She shakes her head: something's caught her eye. With considerable effort she rises, wrenches her body out of the chair and moves arthritically across the cubicle. The smell of wood smoke seeps from her dress. She heads towards the basin and pulls the younger grandchild away from the taps, but he's not happy with the disruption. He was having a blast—his T-shirt's drenched, as is the floor around him—and he yells when Betty takes her seat again and holds him, but soon settles on her lap. I get him a sticker from a nearby drawer—one of those colourful, bright 'I've been brave!' stickers we so frequently bribe kids with—and put it on his arm, which pleases him no end.

'I bet he keeps you busy, huh?' I say to Betty.

'Yeh.'

'All day, I'd imagine!'

She smiles slightly, but still doesn't meet my eyes. 'Yeh. All 'a time.'

As we continue talking I notice that the boy's scalp is riddled with tinea. I make a note to add antifungal medication to whatever other treatment I may prescribe for him, then get back to taking the history.

• • •

I'm halfway through examining the kids when the night's first assault victim arrives. The police help bring the bloodied man into the department but our five cubicles are full. Dave, the nurse on duty with me tonight, quickly shifts another patient to the ward to free up a cubicle, and we lie the new patient down.

'What happened, fella?' asks Dave.

The man groans. The sickly smell of blood and cheap wine sails out on his breath—a smell I ought to be used to, having spent so much time up here, but I'm far from it. I loathe it. Not only the smell: more, what it represents.

'What happened, mate?' we ask again, but he says nothing. The police tell us there's been fighting near the bigger pub—a handful of such establishments grace this little town of just three thousand people—and they'd found him lying nearby. Jackson is his name, but more than that they don't yet know. They'll come back later to see what the extent of the injuries are and to ask him if he wants to make a statement, but for now they've got another job to get to. Dave quickly clears another cubicle.

'Jackson!' I say to the man, rubbing his sternum firmly with my knuckles. No response, so I rub harder.

Jackson groans.

We put a neck collar on and remove his shirt and trousers, covering his lower body with a sheet. Dave and I examine him thoroughly. Jackson's eye movements are all over the place—from alcohol, or due to a severe head injury, we can't tell—and it's times like this that I question my choice to keep working in these remote hospitals. In a big Western hospital we'd put him straight through a CT scanner, and we'd know immediately what we're dealing with.

'Jackson!' I call again. 'Open your eyes, mate. Jackson!'

Groan.

'Jackson! Move your hand. Here—this one. Try to move it.'

He opens it.

'Jackson—can you show me where you're hurt? Show me with your hand. Touch where it hurts, mate.'

Groan.

His hair's matted with blood. I glove up and feel around his skull: there's a large swelling at the back. His face is a dark canvas of old scars and fresh abrasions, and his right forearm is swollen. He cries out when I move it. But his blood pressure is good and his belly and chest seemingly uninjured, and we fortunately have basic X-ray services here. I call in the operator. Dave meanwhile puts in an IV line and rinses water through Jackson's hair, and we locate the large scalp laceration and staple it shut. The bleeding stops immediately. If the X-rays turn out to be okay, we'll watch Jackson closely for the night. The odds are that he'll be fine, sleep off the grog and ask for a sandwich in the morning, then likely go home with a sling and some bandages. Hopefully, that is. Up here, you never do know.

The police are back within minutes. There's been a domestic assault this time, the victim a thirty-something woman. She's had a few drinks but she's sober enough to recall the event and give us a clear history—

'He hit me with 'em fists, a coupla times, here,'

—and fortunately isn't too severely injured. Aside from the lacerations to her eyebrow and upper lip, both of which will need sutures, I find no other problems on examination. According to her notes, the last time she was in here she had a broken jaw, also from a beating. A previous time she'd been knocked unconscious. The police now have the partner in custody, they say, and they'll be back in a few hours to take her statement.

And on it goes.

• • •

It's another hour before I get back to Betty. She's snoozing in the chair, crumpled forward with her plastic bags at her feet and her yellow beanie still pulled on firmly. The grandkids are far from dozing off, though—with all this noise and these new playthings, how could one possibly sleep! They're chattering excitedly, and as I pull back the cubicle curtain I see that they've just taught me a valuable lesson: you don't leave the box of stickers with the kids and then turn your back on it.

'Hey, mister,' says the older one, lifting the front of his T-shirt. 'Look here!' His belly's wallpapered with colour. The younger sister shows me hers as well, revealing an equally dense mosaic of colourful patches on her black skin. No belly buttons on view anywhere.

'Look what we dun!' says the girl.

The older boy lifts up the little brother's T-shirt, too. 'And him!' he says. 'He also got 'em!'

'Nice one, guys,' I laugh. 'I can't see your tummies though. Any stickers left?'

'Nuh!' yells the older boy, pointing to the box. 'We used all o' them!'

I look over. Indeed they have.

With due care not to dislodge any of the adhesives, I get back to examining the children, but I'm soon called away by the arrival of a sicker patient. This happens several more times over the following hours. We run out of cubicles, and I apologise to Betty and ask her to please head back to the waiting room, where the old man in the jeans is still sitting near the door. 'Hey, doc,' he calls, 'how long I gotta wait?'

Could be a while, I apologise.

So continues the night. A feverish child arrives next, then a girl bitten by a dog. Then two more victims of assaults, followed by a thirty-six year old man with end-stage heart disease whom I know well, and who spends at least two nights a week in here. An elderly woman provides a pleasant distraction when she arrives to sell a dot painting she's recently made, asking only for the exact amount due on her electricity bill—a bargain, so I buy it—and at midnight, a semi-conscious man is brought in after being cut down from the sheet he'd used as a noose. It's not the quietest night I've had in this place, not by any means, but neither is it a particularly remarkable one. And who'd ever have believed this was all happening here, in the middle of this country—Australia?

Not me. I still find it unfathomable. Particularly when I return after a break. Granted, I'm obviously seeing the very worst of what happens in this town; such is the nature of emergency departments. The majority of people, who're doing okay and living healthy, productive lives, don't tend to present at these hours, if at all. Nevertheless, tonight speaks volumes. As has every other night I've been on duty.

So why on earth would I work here after everything that happened last year? Why not take a more mundane job, at least for a while?

I definitely didn't seek this when I got home. Dealing with tragedy was the last thing I'd wanted. And I can claim no altruistic reasons in having initially come up here, either. I took the job purely for two reasons: money (doctors like me are paid close to quadruple what we'd make as trainee specialists in Melbourne, yet retention still remains close to zero), and because I thought this would be a sensible, natural transition between medical practice in Africa and a large Western hospital. I was wrong. It's every bit as challenging. Perhaps even more so; that such a burden of illness should exist here, to say nothing of the devastating social issues, seems even more inexplicable given the context.

As for MSF, I'm not working with them for the moment. The Northern Territory government is my employer, and for a while after getting home I'd wanted some space from MSF. Their emails meanwhile arrive weekly. Usually I can't bear to read them, at other times I scan them closely. Always, there are so many positions to fill, and always, a new list of catastrophes. Cholera outbreaks in Zimbabwe; massacres in the Congo; the crisis in Gaza; meningitis epidemics in Chad . . . it goes on. As do they. A part of me expects them to grow tired, to just pull up stumps one day and print something along the lines of *Fuck It, We Tried. Forty years of this: we've done what we can.* But they don't. Nor do any of the volunteers I've stayed in touch with.

I saw Andrea not long ago, when she came to visit a relative in Australia. She'd been based in Africa for much of the time since leaving Mavinga and is doing well, still baking, still exercising and still keen to get back to the field when she can, although finding placements may be a little trickier in the future: she's about to be one half of a package deal, having recently become engaged to another MSF volunteer. (Not Pascal, she assures me.) And on the topic of marrying other field workers, here's a What Are The Chances story. Tim—the same Tim who'd so often bemoaned at our plastic dining table that love doesn't exist—is now married to an aid worker, the *same* one he'd met during those final weeks in Mavinga! They've since had a daughter, and both are still working for aid agencies. I last had a beer with him when I passed through Europe some months ago. He keeps loosely in touch with Pascal, he told me, who's now working with a development agency back in the field. (Pascal and I emailed for a while, but having to run every piece of correspondence through an online translator quickly lessened the frequency. We did at least first manage to solve the debate over glass.)

As for the team in Sudan, Heidi finished her nine months, then took another placement in Nepal. Zoe finished up her contract early and took time off for family. I've not spoken with the others, but I did hear that a volunteer from the Somalia group, a woman I'd met only briefly, subsequently left MSF and joined a different organisation, only to be kidnapped when she re-entered Somalia. (She was later released.) And for now at least, the project in Nasir is still running. I receive the occasional email from a nurse who'd arrived there just as I left, and she says that things remain difficult. Not long after she'd started, a huge gunfight erupted between rival clans due to disputes over a passing convoy of food aid. Forty people were killed, over a hundred others injured, and dozens required surgery at that little hospital. Just imagine the confusion. I can—I can still almost *feel* it. The heat. The shouting. The smell of blood and open wounds, and the desperate uncertainty of it all in those initial moments. I can picture Joseph and Thomas running around to clear beds, to insert IV lines and gather equipment; Peter, loping over to help with a TB mask hanging loosely around his neck; and the new surgeon, wondering what the fuck he's just let himself in for as he steps between patients, trying to get a handle on countless injuries, not a spare moment to even contemplate running to the safe room. I can see the patients on the ward lying low for safety, and, just metres away, those kids from the TB village, patting wads of mud onto little play-*tukuls* when it all began, mercifully far too young to consider what their futures may hold in such a place . . .

Better not to think about it.

So, is there really any point to this line of work? Is there any lasting benefit to the people it tries to help? Or does the aid industry just bumble on blindly, patting itself on the back for 'at least trying', all the while perpetuating its own existence?

I wasn't so sure anymore when I got back. I seriously questioned it. I immersed myself in books on the topic—books discussing the under-lying causes of poverty; why the problem has persisted despite five decades and hundreds of billions of dollars of aid, development and assistance; and where current approaches may be going wrong—and suffice to say such texts tend to be pessimistic. MSF is not blind to any of this, either. Quite the opposite: they're acutely aware. They're a highly introspective organisation, and from what I've seen are far more critical of themselves than any outsider could be. Not long after I'd left Mavinga, they'd printed an internal review on the handling of the cholera outbreaks in Angola, concluding that they could've better managed their response and reduced mortality rates further. When I was returning from Sudan, I came across a book of essays commissioned by them, placed in their lobby, that had been compiled following an open conference they'd hosted on humanitarian issues, and that discussed whether humanitarian intervention hurt the very countries it tried to help. Another book, written by the head of their own research unit and that's widely available, is tellingly sub-titled: *The Failure of Humanitarian Action*. Other examples abound.

For me, though, this is their strength. They know, but they go on anyway, questioning themselves and adapting constantly. I've had my differences with some of their decisions (and they with some of mine) but it's clear that it's not for a lack of insight that they aren't addressing the broader, underlying issues in the field. It's pragmatism. They do what they can. In their own words, they're putting a Band-Aid on the problem, keeping people alive while political actions try and solve it. They're under no illusions.

As for my own answers to any of this? I have none. I'm far more confused than before I first went. I've had no great epiphanies, no profound realisations, but since returning home I've resigned myself to this one thing: that, putting the economics and politics of it all aside—naïve as that may be—what it all boils down to is individuals. It's a simple interaction between just two people: one, a person with opportunities and choices, and who could get a flight out tomorrow should they choose; the other, a person with few options—if any. If nothing else, it's a gesture. An attempt. Food and a tent for Toto. Burns dressing for José. A little operating theatre with car batteries and boiled instruments, where Roberto can ply his trade. Free HIV treatment for Elizabeth, who'll never be cured and will always live in a hut anyway, but who'll have a longer, healthier life because of it. And sometimes it's little more than a bed in which to die peacefully, attended to by family and health workers . . . but hey, that's no small thing in some parts.

My head says it's futile.

My heart knows differently.

I hope to be in the field again sometime soon.

For the moment, though, it turns out I don't have to go far to find people living in devastating circumstances. It's just a few hours' drive from my home.

• • •

Betty's still waiting when I finish. She's eating dry crackers from one of her plastic bags. The kids are sleeping on the floor, the youngest wrapped in his sister's arms. Betty pulls herself out of the chair when I call her back and she wakes the kids, and the sister carries the youngest in. I apologise for the wait and finish examining them all, then give Betty a bottle of children's paracetamol to take home— good treatment for them 'flu—and antibiotics for the younger one's ear infection.

'How you getting home, Betty?' I ask.

She looks at the clock on the wall and shrugs. It's well past midnight.

'Probably a bit far for you guys to walk, yeah?' I say.

'Yeh. A bit dang'rous now, hey.'

'When you got dialysis next?'

'This mornin',' she says.

'I'm really sorry about the wait again, Betty. Come, we'll try and get you guys home quickly.'

I find Dave. He's got a nurse from the main ward giving us a hand in here, and I ask him if either has a moment to take Betty and the kids home in the hospital car. Dave says he can do it, but he reminds me that the Flying Doctor Service will be landing in a few minutes— the man who'd hanged himself needs care in the bigger hospital in Alice Springs, although Jackson fortunately won't need to go there. He's already waking up.

Dave gets the keys and brings the car to the entrance. Betty and the kids squeeze into the back together. No moon tonight, and the stars create a thick veil above, a dense, detailed landscape spattered across a giant vault of sky; only in Mavinga and South Sudan have I seen views like this.

The car pulls out. A police van drives up, and in its headlights I watch the silhouette of three curly-haired kids and one old woman in a yellow beanie huddling together in the back, speaking an

Aboriginal language I know nothing of. I should learn some of it; I always mean to learn more about the people I get to work with because these opportunities are such a privilege, although I tend to lose sight of that; but right now Jackson's yelling for a sandwich, and the police are here with a victim, and the plane's buzzed the runway and the next patient needs to be seen.

SELECTED READING

Bixler, Mark. *The Lost Boys of Sudan: An American story of the refugee experience*, The University of Georgia Press, 2006

Bortolotti, D. *Hope in Hell: Inside the world of Doctors Without Borders*, Firefly Books, 2004

Dau, John Bul. *God Grew Tired of Us*, National Geographic Society, 2007

Deng, A., Deng, B. and Ajak, B. *They Poured Fire On Us from the Sky*, PublicAffairs, 2006

Evans-Pritchard, E.E. *The Nuer: A description of the modes of livelihood and political institutions of a Nilotic people*, Oxford University Press, 1940

Kapuscinski, Ryszard. *Another Day of Life*, Harcourt Brace Jovanovich, 1987

Maier, Karl. *Angola: Promises and lies*, Serif, 2007

Médecins Sans Frontières. *Rapid Health Assessments of Refugee or Displaced Populations*, 2006.

Médecins Sans Frontières. *Violence, Health and Access to Aid in Unity State/Western Upper Nile, Sudan*, April 2002

Médecins Sans Frontières. *Great Upper Nile, Southern Sudan: Immediate health needs remain amid a precarious peace*, March 2008

Oyebade, A.O. *Culture and Customs of Angola*, Greenwood Press, 2007

Pakenham, T. *The Scramble for Africa*, Abacus, 1992

Scroggins, Deborah. *Emma's War: Love, betrayal and death in the Sudan*, Harper Perennial, 2004

Stead, M. and Rorison, R. *Angola*, Bradt Travel Guides, 2009

Terry, F. *Condemned to Repeat? The paradox of humanitarian action*, Cornell University, 2002

Websites

Unicef Statistics: Angola (2011), retrieved from http://www.unicef.org/infobycountry/angola_statistics.html

Websites Central Intelligence Agency, The World Factbook (2011), retrieved from https://www.cia.gov/library/publications/the-world-factbook

World Health Organization, Data and Statistics (2011), retrieved from http://www.who.int/research/en/

ACKNOWLEDGEMENTS

My sincerest thanks to everyone who encouraged me to write this book, and to those who gave feedback along the way. Roxanne Bodsworth, Sean Doyle, Brian Cook, Sam Jordison, Karl French, Alan Wilkinson, and the staff of The Literary Consultancy provided insightful and valuable critiques of earlier drafts. Helping offset the initial trauma of reading said critiques (there can be no more difficult thing for a first-time author than to page through the lists of reasons as to why your manuscript doesn't yet work, as necessary as that may be) were Nicolle Brown, Delecia Bright, Anne Kleinitz, Rich and Sal Kane, Dane and Jules Horsfall, Rob and Alisa Greidanus, Andrew Clift, Theane Theophilos and Erica Cassano. They gave me the confidence to keep writing during the three years it took. Arthur Jackson *insisted* that I pen a book, but demanded, in his own words, at least a mention in it. (So, Arthur: here it is!) And Melanie Thompson and Michelle Lewicki went above and beyond the call of duty, graciously running both their literary and medical eyes over later drafts.

At a time when it seemed that I was likely to spend much of the next decade still working on this manuscript, Selena Hanet-Hutchins came on board as an editor, providing clear-eyed structural advice and helping me find the *real* story. Her guidance has been crucial.

Selwa Anthony, my agent, has been a champion of this project from the moment she came across it, and Rebecca Kaiser, my publisher at Allen & Unwin, has been a dream to work with—and that's despite her having had to contend with grammatical issues that she described, quite diplomatically, as being 'uniquely yours'. Karen Ward diligently helped iron out such issues.

To the staff of the Mae Tao Clinic in Mae Sot, Thailand: your story demands a book of its own, and I can only hope you'll forgive me for glancing over it so cursorily here. Know that it bears no reflection on what it meant to work alongside you.

To the staff of Kafe, the T-House, and Sanctuary: you gave me a home away from home during much of this writing process, and it was a delight.

To my parents, Graham and Denise, who read every line of every draft, and who never wavered in their support of this project, and who endured with unfailing patience the sporadic, siege-like take-overs of their dining area and spare-bedroom by a distracted son and his attendant morass of papers: your support has been invaluable. So too the encouragement. Thank you.

And to all those in the field, both local and expat, who I lived with, worked with, learned from, and laughed with over those months: I'm forever indebted. I hope this book reflects that.

(. . . Oh, as for other ways to stay single?

Move back home with your parents. Then write a book.)